Level Three Leadership

Level Three Leadership

Getting Below the Surface

James G. Clawson

The Darden Graduate School of Business Administration
University of Virginia

Prentice Hall, Upper Saddle River, New Jersey 07458

Acquisitions Editor:	Stephanie Johnson
Assistant Editor:	Shane Gemza
Editorial Assistant:	Hersch Doby
Editor-in-Chief:	Natalie Anderson
Marketing Manager:	Tami Wederbrand
Production Coordinator:	Maureen Wilson
Managing Editor:	Dee Josephson
Manufacturing Buyer:	Diane Peirano
Manufacturing Supervisor:	Arnold Vila
Manufacturing Manager:	Vincent Scelta
Design Manager:	Patricia Smythe
Cover Design:	Bruce Kenselaar
Cover Illustration/Photo:	David Madison/Tony Stone Images
Production/Composition:	Impressions Book and Journal Services, Inc.

Library of Congress Cataloging-in-Publication Data

Clawson, James G.
    Level three leadership : getting below the surface / by James G.
Clawson.
       p.   cm.
    Includes bibliographical references and index.
    ISBN 0-13-010878-2
    1. Leadership.   I. Title.
HD57.7.C545   1999
650.1′3—dc21   98-33824
                                            CIP

Prentice-Hall International (UK) Limited, *London*
Prentice-Hall of Australia Pty. Limited, *Sydney*
Prentice-Hall Canada Inc., *Toronto*
Prentice-Hall Hispanoamericana, S.A., *Mexico*
Prentice-Hall of India Private Limited, *New Delhi*
Prentice-Hall of Japan, Inc., *Tokyo*
Pearson Education Asia Pte. Ltd., *Singapore*
Editora Prentice-Hall do Brasil, Ltda., *Rio de Janeiro*

Printed in the United States of America

10   9   8   7   6   5   4   3

To Alex Horniman,
who declares that excellence is a neurotic lifestyle,
who knows whereof he speaks,
and who taught and continues to teach me much

Brief Contents

Contents

Preface

*L*evel Three Leadership is about learning to make a difference as a leader. In this book, I posit the view that many leaders, especially those raised and trained and experienced in Industrial Age organizations, have learned to lead at Level One, focusing on behavior and often ignoring or undervaluing opportunities to influence people at Level Two (their thinking), and at Level Three (their values and basic assumptions about how the world operates). The result is that many managers have a superficial impact on the people with whom they work. My goal is to provide practical principles of leadership that get beneath the surface, that influence the thinking and feeling of others rather than just their behavior. The perspective of leadership that I present is a practical rather than a theoretical one. This book contains no summaries of common leadership theory, yet bits and pieces of many of them are woven into the story presented here. In preparing the book, I have drawn on the literature, what we say we know about leadership today, but I have drawn more heavily on my own experience and on the experience of several University of Virginia Darden School faculty who have been involved in designing and teaching leadership programs to MBA and executive education students for several decades.

This book is intended for practicing managers who, on their own or in connection with ongoing studies in executive MBA or executive short courses, want to learn more about how to become effective leaders. It is also intended for MBA students thinking about the same issue, yet this book is not a textbook. It is not about summarizing all the leadership theories; rather, it is about integrating theory and practice and about creating a model and a set of related perspectives and concepts on how people can become better leaders in their own lives, in their work groups, and in their organizations.

BACKGROUND

This book is based on consulting, research, and teaching experiences by several faculty of the Darden Graduate School of Business Administration at the University of Virginia in Charlottesville, Virginia, a school whose mission is "to better society by developing leaders in the world of practical affairs" and whose students, we hope, tend to be known for an action orientation, an enterprise perspective, determination, vision, judgment, integrity, and social responsibility. The ideas here have been tested in the MBA and executive education classrooms of the Darden School over the last 10 years.

The Darden School faculty take a student-centered, practical approach to education; that is, we believe that each class should begin with and build from the level of the students' understanding of the issues and intricacies that are presented in a series of cases. Cases are descriptions of actual business situations in which the authors focus on the situation rather than on demonstrating any particular theory or point of view. Real (as opposed to armchair) business cases form the basis for almost all the class work at the Darden School.

Students, all with more than two years of work experience after college, are required to prepare, on average, one case for each of three 85-minute classes each day. Classroom analysis of those cases typically begins with a student speaking to the case as well as he or she can and is followed by an active and ranging discussion by all members of the class. We have not included any of the cases from our various programs in this book, although several are referred to. The cases used in class are not intended to be used as illustrations of theory as orchestrated by an instructor or as presented by student study teams. Rather, they provide data and situations that invite personalized discussion and that demand decisions and action plans—so that students can confront and learn to deal with actual business situations (as presented in the cases) as viewed by a group of highly active, intelligent peers.

Typical discussions include overviews of the key issues and problems, analysis of the underlying forces and realities, choices of action, and suggestions on how to implement action decisions. Business-related cases are available from Darden Educational Materials Services (DEMS) at the Darden School, from Harvard Case Services at the Harvard Business School, from the Ivey School in London, Ontario, Canada, and from other sources, including the *Case Research Journal.*

To assist the students in their struggles with these business cases, faculty often write and disseminate technical notes, which are short briefs of relevant theories, concepts, frameworks, and principles. We expect the students to read these notes and sort out that information that is useful and that which does not fit their experience. These technical notes help students sift through the current literature and consolidate current thinking on a number of topics. These notes are intended to provide frameworks for the students to use to help them make sense of cases or a series of cases.

Students read these conceptual treatises and choose whether to apply them to any succeeding case that they may encounter. The case method avoids rote memorization for the sake of an exam. The use of technical notes avoids "reinventing the theoretical wheel," a common criticism of case method, so that students can wrestle with the practical applications. Technical notes also offer students a flexibility that text assignments cannot: Students can pick and choose the conceptual frameworks they want to use without having to read an assigned book for each.

We desire to have students develop their own theories-in-use that will *stick with them* over time. Thus, although the technical notes tend to focus less on abstractions and more on practical applications, they are decidedly *not* atheoretical. The notes are filled with theories, portions of theories, concepts, and principles gleaned from multiple sources, including the academic literature, our faculty's own research, and the faculty's practical experience in working in and consulting in industry. This book is derived in part from these technical notes.

This book also draws on the work of a wide range of scholars and authors in the field of leadership and managing change. I do not intend for this book to be a substitute for those primary sources; I only intend to summarize, where appropriate, for those readers who want the core concepts without the supporting discussion and databases. Consequently, most chapters have notes for further references that readers may pursue if they wish.

STRUCTURE AND THEMES IN THIS BOOK

This book does not purport to present a summary of the various theories of leadership. Other volumes, notably Gary Yukl's *Leadership in Organizations* (Upper Saddle River, NJ: Prentice-Hall, 1994), do that task very well. Rather, my goal here is to present a set of practical principles of effective leadership as they emerge in these difficult times that mark the transition from the Industrial Age to the Information Age.

The book follows the structure of the general leadership model presented in chapter 2. This framework incorporates aspects of many previous leadership theories into a single, broad structure that can be examined in part or in whole and that provides the largest overarching theme of the book. This model includes four basic elements—*leader, task, others,* and *organization*—and various relationships among them. All these elements and their relationships appear in an environmental context and combine to produce a set of leadership outcomes.

Structure of This Book

This book follows the rough outline suggested by the diamond-shaped general model of leadership. Part I introduces the major paradigm shift between the Industrial Age and the Information Age, the general model of leadership employed in the book, and some important concepts on ethical behavior in leadership. Part II focuses on characteristics of individual leaders that are important to positive leadership outcomes. The short part III addresses strategic thinking and the importance of a prospective leader developing strategic thinking skills. Part IV explores the connection between the leader and the followers and introduces concepts of leading others and leading teams. Part V examines the importance of leadership as manifest in the design of organizations and their systems and of leadership in managing change. The book ends with a conclusion chapter, a few exercises that readers may wish to use in conjunction with a classroom experience to deepen their insight on several concepts introduced in the book, and some recommendations for additional reading.

At the end of each chapter is a summary list of the principles of effective leadership introduced in that chapter. These lists include summaries and concepts as well as "if you do x, then y will occur" principle statements. Although these lists may tally what I see as the important ideas in each chapter, they do not provide a substitute for the logic and reasoning in the chapters themselves. This book, like the classroom activities, is not about memorizing ideas; rather, it encourages readers to think more deeply about leadership and about how they might become better at it.

Each chapter also includes a series of questions for the reader's personal reflection. These questions are intended to help the interested reader think about the key ideas in that chapter. These serious questions become a series of exercises from which readers can learn more about themselves and their leadership philosophy. The questions provide a gateway to a deeper level of thinking about leadership than simple reading might yield.

Themes in the Book

The major theme running throughout this book is what I call Level Three Leadership. I describe how management for the last hundred years has focused on behavior, on what I call Level One, to the exclusion of followers' values and basic assumptions, or what I call Level Three. Level Three Leadership attempts to go below the surface in leading and managing others. This effort, and it is an effort, means, first, an awareness of some of the complexity of human behavior and, second, an engagement in trying to use that complexity to have a deeper, longer-lasting impact on others. Level Three Leaders think about how people think and about what they value and about how that influences their behavior—Level Three Leadership is much more than just telling people what to do. I assert that effective leadership is Level Three Leadership; that is, effective leadership is aware of and able to deal with basic beliefs and values of employees.

Because leaders work at influencing the basic values and assumptions of others, leadership has a markedly moral aspect. We find it difficult to discuss leadership with our students and executive program participants without addressing the ethical and moral overtones. The Darden School was one of the first in the country to require an ethics course in its MBA program and has long been a leader in ethical research and teaching in business. The Olsson Center for the Study of Business Ethics has been at the forefront of this field. Chapter 4, on ethics and leadership, summarizes some of the concepts and principles that we have used successfully for many years at Darden and that relate powerfully to most people's intuitive understanding of what it means to be an effective leader.

A fourth theme that appears in the book is the integrative nature of leadership. We do not believe it is accurate or effective to talk about leadership in isolation; any discussion of leadership must address questions of strategy, managing change, and ethics. For several years, our required capstone course in the MBA program was called *Strategy, Leadership, and Change,* and then *Leading Strategic Change.* We strongly believe that when we talk about leadership, we have to talk about strategy, about managing change, and about the ethical underpinnings of both. Readers will find here, then, forays into each of these areas as it closely relates to leadership. These explorations do not by any means constitute complete courses or examinations of strategy, managing change, or ethics, but they are intended to signal clearly the interrelatedness of these areas.

Finally, a fifth theme is a very personal one. Consistent with the notion of Level Three Leadership, I invite the reader to engage the leadership process personally and to consider the demands and consequences of leadership behavior. I am more interested in contributing to those who want to work at *becoming better leaders* than in talking *about* leadership in the abstract. Our course work always includes many descriptions of individual leaders that consist not only of their business activities, but also of how they manage their lives and the balance between self, family, work, health, and social activities.

Readers may ask if the principles presented here are uniquely American and are not relevant to Europe, Latin America, Africa, and Asia. I can only say that, having lived abroad in Hong Kong and Japan and having worked off and on over the years in South Africa, England, France, Australia, and Southeast Asia, the models, concepts, ideas, and thoughts contained here have proven to be stimulating and provocative for all those audiences. Certainly the application of these concepts varies from country to country and from region to region. My goal here has been to present ideas in a general framework that works like a four-wheel drive vehicle, able to negotiate rough terrain in various parts of the world but rugged enough to stand the strain. For example, the concept of Level Three Leadership, leadership that intends to influence the values of followers, does not specify what those values might be, yet it does invite Asians, Latins, Europeans, and Africans as well as North Americans to consider the potential impact leaders might have if they are able to connect with others at this deeper level. In this sense, I believe the framework introduced here to be sturdy enough to work around the world. So far, for me, it has.

ACKNOWLEDGMENTS

Many of my colleagues have contributed ideas and frameworks to the thinking that resulted in this book. Although the book draws on their experience, I wish to make it clear that I do not speak for them nor presume to put words in their mouths. By teaching together, consulting together, and working together, we share ideas and approaches. I wish to acknowledge the tremendous impact these people have had on me. This list would include but not be limited to Alex Horniman, Bill Zierden, Eileen Hogan, Paul McKinnon, Jack Weber, Lynn Isabella, Robin Johnson, Jay Bourgeois, Jeanne Liedtka, John Rosenblum, Ed Freeman, Sherwood Frey, Elliott Weiss, and Robert Carraway. To a large degree, the conceptual material contained herein is the product of being in their midst. Somehow, in that context, writing "I" seems inappropriate. I have learned too much from them and benefited too much from their experience to claim ownership of many of the ideas presented here. Early reviewers took exception to the use of "we," so when I felt it necessary to assert an individual point of view, I have used "I." Any faults of the book and in the way the principles and concepts are presented lie with me; any strengths of the concepts are the result of collaborative effort in an unusual community of scholars and teachers.

Can leadership be taught? I do not suppose it can in its entirety; surely some qualities are inherited or well developed by the time students arrive at college or graduate school or have spent 10 to 20 years in business settings. Yet our experience with these materials over the last 10 years suggests that students can learn a lot about what leadership is and is not, can develop skills that will help them be more effective in leadership situations, and can create developmental plans that will continue this development after a course (long or short) is finished.

As you know, the literature on leadership is enormous and growing rapidly. If this book can distill some practical personal and professional leadership concepts and can help students and practicing managers and leaders develop a stronger desire to make a difference in society in a powerful, Level Three, ethical way, then this book will have served its purpose.

In addition to my Darden School colleagues in general, I would like to acknowledge many people over several years who have contributed specifically to this project. I am grateful for their effort and contributions. First, I would like to thank Bill Zierden and Alex Horniman, who invited me to join this remarkable community, for their contributions to my life. Next, my thanks go to Paul McKinnon, presently the vice president of human resources at Dell Computer, with whom I worked for three years and in conversations with whom this book was conceived. The work of secretaries and research assistants over the years may not be obvious, so I would like to thank, in particular, Mary Darnell for her years of unflagging support and assistance; Christine McCabe and Maki

DePalo for their help on various aspects of the manuscript; the Darden School editing department, Steve Smith and Elaine Moran, for their timely support; and the Darden School and the International University of Japan for their support while I was writing this book. My thanks also to Stephanie Johnson and Maureen Wilson, text and production editors at Prentice Hall, for guiding me through an aggressive schedule. A big thanks to Karen Dorman for her hard work in editing word by word. Thank you, too, to Kevin McCarthy for his encouragement and for his ability to crystalize a process that finally worked for me. Most of all, I wish to acknowledge the consistent support and encouragement of my wife, Susan, whose love and dependability and willingness to fill in elsewhere made this book even possible.

James G. Clawson
Charlottesville, Virginia

Level Three Leadership

CHAPTER

The Changing Context of Leadership

1

Chapter Outline

■ The Aristocratic Society

■ The Industrial Revolution

■ The Present Paradigm Shift

Things are not what they used to be, especially when it comes to understanding what it means to be an effective leader. Most observers agree that the industrialized world is in the midst of a major managerial paradigm shift that is changing the way that we think about business, the way that we organize to do business, and the problems and dilemmas that business presents.[1] These changes are as significant as those experienced during the last major paradigm shift during the Industrial Revolution, when the western world moved from agrarian to manufacturing-based economies. Now, two hundred years later, we are in the midst of another similarly significant and fundamental transition as we move from the Industrial Age to the Information Age.

Understanding, and becoming effective in, this third and emerging new context requires a fundamental shift in management thinking and modes of leadership. Principles of organization and leadership that worked well for the last one hundred years are being replaced with new principles, principles based on new assumptions about people, economies, and how to organize. Understanding this new paradigm is essential to becoming a leader in the world of today leading to tomorrow. Many of the basic assumptions about leadership and management that you may have been taught earlier may be ill suited to the emerging information age business world. Your perspective on the world around you and the way in which you plan and execute your business in that world will surely determine your success. This book suggests that, if you do not understand the new emerging realities, you will be at a disadvantage compared with your peers and competitors.

Because we were all born in a world dominated by the bureaucratic mentality, filled with pyramidal organizations that operate on such principles as "one man, one boss," "follow the chain of command," and "success means climbing the corporate ladder," it is often difficult to grasp and appreciate the nature of the changes taking place around us. The bureaucratic mind-set is the one that most of us learned at an early age and have had reinforced over years of experience. At one level, we can see corporations combining and dividing, growing and dying, much as they have done for a long time. At a second level, we can observe that the reasons for those combinations and divisions, for the growth and decline, are changing. And at a third level, we can begin to identify the fundamental differences that underlie the belief systems that support those causes. Despite the common difficulty of "seeing" what is happening in the larger picture of today's world, if you desire it and if you are willing to extend yourself—perhaps being willing to reexamine some long-held beliefs—you have a chance to add new concepts, new principles, and new ideas to your present skill set: concepts, principles, and ideas that will enhance your efforts to lead. If you take that opportunity, you will be a more effective leader.

There have been two major worldwide paradigm shifts in management, one caused by the Industrial Revolution and the second caused by the Information Revolution. We are living in the midst of this second shift, a transition period between the Industrial Age and the new, emerging Information Age. If you understand the dynamics and implications of this turbulent period and can put your personal efforts at leadership in that context, you will be better prepared for making the transition, for understanding the seeming chaos about you, for influencing those around you, and for helping, not hindering, your organization's efforts to make the transition as well. And that is what this book is about: enhancing your ability to influence others amidst changing times. I begin, therefore, with an overview of the changing context of leadership.

THE ARISTOCRATIC SOCIETY

Before the nineteenth century, much of society was stratified according to the aristocratic model.[2] The word *aristocracy* comes from Greek and means "rule by the best"—which means those born to noble families. With few exceptions, societies around the world prior to 1800 assumed that royal birth meant royal abilities and royal rights to power and authority. People's births determined their likely standing in society, their wealth, and their ability to influence events. This meant that societal and organizational power and authority were largely distributed according to family lineage. The random process of birth picked the next generation's kings and queens and emperors and empresses. In the effort to consolidate power and authority, great houses in Europe and Asia sought alliances through political means, military means, and arranged marriages, hoping to bind their fortunes and build greater stability in society.

Structurally, on a basic level, the aristocratic model meant that certain families tended to rule and dominate the social and political landscape. At a second, mental level, it meant that people thought that this was normal and that the noble families were rightly ruling. At a third level, the tacit, central assumption in the aristocratic paradigm was, practically speaking, "father knows best." Royal fathers were the center of political and economic activity in most of the world. Fathers who were also heads of states, nations, and great estates made the decisions and the laws, arbitrated disputes, and administered justice and punishment. Fathers dreamed dreams of conquest, alliance, or economic expansion and then established the funds for and recruited others to fulfill those dreams.

TABLE 1-1 Characteristics of the Aristocratic Era

- Orderly Society
- Limited Information
- Limited Transportation
- Homogeneous Followers
- Limited Opportunities
- Limited Education
- Limited Technological Advances
- Dominated by Males
- Limited Resources

The sons, the princes, held hopes of ascending to the father's throne by right, a right recognized by the people.

There were many positive aspects to the aristocratic model. It gave stability to society in that people knew their place in the world virtually from birth and were molded and educated to accept and grow in that place. With enormous wealth and lots of leisure time, monarchs and royal families searched for interesting employment and entertainment. Artists, musicians, sculptors, and writers all benefited from this search and thus were able to add to the world's treasures. The aristocracies supported the development of some of the world's greatest literature, philosophy, art, and music. The major characteristics of the Aristocratic Era are summarized in Table 1–1.

Despite these advantages, the aristocratic model had many disadvantages. The aristocratic system tended not to recognize individual talents if the person possessing these talents was not in the proper class. It limited education to a few; restricted the movement of talent into key positions in a multitude of organizations; inhibited the distribution of wealth in a fair and equitable way; and, importantly, was not flexible enough to adjust to the changing times. All these factors contributed to the burgeoning dissatisfaction among the underprivileged classes. Millions of people felt disenfranchised. Although many accepted their societally defined "natural" position as servants or subjects, others longed for a more fluid, free society.

THE INDUSTRIAL REVOLUTION

The revolutions for freedom and independence in the eighteenth century, including the revolutions in France and the Americas, were manifestations of humankind's dissatisfaction with a model of society that had worked in the past but was beginning to feel increasingly confining, unfair, and anachronistic. Powerful as the political changes were, an equally profound, but quieter, change was gathering momentum. In the second half of the eighteenth century and the first half of the nineteenth century, the invention of the steam engine, the discovery of petroleum, and the development of new, mass manufacturing techniques for clothing, guns, shoes, utensils, and tools revolutionized the economic world. This transformation made a host of durable goods available to an ever wider subset of the population and created a new, more powerful merchant class. The Industrial

Revolution also caused a major shift in the nature of leadership in organizations as it became clear that the aristocracies could no longer keep up with the changes that were occurring nor could they be counted on to provide the best leaders for the new organizational forms that were taking shape.

These realities, along with the increasing economic and political gaps between the noble class and the working classes, created a tension between the old system and the emerging new reality. Wars of independence in the United States, France, and Russia were the earthquakes that occurred along the fault line of this tension between the old and new ways of thinking and were symptomatic of an aristocratic paradigm giving way to a new worldview.

Another significant precursor to the bureaucracies that we know today were the efforts of Frederick the Great, who needed to find quick and efficient ways of molding uneducated, poor people into effective fighting units. His efforts at assigning specific jobs to members of teams, developing uniforms and systems of rank, and centralizing decision making all provided strong models for future organization designers.

The Industrial Revolution forced a paradigm shift to a new model of management for society in which "common" people were given authority and power by virtue of their abilities and skills. The powerful positions in the new companies began to be occupied increasingly by people who were more familiar with the techniques of manufacture and wealth creation rather than with the political and societal niceties of the elite. Power began to be distributed according to the office one held, not one's birthright. The French word *bureau,* meaning "office," was joined with *-cracy* to convey the novel idea that power was fixed to the office one held and not one's last name. This concept was a key difference between the old and new paradigms: power accrued to the office, not to the individual. There are yet today, of course, vestiges of the aristocratic model, although in both England and Japan as well as elsewhere, these vestiges are under increasing scrutiny and are more and more considered outdated and expensive residues of a previous world order.

This transition from the Aristocratic Age to the Industrial Age was a major paradigm shift. Although we speak of a paradigm "shift," the process seems painstakingly slow when viewed from the vantage point of the span of a single lifetime; most people are born, live, and die in one dominant model. When we look at the structure of society over several generations, however, paradigm shifts represent dramatic disruptions in the stability of society and dramatic changes in its thinking and organizational forms.

Ironically, one of the best summaries of the new bureaucratic system was written by a man born into the highly cultured, upper middle class in Europe in 1864, the German sociologist Max Weber. By that time, the Industrial Revolution had been gaining momentum for almost a hundred years so that the world into which Weber was born was already largely "industrialized." Weber summarized the key assumptions that represented a break with the aristocratic system and clarified the way that the bureaucratic system had already begun to take hold. In *The Theory of Social and Economic Organization,* Weber took great pains to describe carefully his view of the new "legitimate" authority as opposed to aristocratic authority. His writing was considered a milestone in describing the shift from aristocratic thinking to bureaucratic thinking because it clarified the view of what largely had already happened.

In describing the new bureaucratic system, Weber concluded that a new order of society was growing out of a widely accepted set of laws "which are formally correct and have been imposed by accepted procedure"[3] and were very distinct from the aristocratic view. The key components of this new idea of legitimate authority were:

1. Legal norms or laws or "rules" are established by mutual agreement.
2. Laws should be equally applied to all.
3. People in authority occupy an "office."
4. Members of societies or organizations obey the laws, not the whims of the office incumbent.
5. Members are free and owe obedience only to the impersonal order of laws, not to the individual incumbent.
6. Organizations and their offices have spheres of competence and authority and can only compel people within those bounds.
7. The offices in the organization are arranged hierarchically so that higher offices have more authority or legitimate power than lower offices.
8. Appointments to office should be based on expertise.
9. Reward for work comes in the form of a set salary. (Weber waffled a little here by noting that salaries should be related to a person's office *and* to their "social status.")
10. Management should be separate from ownership.
11. Individuals do not carry rights of office; when they leave office, their authority is gone.
12. The authority of an office must be documented.
13. The incumbent of each office is subject to "strict and systematic discipline" in the control and management of his office.[4]

The institutionalization of the bureaucratic model produced, as institutionalization did for the aristocratic model, enormous momentum and commitment throughout societies worldwide. Whereas aristocracies depended on the good health and skills of the heirs, bureaucracy allowed organizations to continue even without a particularly key family member or individual. Bureaucracy changed the aristocratic handing down of power by allowing nonfamily members to fill the offices of power, subject to the rules of the organization. Hence, institutions could be created and continue in existence even though their individual members and surnames changed with time.

In bureaucracies, power and authority were distributed according to the office or the structural relationships of the offices in an organization. When promoted, a person received additional power, authority, and usually wealth. Decision making was often consolidated at the top of these organizations and implementation of those decisions was assigned to the middle and bottom. Organizations continued to come and go as they did in the aristocracies, and people continued to think of the established organizations as the "right" ones. However, the basic assumption underlying the bureaucratic model, although parallel to the third level basic assumption in the aristocratic model, was quite different, namely, "the boss knows best."

Although similar to the aristocratic model in some respects, the bureaucratic model expanded the range of individuals who could fill the power roles. As in the aristocracies, new bosses were primarily men, but now not necessarily the sons of previous bosses. The new leaders were better educated than others and often more experienced, thus lending a general credence to the underlying assumption that "the boss knows best." Employees and middle managers in most bureaucracies looked to the executive ranks for vision, guidance, control, encouragement, rewards, and information about the nature and status of the organization. Raw data flowed up, analysis and decision making took place at the top, and instructions and orders flowed down.

This common pattern spawned a range of bureaucratic phrases like "We don't pay you to think, just do it" and "That's on a need-to-know basis only" that have become, for most of us, common everyday expressions, so much so that, even today, we seldom question them. People at lower levels in the early days of the age took similar phrases for granted, accepting them as the way things were. This taking for granted, in fact, reflected the reality that the new paradigm had taken hold and was no longer thought of as a change.

Bureaucracies, which worked very well for more than a century, were a powerful influence and produced many positive changes. Talented people had greater freedom of upward socioeconomic movement than in the aristocratic model. Bureaucracies provided a structure for mobilizing large labor pools. The development of new industries was no longer dependent on the whims of aristocratic individuals. Bureaucratic society as a whole was more flexible to meet the challenges of changing times. Bureaucracies dampened the effects of ignorance improperly promoted and, importantly, reduced the dissatisfaction associated with the aristocratic model (although supplanted it in many ways with a new resentment for those with "new" money).

Bureaucracies also generated a stream of organizational research and theory building, much of it based on a desire to reduce the variance between job descriptions and human performance. Much of Frederick Taylor's work on scientific management, along with his work on dominant leadership models of the bureaucratic era, revolved around finding ways to fragment, prescribe, and control human behavior.[5] The goals of management during those times included standardizing human behavior and minimizing variance in human work. It was, in Gareth Morgan's term, the machine company.[6]

With bureaucracies, as with many systems, sources of historical success became the seeds of future decay. The system of assumptions and principles that formed bureaucracies generated some unfortunate outcomes. The ability to continue business without a particular individual and eventually to create institutions as more or less fixed parts of society led some organizations to focus more on survival as an objective of their existence—diverting their efforts from customer service goals and purposes. The fitting of people into predefined job descriptions tended to alienate them from their work, to encourage a one-way, top-down communication pattern, and to discourage learning activities. In their worst form, bureaucracies came to serve few, if any, beyond their employees. Bureaucracies also, as they grew, allowed moderate or lesser talents to remain and hide within the labyrinthine structures of the organization. Sometimes, the new, prescribed, legal order of things codified by Weber blurred the view of good people properly promoted, so that they could not *see,* much less contribute to, customer needs. Bureaucracies also had the propensity to discourage creativity and entrepreneurial behavior in favor of low-risk, previously conceived of and planned for, action. These problems of bureaucracies have come to the fore recently with a vengeance as North American and European firms wrestle with the underlying principles, technological breakthroughs, and ferocious competition in the new, emerging paradigm.

THE PRESENT PARADIGM SHIFT

Today, rapid change is the order of things. In many respects, this is a function of the turbulence as we move from the Industrial Age into the Information Age. During the twentieth century, we have seen the development of electricity, petroleum products and fuels,

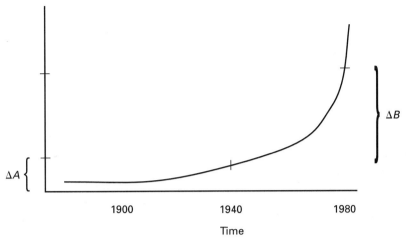

FIGURE 1–1 The Changing Context of Leadership

nuclear energy augmented by wind and sun, and unanticipated volumes of technological breakthroughs in chemistry, physics, machinery, biogenetics, biochemistry, miniaturization, nutrition, energy use, data transfer, computers, and hundreds of other fields. The pace of change represented by these breakthroughs and innovations seems to have accelerated in the last 50 years. Most managers agree that the relationship between time and change in our society is exponential, as shown in Figure 1–1; that things are changing at an ever-increasing rate. Of course, no system can maintain an exponential rate of change because eventually it will approach a vertical line, but during the transition period between Industrial and Information Ages, the rate of change is enormous.

The task of keeping current in any field has become overwhelming. There are more books to read, theories to comprehend, sensors creating more data, observers making more conclusions, TV channels, and access to political, scientific, and socioeconomic situations than ever before. Citizens of many countries can watch at their leisure the inner workings of foreign governments around the world as they happen. Our ability to integrate the disparate tidal waves of information and new knowledge is overtaxed.

The implications of this information and change explosion for our generation and succeeding ones are many and enormous. Perhaps first on the list is the realization that, although our parents may have had the luxury of continuing their careers in the same fields over the course of a 40–year career, our generation does not have that luxury. We cannot expect to finish our careers doing the same kind of work that we began with. In almost every field, new materials, tools, theories, techniques, substitutes, and ways of organizing mean that *we must all be constant learners* or soon be obsolete and out of work.

Now, more than ever before, lifelong learning is critical to survival. Expect that whatever you learn now will soon be displaced and replaced and that you must be engaged in learning, not passively but actively seeking to gain an advantage by learning faster than others. Reading, thinking, ingesting, digesting, pondering, struggling, skimming, researching, investigating—and all with a sense of urgency—have become the *normal* way of life, the necessary means of keeping up. This learning is especially true in leadership, in growing in the ways you think about and manage your influence on others.

A new framework for organizations that differs significantly from the bureaucracy is emerging in response to these dramatic changes. Organizations are reforming around information systems and communication systems that support them. Power now is emanating from people who have access to and can digest volumes of information. As with the previous paradigm shift, this shift has not been instantaneous, although it is happening much faster than the previous shift from the Aristocratic Age to the Industrial Age. The causes for this new shift, like the last one, are rooted in technological change.

Many aspects of this new Information Age shape our thinking about organizations and leadership. In this new age, power revolves around the people who coordinate resources to meet customer needs. Information becomes the key competitive and managerial advantage as markets and customer demands change much more rapidly than ever before. Companies such as Wal-Mart and Banc One have used information systems as powerful strategic weapons in building competitive positions that are difficult for others to assail. With increasing size and shortening time lags between customer orders and expected fulfillment, internal cycle times of developing products and then of getting those products to market are much shorter than before. These phenomena, in turn, create the realization that management can no longer know and understand what needs to be done at each interface between the organization and its environment.

Managers are turning increasingly to other employees to get relevant data and to make decisions in order to respond to demands and challenges more quickly than bureaucratic structures would allow. This trend has given rise to the popular term of the late 1980s and early 1990s: *empowerment.* Organizations unable to wield bureaucratic structures effectively to compete are turning to their employees and empowering them to make decisions, to take responsibility for corporate results, and to show initiative in recognizing and solving the problems confronting their firms. Although this flattening of organizations is a natural outcome of the Information Revolution, many managers still see it as an isolated fad that they can choose to ignore or treat superficially. Those people do not understand the larger context in which these changes are occurring.

As information networks proliferate, the boundaries of any organization begin to blur so that recent writers have begun describing the emergence of boundaryless, or virtual, organizations that exist primarily in concept but whose boundaries or edges are hard to find. Large numbers of part-time employees, commingled computer systems that automatically place orders to stock shelves, and alliances between competitors and vendors of all kinds are examples of this emerging boundarylessness in corporations. In an interview in *Industry Week,* Mike Malone, coauthor of *The Virtual Organization,* described the redistribution of power that takes place in these new organizations this way:

> The biggest [example of the disappearing perquisites of power] is position at the top of the corporate hierarchy on a permanent basis with levels of people reporting to you, that very set pecking order. In this sort of fluid organization [the virtual organization] a lot of that disappears. The idea of empowering the people out there on the edges of the company to deal with the suppliers and deal with the customers, you're stripping power away from yourself, but you're still retaining a lot of responsibility. And you have to know what's going on out there, but you may not have much ability to control what's happening because you have to trust those people to make the right decision. And it's a very difficult position to find yourself in. The trade-off is that managers always talk about how they wish they had more time to spend on being visionaries; well, now they're going to get the chance. Long-term strategic planning suddenly becomes the primary job of people at the top, along with holding this amorphous company together.[7]

One concern in these new emerging organizational forms is the danger that employees will lose a sense of being, a sense of participation, a sense of being part of a large organization. If people do not see who they work for and do not understand the larger picture of how their work fits into an ethereal, virtual organization, they may not be able to commit enough energy to contribute world-class work. Effective leaders in these new organizations will be able to find ways to hold the people in these organizations together. Traditional kinds of organizational "glue" are becoming less adhesive. In this respect, many private sector companies are learning from nonprofit organizations, which historically have pioneered structures that deal with fluid employees and fuzzy boundaries.

Another symptom of this paradigm shift is the wave of *delayering* or *flattening* of organizations that we have seen in the 1980s and 1990s, in which the ranks of middle managers are being eliminated. Nineteenth-century railroad companies had a big impact on the rise of the bureaucracy. They built multiple layers of management, primarily to process information that was coming in from a geographically diverse organization, move it up through the organization, process it, refine it, summarize it, and pass it on to the top. A decision was made, which then traveled back down through these organizational layers and was disseminated to the ranks. However, modern information systems are rapidly replacing these vertical organizational forms. Customers' use of similar systems in dealing with competitors also means that an organization does not have the time to follow that involved chain; rather, many organizations are learning to become instantaneously responsive. As a result, the need for a vertical hierarchy of decision makers is disappearing.

These pressures are causing more and more companies to experiment with and deploy empowered, team-oriented structures. People at lower ranks of the organization are gaining authority to commit the resources of the firm to meet customer needs as the middle levels are being cut out. Not coincidentally, this trend parallels a similar one in the political realm, in which so many countries recently have exerted their independence from former "protectors" and dictatorships. Centralized systems are breaking down all over the world as people at all levels are confronted with frenetic technological change, instant information, and the need to act.

As we saw in the transition from the Aristocratic Age to the Industrial Age, on the surface, organizations are continuing to come and go and reform. Further, most people are beginning to accept mentally the emerging reality that change is a fact of life and that the new, flatter organizations are the "right" ones (although many people still, early in this transition period, resist this recognition). But at the third level, the newly emerging assumption about management is not that "father knows best" nor that "management knows best," but rather that "people close to the work know best." These are the people who are closest to the central processes that directly serve customers. These *key process contributors* (KPCs) are the people who know the key customer serving processes best and who know what needs to be done to manage those processes to the best effect. Although some executives and managers who still adhere to the bureaucratic mind-set are resisting this realization, the de facto reality is that the power to make effective decisions is migrating to the key process contributors, who are closest to the systems and processes that serve customers.

Organization designers are struggling to find structures that recognize and accept this new reality. Business executives in the nation's largest corporations are now talking about speed, boundaryless organizations, project teams, concurrent engineering, and the importance of listening rather than telling. In the late 1980s for instance, Jack Welch, CEO at General Electric Company, initiated an enormous corporate change called "WorkOut," intended to help the business leaders of his divisions learn to get in touch with the ideas and perspectives of people at various levels. As one of 24 national consultants hired to assist this effort, I saw how Mr. Welch was working to transform his company from an Industrial Age bureaucracy into an Information Age organization. Welch has not been alone in this effort; more and more of his peers in industry after industry have sought to do the same.

Everywhere there is a new interest in the key information-based processes that produce goods and services and in the organizational structures that support them. Enlightened corporate executives are examining how these processes function and are looking for flaws, for ways to speed up the production and creative processes or to help management find new processes that work faster with higher quality *and* increased levels of customization to meet customer needs. Those executives who were raised in bureaucracies and are uncomfortable with the new context tend to be reluctant, recalcitrant, and resistant to understanding what they must learn to be effective in the new surroundings.

Observers call this new context the Information Age or the Post-Industrial Era. One wonders what the emerging organizational forms for distributing power will be called—because they are not bureaucracies. Although they have some lingering bureaucratic characteristics, they look more like neural networks. Whether they are called "team forms," "empowered organizations," "circles of influence," "virtual organizations," "infocracies," "custocracies," "boundaryless organizations," or "fluid collections of processes," they will be the face, the image, the visage of the new paradigm. It may be that we will settle on Peter Senge's simple but powerful term, the *learning organization*.[8] For me, the term *infocracy* seems to capture much of the reality that information has become the basis of power in these new forms. It is no longer the family or the office that is the source of the power that determines organization. Rather it is the information explosion that has caused the shift in the distribution of power in these new organizations. Whatever the new approach is called, it will be characterized by widely distributed power and structures that recognize much better the value of all organization members receiving, processing, and making decisions from new and exploding oceans of information.

In these new structures, leadership power will migrate in what will seem to older managers like chaotic fashion to the people who are close to the key challenges of each organization and who have the talent and abilities to resolve them. Employees in surviving companies will ignore and avoid the historical, formalized ways of functioning, titles will become less meaningful, and relationships between people assigned to different areas or functions will become more so. Management will support rather than direct teams, and the artifacts of steeply stratified bureaucracies (such as executive parking places, dining rooms, washrooms, suits and ties, isolated offices, one-way performance evaluation, and disparities between employee and executive compensation) will continue to shrivel and disappear. Organizational boundaries will continue to blur as vendors and customers alike demand and tolerate organizational representation, data, mainframe access, team membership, and influence on what used to be "internal" decisions. Alliances made possible by vastly superior communications will continue to grow in number around the world. The very notion of what is "internal" and "external" to an organization will continue to fade.

The paradigm shift from bureaucracy to infocracy has been described and predicted by many others, one of the first being Warren Bennis, who, in a 1966 article in *think* magazine, wrote about "The Coming Death of Bureaucracy."[9] He characterized bureaucracies as having well-defined chains of command, standardized operating procedures for dealing

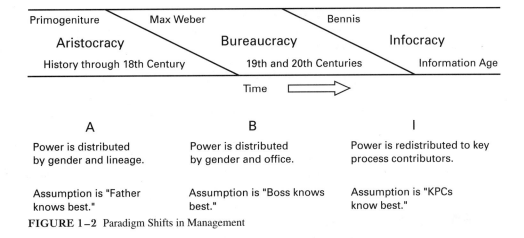

FIGURE 1–2 Paradigm Shifts in Management

with virtually every contingency, divisions of labor based on specialization, selection and promotion systems based on technical competence, and high levels of impersonality when dealing with employees. Bennis identified four threats that spelled the demise of bureaucracies: rapid and unexpected changes, growth to the point that historical procedures would no longer work, increased complexity in modern technology, and growing discontent with the impersonality of management/employee relationships.

The new organizations replacing bureaucracies, Bennis said, would be temporary in nature and shift rapidly to meet changing demands. He called them "organic-adaptive" structures. In these structures, employees would be highly motivated but have less commitment to a particular work group because these connections would change rapidly. Organizational designs would evolve to the point that, rather than repressing ideas and creativity, they would encourage play and creative thinking as organizations struggled to keep pace with environmental changes. Today, as we watch the changes taking place in organizations around us, we cannot help but be impressed with Bennis's 30-year prescience. Others have described this transition as well.[10]

A visual representation of the paradigm shift that we have been discussing is shown in Figure 1–2. The diagonal lines separating the three major paradigms described here are intended to show the gradual nature of the shifts; however, the shift from bureaucracy to infocracy will surely happen much more quickly than the shift from aristocracy to bureaucracy. The impact of new fuels and new sources of information are key stimulants to the shift. The models used to distribute power in organizations are shown at the bottom of the figure with the key assumptions about "who knows what to do."

The new information-based paradigm requires new thinking, values, systems, skills, and kinds of leadership. Members in the new organizations also will have to develop broader ways of thinking about their work. No longer will they be able to say "that's not my job" and expect to have either a job or a company that will survive. They will have to find ways of sending information from the bottom up as well as from the top down. Managers and employees alike will have to realize that every employee has something to contribute that may go beyond the formal job description. Less and less will leadership be an exercise in conveying the message, "Listen up, folks, here's how we're going to do this!" We will have to think about the inclusive answers instead of the exclusive ones. We will learn in organizational terms and in leadership terms. We will find "fuzzy logic" and "and/also" answers instead of "clear logic" and "either/or" answers. Employees and leaders who will thrive in these new organizations will be comfortable with these less certain kinds of influence.

The new paradigm also demands that its leaders develop some new core values and skills. The new leaders will have to place greater value on listening compared with talking than in the past. Leaders will have to learn to value cooperation more than competition. They will have to value talent more than title. They will have to value team work more than individual effort and glory. They will have to value service to customers more than (but not at the exclusion of) profits and accept, deep down, the fact that customers come before profits, that profits come after customers, and that without customers there are no revenues or profits. Collins and Porras in their soon-to-be-classic book, *Built to Last,* call this orientation "purpose beyond profit."[11] Many of us, striving for positions of leadership, will have to, as Davidow and Malone put it, "reverse our thinking" so that rather than trying to create customers for our present products in order to create revenues, we will have to value and understand customer needs and then reorganize our firms to meet those needs faster and with higher quality than others.

The new leaders in this new context will have to learn to value fixing things that are not yet apparently broken. This is what Hal Leavitt means in part by introducing the notion that new leaders will be problem creators as much as problem finders or problem solvers.[12] The new leaders will value anticipation. They will value risk taking. They will value new ideas. They will have to *develop a value for change,* a deep-seated belief in and trust in the change process and an enthusiasm for embracing it. Hugh McColl, CEO at NationsBank, has taught the motto, "We will savagely embrace change."[13] It is a philosophy that effective leaders in the new paradigm will understand and live by. They will have to relinquish their values for stability and control and the present distrust for surprises and learn to love learning, change, diversity, and the feeling of having to be alert and ever present in order to see and respond to surrounding changes.

The new paradigm will also require the design and implementation of new organizational systems. The new leaders will implement and experience new organizational forms like the spaghetti organization in Denmark reported by Tom Peters.[14] They will implement "spherical" performance evaluations (that go beyond the groundbreaking 360–degree evaluations done in some companies now) done by team members, subordinates, *and* customers, suppliers, and community citizens rather than single superior officers. These spherical evaluations will include relevant data from all who have stakes in a person's or a team's contributions to the organization. We will see working hours shift to meet the needs of customers and team members, not predictable working hours in our time zone as standardized by bureaucracies. We will see computer data links worldwide at all levels of organizations, not just at the pinnacles.

The new paradigm is dependent in many ways on speed of travel and speed of information transfer. Without these, the knowledge necessary to build loyal and trustworthy alliances and partnerships would break down. We will see increasingly sophisticated cost accounting and tracking systems that match cost causes with total costs rather than spreading costs across departments. We will see promotion systems that allow for changes in the strategic and competitive tactical demands facing firms. We will see recruiting systems that focus increasingly on social skills as much as or more than on technical skills, which can be taught and developed more easily.

Infocracies will require new internal organizational skills. Employees and managers alike must be better at listening, eliciting, discussing, encouraging, recognizing feelings, informally influencing, persuading rather than commanding, speaking foreign languages, using computers, focusing on customer-oriented priorities, searching out causes, and paradoxically, attending to more by attending to less, that is, by *focusing* in a way that one can see *more* of what is happening. The new paradigm will require employees and managers who are more facile at intercultural understanding and communication, better at seeing what people have to offer rather than what they look like. We will have to become better at sharing, at taking personal risks in order to model, at praising rather than criticizing, at helping rather than telling; we will have to become better at process observation and intervention. We must learn how to be patient up front in order to be more effective later on. We will require more empathy, that is, we must be able to see the world the way others see it, and less sympathy, that is, we must not try to solve others' problems with our own core of beliefs and values.

The new leaders will be learners, people who are open to new ideas, who value change. The new leaders will be trustworthy, respectworthy, and changeworthy. We will value what others can do and know how to highlight and build on that. We will be clear on who we are and what we stand for, for without a central pool of guiding principles the changes ahead of us would overwhelm. Unlike most aristocratic and many bureaucratic leaders, we will be deeply respectful of the value and dignity of individuals in and near our organizations.

The new leaders of tomorrow will be systems thinkers, able and eager to see ever larger pictures of systems within systems. We will respect individuals regardless of race or gender or religion for what they can do and how they do it. We will be designers and initiators, people who are always looking for a better way, always willing to fix things that are not yet broken, but with a specific purpose in mind. The new leaders will be "and/also" thinkers instead of "either/or" thinkers.[15] The new leaders will be coaches and caretakers, teachers and students, workers as well as managers, and role models as well as instructors.

Timing is important in all of this. Moving too soon is as deadly as moving too late. Remember, if you can, the Nash Metropolitan, which was a compact car designed for urban traffic and ease of parking, with lots of storage space, high gas economy, and sturdy construction. Unfortunately, it was introduced in the early 1950s rather than in 1973, when the oil shock taught people worldwide the value of such cars. The picture telephone was introduced about the same time but is only now coming into its own as a desired technology. Companies who succeed in the new paradigm will have a good sense of timing and be able to take account of the parameters in their industries that either facilitate or inhibit the introduction of the new paradigm. Unfortunately, too often the usual error will be changing too late, and the usual inhibiting factor will be senior or middle level management.

Conclusion

The world around us is changing rapidly. This rate of change is not going to slow down in the near future. Organizations are scrambling to invent new structures and systems to respond and are discovering that the changes are so profound that they require new thinking, values, skills, designs, and leadership. This book is about what that leadership might look like. Our goal is that you will begin to prepare in earnest for the changes that you will encounter during your career and lifetime. The next chapter introduces a simple conceptual framework to help provide a structure for the book and help you to think about how to plan for and develop new skills of leadership.

Principles of Level Three Leadership

1. As the millennium turns, we are in the midst of a major paradigm shift in the way business is done, the way organizations are structured, and the way leadership is working.
2. The Information Revolution is creating new organizational forms that are flatter; are more dependent on fast, accurate information; demand more participation from all members; and must respond more quickly than ever before.
3. The Information Age demands new kinds of leadership that are substantially different from the leadership of the bureaucratic Industrial Age.
4. Many leaders trained and experienced in the Industrial Age will find it difficult to let go of old leadership habits and to learn new ones.
5. Effective leaders in the new Information Age will understand and be masters of the change process.
6. Effective leaders in the new Information Age will be able to coordinate diverse subunits of ethereal, boundaryless organizations that often defy description.
7. Effective leaders in the new Information Age must learn new skills and develop new perspectives.

Questions for Personal Reflection

(These questions are designed for those students who have worked or are working. For those of you taking this course prior to working, these questions may help guide your thinking when you join the workforce.)

1. What kinds of changes have you noticed in your work and organization over the last several years?
2. What role does accurate, current information play in your ability to do your job, to become a more effective leader, and to shape your organization in the future? How well are you able to collect, understand, and utilize that information?
3. Which people in your organization seem to be working on an old, bureaucratic paradigm and which seem to be moving ahead with fresh thinking?
4. Where does your organization rank with the competitors in your industry in terms of moving into the Information Age? Are you ahead? Middle of the pack? Behind?
5. What is your emotional reaction to the changes you see taking place around you? Do you feel threatened or invigorated? Why?
6. What would it take to get your organization moving firmly into the Information Age?

Notes

1. Although many writings support this premise, one good one is *Intentional Revolutions* by Edwin C. Nevis, Joan Lancourt, and Helen G. Vassallo (San Francisco: Jossey-Bass, 1996), p. 6.
2. Human groups, like chickens with their pecking order and many other groups in the animal kingdom, always stratify themselves. We have yet to find a human group that is not stratified. The

only question seems to be "along what criteria?" We will discuss this in greater depth further on in the text.

3. Max Weber, *The Theory of Social and Economic Organization* (New York: Free Press, 1947), p. 131.

4. *Ibid.,* pp. 332–334.

5. Frederick Taylor, *Principles of Scientific Management* (New York: Harper, 1911).

6. Gareth Morgan, *Images of Organization* (Newbury Park, CA: Sage, 1986).

7. "Think in Reverse," *Industry Week,* July 19, 1993, 14. Interview with Bill Davidow and Mike Malone, authors of the book *The Virtual Organization* (New York: HarperBusiness, 1992).

8. Peter Senge, *The Fifth Discipline* (New York: Doubleday Currency, 1990).

9. Warren Bennis, "The Coming Death of Bureaucracy," *think,* IBM, 1966.

10. See, for example, Gifford and Elizabeth Pinchot's book, *The End of Bureaucracy and the Rise of the Intelligent Organization* (San Francisco: Berret Kohler, 1994).

11. James C. Collins and Jerry I. Porras, *Built to Last* (New York: HarperBusiness, 1994).

12. Harold Leavitt, *Corporate Pathfinders* (Homewood, IL: Dow-Jones Irwin, 1986).

13. From a private conversation with a NationsBank executive.

14. Tom Peters, *The Tom Peters Seminar* (New York: Vintage, 1994), p. 29.

15. See, for example, Charles Handy's *The Age of Paradox* (Boston: HBS Press, 1995).

CHAPTER

General Model of Leadership in Organizations

2

A Diamond in the Rough

Chapter Outline

- Leading Strategic Change

- Key Elements of Leadership

- A Diamond in the Rough

- Relationships Are the Key

- How the Diamond Model Relates to Other Models of Leadership

- Leadership Potentialities

- Leading Ethically

- The Diamond Model and What CEOs Do

- Basic Definitions

- Target Levels of Leadership

The chief executive officer of a Fortune 500 company realizes that the way his company has been managing its hundreds of thousands of employees is not working anymore. The woman in charge of a major telecommunications company seeks to revise the culture of her firm so it can compete in the next

Adapted from "Leadership in Organizations," UVA-OB-380, prepared by James G. Clawson. Copyright © 1997 by the Darden Graduate Business School Foundation, Charlottesville, VA. All rights reserved. Reprinted with permission.

century. An Asian member of a global project team developing a new product worries that the approach the team is taking will not work. A single parent facing evening responsibilities wonders how to manage homework and "life's lessons" conversations with headstrong teenagers.

Each of these people faces a similar set of challenges. They are surrounded by the turbulent environment described in the previous chapter; they need to find ways to influence people who may not be interested in being influenced; they operate inside of structures that have a history and a momentum; and they need results. Each of these people needs to find ways of developing influence. Although the scope of their influence varies widely, many of the characteristics they need to develop are the same. Together, they all need to become more effective leaders. It would help if they had a simple, powerful, and generally applicable model of what leadership is and of how to improve their own leadership abilities. Finding this model may not be easy; there are many from which to choose.

Leadership studies over the last one hundred years have focused on various aspects of leadership. Some studies have looked at the traits of well-known leaders in various fields and tried to find the commonalities. After this effort led to lists of traits several hundred items long, researchers focused on the fit between leaders and the situations they were in, the so-called contingency theories. Recently, writers have commented on the importance of values, on the ways in which women lead, on leadership that recognizes diversity, and on the relationship between leadership and a firm's strategic challenges. As we move into a new millennium, we need a model of leadership with an eclectic approach that includes the major leadership principles we have discovered in this century and yet provides for a powerful, flexible application of those principles in a range of settings. This chapter presents such a model.

Why would we need yet another model of leadership? Well, first, we live in a rapidly changing world that needs leaders at every level of society. We need leaders at the international, national, local, neighborhood, and family levels. We need leaders in businesses at all levels regardless of their overall size. We need these leaders because until we all become perfectly and uniformly able to perceive the meaning of present and future events clearly and to act on them effectively, leaders help us see things differently, help us organize our efforts, and help us accomplish things that we might not be able to accomplish otherwise. Yet the leadership models available seem to omit various aspects of leadership that are needed in today's environment. Some models emphasize individuals, others emphasize situations, others emphasize coworkers, others emphasize strategies, and still others emphasize organizational design. We need a model that can allow for all these various aspects of leadership. The model presented here is more of a Jeep than a Cadillac, designed for flexibility, rough terrain, and alternative explorations and tough enough to take the impact of various settings and situations.

Before I introduce this model, let me inquire about your motivation. You may or may not desire to be a leader. This question bothers some people who do not think of themselves as organizational leaders. Perhaps you feel uncomfortable trying to influence others; you are too shy or more interested in doing your work than in getting involved in "office politics." Let me suggest an alternative way to think about this question, and that is to ask whether you would like to have more positive influence on those around you.

You may be thinking of thousands of employees, a few team members, colleagues in a professional firm, other citizens on a local committee, or members of your family. If the answer to that question is "yes," then you can learn something here that will help you develop that influence. Having a flexible but powerful approach to developing that influence will guide your efforts.

LEADING STRATEGIC CHANGE

Our model begins with a key concept, that leadership only has meaning if it has a direction and a means of achieving that direction. In other words, leadership without a strategy is aimless, and leadership without the ability to manage change is powerless. To address leadership, we must address the questions of strategic thinking and of managing change. In essence, leadership is really about leading strategic change. The first question that the leader or leader-to-be needs to answer is "leadership for what?" That is the strategic question. Once that answer is developed, the next question is "how can we get there?" This question usually involves two domains: others, that is, the potential followers; and the organization or the setting in which the leader and the followers work. One way to diagram this three-way view is shown in Figure 2–1. Potential leaders must address all three directions, or vectors, to solve the fundamental problems of "what?" and "how?" These three "directions of attention" provide the basis for a comprehensive, four-wheel drive, utility model of leadership.

Thus, while we speak of leadership, of strategy, and of managing change, we could also speak of, and, I argue, should speak of, *leading strategic change* as a more comprehensive concept. A simple illustration of the overlap of these domains is shown in Figure 2–2.

KEY ELEMENTS OF LEADERSHIP

If we begin with the characteristics of the leader, add that leader's view of the strategy that the organization should follow, and then add the followers and the organization they all work in as shown in Figure 2–1, we have a group of elements that resembles a dia-

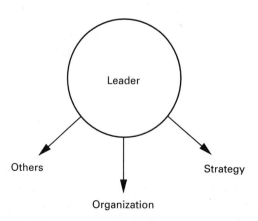

FIGURE 2–1 Three Key Leadership Directions of Attention

FIGURE 2–2 Interconnectedness of Leadership, Strategy, and Managing Change

mond. If we examine the relationship among those four basic elements, we can say that leadership is not just a result of any one of them but of how all the elements work together. In other words, leadership is about much more than the qualities of the leader: It is also about the strategy envisioned by the leader, the leader's relationships with the followers, and the organizational context in which the leader will attempt to influence those followers. In this view, leadership is the result of a confluence of the characteristics of these four main domains and the relationships between and among them, resulting in a total of at least 11 essential factors. Each of these factors—the four basic elements and their relationships—will influence the outcome of a situation as much as the traits of any potential leader would and will help determine any positive results. These four elements and their connections are shown in Figure 2–3. Let us examine each of the elements.

Leader: The Individual Leader

Clearly, the leader, the person—*you*—have characteristics that will influence your ability to create a successful leadership outcome. Each individual leader brings to a situation a variety of personal characteristics, including preferences, skills, values, goals, education, interpersonal style, and a psychological makeup. These attributes shape a leader's abilities to observe, to make sense of and deal with the environment, to understand and relate to followers, to manage change, and to define and work toward a goal. Many leadership theories focus on individual characteristics, but the approach here is that what a leader brings to the situation is only one set, albeit an important set, of factors that will affect the outcomes of that situation.

Task: The Strategy of "What Should We Do?"

Another key domain or element is the set of tasks that confronts the organization. The individual leader's *view* of those tasks, of what the organization should be working on, sets the agenda for an organization and is critical to the leadership outcomes in that situation. Clearly, one person's view of those tasks can vary from another's. Outside observers may see a different set of tasks or challenges that the organization "ought" to be addressing. An individual's ability to read and assess what is taking place around him or her guides

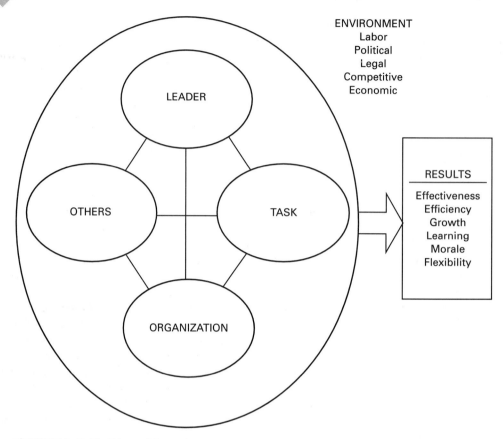

FIGURE 2–3 The Diamond General Model of Leadership

that person's conclusions about what is important and what the organization could do and should do. This view, or vision, of what *needs* to be done, what *can* be done, or what *should* be done will shape virtually all of the person's behavior and, if the person is a leader, will shape the agenda for the rest of the organization. How a person views the challenges facing an organization is clearly a function not only of that person's vision but also of the "realities" facing the organization. I have put the word *realities* in quotation marks because those issues only become realities when the leadership recognizes them and places priority on them. I will continue this discussion in more depth later in this chapter.

Depending on what the leader sees, on what the leader believes he or she can do, and how the leader behaves, the situation might be transformed from a no-change situation into one in which dramatic and positive things begin to happen. Leadership has a lot to do with sensing, seeing, and *appreciating* what is taking place around us.

Others: Working Together with Followers

Leadership does not happen without followership, so any map or model of leadership must include the "others," or followers. The employees and colleagues of the leader also bring to the situation their sets of characteristics, values, preferences, experience, skills, goals, educational background, and concerns. Environmental pressures affect them as well as the leader, but perhaps in different ways. Their personal and collective characteristics help determine whether the leader will be able to develop an influential relationship with them. The quality of that relationship will determine in large part whether the followers will develop a view of the tasks facing the organization similar to the view held by the leader. If the others do not trust or respect the leader, it will be difficult for them to develop commitment for and energy to work on the leader's view of what can be or should be.

Organization: Designing the Right Context

As the leader and employees develop convergent views of what the firm should be doing, the structure of the organization and the systems that hold it together become increasingly important. This organizational subcontext can either enable the leader and the employees to move ahead on their objectives or constrain them from realizing their vision. If the organization's structure and systems do not fit the demands of the task that has been defined, the organization and its leadership will be at a severe disadvantage. Effective leaders are constantly working with questions of whether the organizational context is favorable to the task or mission they have defined. Stan Davis, in his book *Future Perfect,*[1] asserts that *all* organizations are obsolete by definition because of the time lag between the development of a strategic vision and its implementation by an organization. By the time the organization is in place, he says, especially in a turbulent environment, the strategic picture has changed and the organization must be changed again to try to keep up. Peter Senge reinforces this message with his concept of the learning organization in *The Fifth Discipline.*[2] Unless an organization is a learning organization, he notes, it will be unable to keep up with the rapidly changing world as we now know it. Similarly, if the attitudes and abilities of the employees are not matched to or aligned with the systems and structure of the organization, their efforts to achieve the goals of the firm will be diluted and diffused.

A DIAMOND IN THE ROUGH

These four elements—the leader, the followers, the task, and the organization—can be arrayed in the shape of a diamond, as shown in Figure 2–3. An effective leader needs to understand each of the four elements and its characteristics. This basic four-point mental model, or map, of leadership provides the basis for our four-wheel drive vehicle, one that can be applied to a variety of settings and used to understand a multitude of situations. This model is a diamond in the rough because I do not specify exactly which characteristics need to be addressed in each element. As times change, as knowledge increases, our understanding of the importance of different dimensions in each element might evolve. Also, the context in which these elements combine may change.

Environment: The Context

All leadership situations occur within an environmental context that includes political forces, legal forces, labor market realities, financial vicissitudes, increasingly diverse demographics, advancing technology, investor inquiries, and competitive pressures. Although these forces are often overlooked or only given cursory attention, they impact all other elements of a leadership situation, individually and in concert. Effective leaders are adept at scanning and interpreting these external forces and their impact. The previous chapter described how important these environmental changes are in setting a context for one's attempts to lead or influence others.

Results: Outcomes of Leadership

In the end, leadership is about results, about outcomes. The outcomes we see from a leadership situation might include effectiveness, efficiency, growth, learning, and morale. Effectiveness is an important outcome measure because it tells us whether we have accomplished our purpose. Effectiveness measures might include profitability, new product development, client studies completed, and so on. Efficiency is a useful measure because it reminds us of the costs associated with every outcome and encourages a consideration of the value of the cost/benefit perspective. Growth and learning are indicators of health. If the people and the organizations in the leadership situation are not larger and better educated as a result of the leadership experience, we might question the effort. Finally, if people are not engaged in and feeling rewarded by the experience, we might ask whether the effort was worth it. Selecting the right measures of leadership situation outcomes becomes an important issue in and of itself, which I discuss in chapter 11, "Leading Organizational Design."

RELATIONSHIPS ARE THE KEY

Set in an environmental context, the four basic elements—the leader, a set of strategic challenges or tasks, the followers, and the organization—form the key building blocks of leadership outcomes. But although the characteristics of these elements provide the basic raw materials of a leadership situation, it is the *relationships* among them that determine how the situation will turn out. Consider again the diamond-shaped model shown in Figure 2–3.

On the northeast corner, the line between the Leader and the Task represents the relationship between the leader and the challenges facing the organization. This relationship is the substance of what the leader *sees* as critical and forms the crux of the leader's vision of what the organization should be doing. If this axis is broken (that is, if the leader has not developed a vision of what needs to be done and has not set some priorities for self and the organization), the leader has no purpose, no direction, no outlet for attempts to lead or influence. In short, leaders cannot get somewhere if they do not know where they want to go. The relationship between who the leader is and the array of tasks from which the leader may choose defines the leadership agenda, what the leader will choose to focus on and work on.

On the northwest corner, the line between the Leader and the Others represents the relationship between the leader and the followers. The quality of those relationships can be analyzed and examined to determine if they are healthy or "broken." If they are broken, that is, if the leader does not have influence with the followers, not much in the way of leadership will happen no matter how clear the vision (northeast axis) is.

On the southwest corner, the line between the Others and the Organization represents the quality of the connection between the followers and the organization. If this relationship is basically a mercenary one in which people trade time and talent for money, it will be more difficult to lead toward world-class performance, for instance, than if that relationship is a committed one in which the systems and processes of the organization encourage a deeper attachment to the organization.

On the southeast corner, the line between the Organization and the Task represents the match between the various aspects of the organization (structure, systems, processes, culture, etc.) and the strategic challenges facing the organization. If the organization is ill-structured to meet those challenges, it will be difficult to create a positive leadership outcome.

On the east-west axis, the line between the Others and the Task represents the view that the followers take of what they are trying to do. If there is a gap between what the leader sees (the northeast axis) and what the followers see (the east-west axis), it will be difficult to have a positive leadership outcome. If the leader's view of the task (northeast axis) is strong and the leader's relationships with the followers (northwest axis) is strong but the east-west link is broken, it will be difficult to get a positive leadership outcome.

Finally, on the north-south axis, the line between the Leader and the Organization represents the leader's connection to the organization. If the leader's style and skills do not match the way the organization is formed, one or the other will have to change. If the leader is a good organizational designer and a master of managing change, this north-south link will be strong. If the leader comes from the outside and has a style that is at great variance with the characteristics of the organization, it will be difficult to create a positive leadership outcome. I have seen a situation in which an outside leader came in and was clearly at odds with the culture, structure, costing systems, and other features of the organization, and even though he was hired to make changes, the organization eventually rejected him as a body might reject a poorly conducted transplant.

Each of the circled elements portrayed in Figure 2–3, including the environment that surrounds the whole of it, has a variety of features or characteristics that affect the outcome of the leadership opportunity. Leaders who ignore any of elements may not get the results they hope for. Further, understanding the relationships between and among those elements is essential to understanding leadership.

Margaret Wheatley, in her provocative book *Leadership and the New Science,* made an important point:

> One evening, I had a long, exploratory talk with a wise friend who told me that "power in organizations is the capacity generated by relationships." It is a real energy that can only come into existence through relationships. Ever since that conversation, I have changed what I pay attention to in an organization. Now I look carefully at how a workplace organizes its relationships; not its tasks, functions, and hierarchies, but the patterns of relationship and the capacities available to form them.[3]

Although Wheatley was speaking of human relationships, I am convinced that the observation holds as well for the relationships between elements of the diamond model outlined here. The connections are where the interesting insights into leadership effectiveness lie.

HOW THE DIAMOND MODEL RELATES
TO OTHER MODELS OF LEADERSHIP

The diamond framework presented here is flexible enough to incorporate many of the features of the main leadership models popular today, but in a way that is simple and useful for the practicing manager. The diamond model allows a focus on the individual characteristics of the leader, giving room to include the useful elements of the great leader theories. It allows a focus on leader-follower relationships (northwest axis). It also contains a strong contingency flavor in that it asserts that the fit between the leader and the surrounding situation is a critical part of a positive leadership outcome. The model includes the importance of leaders as designers in shaping their organizations. Although the model does not give all the details related to each element or all the relationships that connect them, it does point out the key areas of attention that leaders need to be aware of and understand.

LEADERSHIP POTENTIALITIES

Leadership situations or opportunities can be viewed from another important perspective. Margaret Wheatley, again, notes that every situation in relationships and in organizations can be seen in a number of different ways, and in fact, the way you view the situation can determine its outcomes. Wheatley compares these organizational or relational situations to photons, the tiny particles of light that emanate from the sun. Photons are remarkable in that how you look at them determines what you will see. If you conduct an experiment that tests to see if they are waves of energy, they look like waves of energy. If you look at them expecting to see tiny particles of mass, you will see tiny particles of mass. Physicists speak of photons as having different *potentialities;* that is, they have the potential to be seen as energy or matter.

Like photons, each leadership situation contains a myriad of potentialities. Which one will emerge depends on how the people in that situation see, understand, and behave in that situation. This factor makes leadership that much more important. If a leader is able to see a different potentiality in a situation than others do and is able to convince them of the possibilities, then a different outcome may result. This view is consistent, by the way, with long understood and accepted perspectives on how humans create their own realities. We know that people filter what they see and accept from among all the sensory stimuli that surround them. That filtering process determines what people will pay attention to and spend their energy on.[4] The challenge of the potential leader is to see various potentialities rather than one or two and to find ways of helping those potentialities come to life.

Our basic model allows for that variety of potentialities. We can see the situation from the eyes of the leader, the eyes of the followers, from the context of the organizational structure and other systems, from the point of view of the various tasks that lie in front of the organization, and so on. Depending on what we see and where we focus our energy, we can envision and perhaps create many different leadership-based outcomes to almost any situation.

LEADING ETHICALLY

I have already said that leadership is not an isolated phenomenon. Rather, it occurs in connection with other aspects of organizational life, namely, strategy and managing change, and these three domains—leadership, strategy, and managing change—are all part of the same overall phenomenon. We must add ethics to that picture.

   The relationship between leader and followers always takes on significant moral and ethical dimensions. In fact, I argue that every leadership situation is an ethical situation. Leadership involves the use of power and influence, and this fact raises a long series of questions about when, how, and why a person seeks to gather and to exercise this influence. Who agrees that it is one person's right to influence others? Who decides what kinds of influence are acceptable? How do the followers view the efforts of the leader to influence them? Is it right or wrong for the leader to exert this influence? Do we have the right measures for assessing the outcomes of attempts to lead? Who decides what the right measures are? To what extent do we attempt to influence our environment or allow it to influence us? These and other questions relate to the very important issue of the ethical side of leadership. Figure 2–4 shows how these three domains—strategy, managing change, and ethics—might map onto our general leadership model.

FIGURE 2–4 The Relationship of Strategy, Change, and Ethics to the General
            Model of Leadership

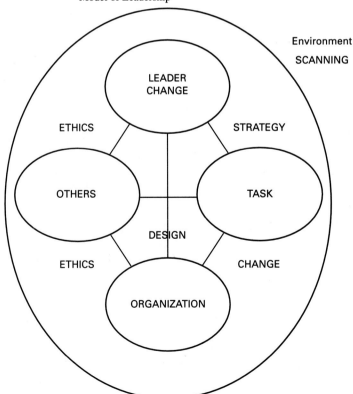

THE DIAMOND MODEL AND WHAT CEOS DO

If the diamond model is an accurate depiction of leadership activity, it should map well onto empirical studies of what leaders do. An important corroboration of this idea comes from a study by Farkas and Wetlaufer as reported in the *Harvard Business Review*.[5] The authors studied 160 chief executive officers (CEOs) of major companies on several continents and concluded that the CEOs used five basic leadership foci. The authors characterized these five foci as strategy, box, human resources, change, and expertise. The *strategy* CEOs emphasized the importance of setting a strategic direction for their firms. The *box* CEOs focused on building organizational control systems and measurements that defined what employees could or could not do. The *human resources* CEOs focused on building human relationships and developing mini-CEOs through their relationships. The *change* CEOs centered their attention on managing change in their organizations in the attempt to keep current with their environments. The *expertise* CEOs focused on developing particular expertise in their organizations to create a competitive advantage.

These modern CEO styles map easily onto our general model as shown in Figure 2–5. The strategy focus aligns with the northeast axis in the model. The human resource

FIGURE 2–5 CEO Styles and the General Model

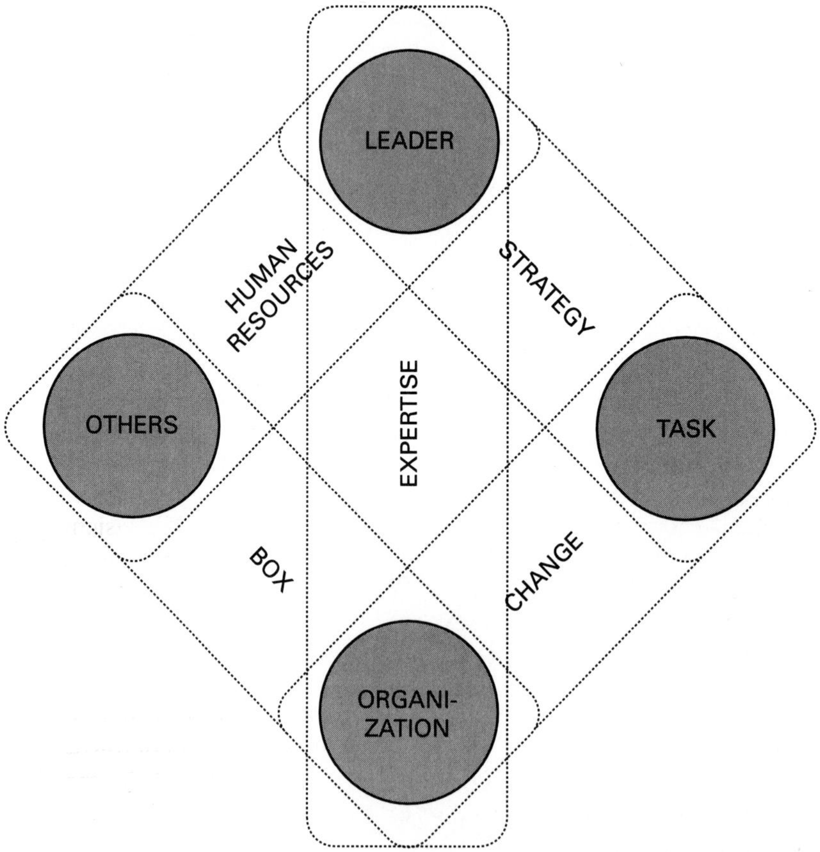

focus maps onto the northwest axis. The box approach parallels our southwest axis, and the change approach gives attention to the southeast link (redesigning the organization so that it fits the demands of the strategy tasks chosen as priorities). The expertise approach maps onto the north-south link because these CEOs built expertise into their organizations. This high degree of overlap suggests that the diamond model of leadership is flexible enough to relate to and help explain the skills needed in leadership situations as defined and implemented by chief executives all over the world.

BASIC DEFINITIONS

Before we continue, I need to establish some working definitions that will help you understand what I mean by leadership and help me be more clear in talking with you about what leadership is and is not. Let us begin with power and leadership. First, I assert that **power** is the ability to make something happen. Power in organizations is the ability to get others to do what you want them to do. There is nothing fancy about this definition; it simply states that when you make a change in something, you are exerting power in that thing. Allow me to return to the physics theme I used earlier and say that the definition of power is similar to the definition of work, which is mass times acceleration. If you exert power, you get something done, you move a person, an organization, a project from here to there.

> **Leadership** is the ability and the willingness to influence others so that they respond willingly.

Leadership, I say, is something different. **Leadership** has three key components: first, the ability to influence others; second, the willingness to influence others; and third, the ability to influence in such a way that others respond *willingly.* Thus, although leadership includes the use of power, not all uses of power are leadership. Consider the three components of this leadership definition.

The first component is the ability to influence others. This ability can be taught. In fact, in *The West Point Way of Leadership,* the author notes that one West Point commandant once said that he could make a leader out of anyone who was not a schizophrenic.[6] Leadership skills cluster around three areas: visioning, garnering the commitment of others, and monitoring and measuring progress toward the vision. The visioning cluster includes gaining a historical perspective, identifying trends in the present, and perceiving the outcomes of those trends in the future. This cluster includes a concern for what might be and could be. It includes the ability to identify signposts along the way. It includes the ability in some sense to dream, to see clearly a desirable picture of the future and to articulate that picture to others.

The skills that cluster around garnering the commitment of others include your communication style, patterns, and abilities. It includes your level of trustworthiness and the quality of the relationships that you develop with others. It includes the ability to listen, that is, to understand and respect the goals and dreams of others so that you can find ways to match those goals with your own.

VCM CLUSTERS OF LEADERSHIP SKILLS

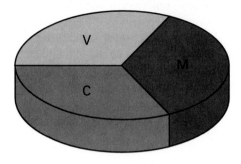

FIGURE 2–6 Vision-
Commitment-Managing Model
of Leadership Skills

The monitoring and measuring skills cluster includes the ability to design and follow measures of progression toward your vision and the ability to praise and to celebrate those who contribute to that progression.[7] This tripartite view of leadership skill development, what we could call the VCM perspective (for visioning, commitment gathering, and monitoring and measuring), is shown in Figure 2–6. Each of these skill clusters include specific skills that you can learn. If you wish, you can, by studying these skills and practicing them, increase your ability as a leader. Whether your increased ability will have the desired effect depends on other factors that we will discuss later.

The second element of our leadership definition is **willingness.** Some people who have the ability to be leaders choose not to exert influence. There are a variety of reasons for this reluctance. Sometimes people are uncomfortable being in center stage and laying out their thoughts and beliefs for others to accept or reject. Sometimes reluctance is based on an ethical conclusion of self-determination above all else. Regardless of the reason, each of us has to decide whether we will accept or seek leadership responsibilities.

Working for seven and a half years as the chief operating officer of a large nonprofit organization involving 2,800 people and eight different operating units, I learned a lot about the practical aspects of leadership. One thing I learned was that in some respects, leadership is like a crucible that either refines or incinerates a person's soul and being. At times you feel like the figurehead on the prow of a clipper ship: Your arms and legs are pinned back against the hull, your face and chest are exposed to the elements and to the flotsam and jetsam of the sea, and you are crashing repeatedly into the waves with nothing to buffer or protect you except your own determination to persist and reach your goal. This aspect of leadership—the loneliness and vulnerability to attack and criticism, justified or not—often causes otherwise capable people to shrink. Even in smaller group settings, the process of exposing your thoughts and feelings and beliefs and analyses to others can be daunting. Clearly, to be a leader, you must develop some mental toughness and ability to endure criticism. Ultimately, to be a leader, you must be willing to attempt to influence others.

The third key element of this definition lies in the willingness of the followers to follow. When the agency of the followers is compromised or removed, that is, when followers are forced or coerced into doing something, leadership ceases to exist and something else takes its place. If you threaten people with their jobs and thereby force them to do what you want, you may indeed be exerting power, but by this definition, you are not leading. If you get people to do what you want them to do but they do not know about it, you have moved into the realm of manipulation. And that, I say, is not leadership. If people feel that they *have* to do what you want them to do for fear of their jobs or their well-being, you have moved out of leadership into coercion. Leadership is not about dictatorship. It is not about force. Leadership is about winning more than the behavior of people, it is about winning their minds and hearts.

People in positions of potential leadership, like chief executive officers or vice presidents or supervisors, sometimes borrow authority from their titles and order people to do things on threat of their livelihoods. My first business school instructor, Stephen Covey, many years ago likened this use of authority to using a crutch to walk; unable to influence on their own merits, people who borrow power from their title to force others to do things are using a leadership crutch. Although they may see short-term results, they are not using leadership, they are using intimidation and coercion, and in the end, such tactics undermine their ability to lead others.

I made a distinction earlier between manipulation and leadership. The deceit involved in manipulation removes the element of follower willingness. If people do not know what you are making them do, how can that be leadership? The question becomes, "If the followers knew what you were doing, how you were doing it, and what your motives were, would they still follow you willingly?" If the answer is "yes," then you do not need to use manipulative techniques and you can claim to be a leader. If the answer is "no," I would not consider you to be a leader, and, I argue, neither would your "followers."

TARGET LEVELS OF LEADERSHIP

I want to introduce now one more important aspect of leadership, what I call *target level*. When we talk about leadership, we usually think of the organizational or institutional level, and we refer to the titular heads of companies or foundations or institutions as their leaders. True, organizational leaders have a broad impact; their decisions can affect thousands of lives. Yet much research and experience suggest that we need leaders at many levels in organizations.[8] Each of the people introduced in the epigraph of this chapter are potential leaders. They all will surely continue in their responsibilities, but to what level of effectiveness and influence? Each work group within an organization needs leadership to guide and manage its daily activities. Think also of individual leadership or self-leadership.[9] If we are unable in some sense to lead ourselves, how can we presume to lead others?

> Leading Strategic Change can occur on at least three levels: organizational, work group, and individual.

The general model in Figure 2–3 applies to organizations, to work groups, and to individuals. These three levels of attention are important to remember throughout the remainder of this book. Later discussions about the ethics of leadership, the need for strategic thinking, the ability to influence others and to redesign structures to unleash potential all relate to each of these levels—the organization, the work group, and you, the individual.

Conclusion

As you reflect on the model in Figure 2–3 and contemplate your own goals and aspirations of leadership, please note that leadership is the *result* of a situation in which people have worked together voluntarily with energy to accomplish some purpose. In this view of leadership, leaders respect the dignity of their followers and recognize the importance and power of self-determination. Leaders work openly rather than covertly to convince, persuade, and guide others to a view of what needs to be done, and, in so doing, build commitment to that view. There are necessary and strong underlying ethical foundations in this approach. Further, leaders often face environmental and organizational contexts that can severely handicap their efforts.

The view of leadership presented here has a respect for various forces at play—including the characteristics of the leader, the characteristics of the followers, the characteristics of the organization, and the characteristics of the environment including the array of strategic possibilities it presents. This view is optimistic about the internal capacities of the followers and about the leader's confidence in and acceptance of his or her own role in guiding those capacities. This view asserts that leadership begins to happen when a person recognizes all the elements of the situation and is willing to work to unlock the potential in each of those elements to make something happen. This view asserts that leadership requires significant, assertive personal attributes, intense effort, and a deep sense of respect for the environment and people. Leadership requires an ability to see and formulate strategy. It requires an ethical foundation on which to build relationships. And it requires a clear sense of appropriate measures and the ability to manage change.

All these features take place at three levels—the individual, the work group, and the organization. Effective leaders understand this and are aware and active at all three levels, are willing to influence organizations and work groups around themselves, are willing to lead strategic change, but are also willing to initiate equally disruptive change in themselves.

Principles of Level Three Leadership

1. Leadership is the result of much more than the personal characteristics of the potential leader. Leadership includes defining a task (setting a strategy), developing influential relationships with followers, designing organizations, and managing change within the organization and with followers in order to achieve the outcomes desired in the task or strategy.

2. Exercising leadership is different than exercising power. Power is getting others to do what you want them to do, but leadership involves ability (skill in influence), willingness to be in the leadership role, and influence that creates voluntary response. Many people who have the skills to lead choose not to because they do not want the leadership role with all its pressures and difficulties.

3. We cannot talk about leadership without talking about strategic thinking, managing change, and ethics. Effective leaders are strategic thinkers, masters of the change process, and ethically grounded.

4. Leadership involves a cluster of skills around creating a vision, another cluster of skills around garnering commitment, and a third cluster of skills around managing progress toward the vision.

5. Leadership occurs at three levels: externally in the organization, externally in the work group, and internally in the self.

Questions for Reflection

1. To what extent do you rely on your position or title to influence others (exercise power)? If your title or position were taken away, would others listen to you? Why or why not?

2. How much time do you spend in strategic thought, in creating a vision for yourself, your work group, or your organization? How could you increase this time?

3. How comfortable are you with the change process? Do you understand it? Do you feel like you are a master at managing it?

4. Why is it important for a potential leader to have a clear vision or dream in order to become an effective leader?

5. Recall an authority figure in your past who influenced you through power rather than leadership as defined here. How did you respond to that person? What were your thoughts about that experience? What did you learn from that experience?

Notes

1. Stanley M. Davis, *Future Perfect* (Reading, MA: Addison-Wesley, 1987).

2. Peter Senge, *The Fifth Discipline: The Art and Practice of the Learning Organization* (New York: Doubleday, 1990).

3. Margaret Wheatley, *Leadership and the New Science* (San Francisco: Berrett-Koehler, 1992), pp. 38–39.

4. See *The Social Construction of Reality* by Peter L. Berger and Thomas Luckmann (New York: Doubleday, 1966).

5. Charles M. Farkas and Suzy Wetlaufer, "The Ways Chief Executive Officers Lead," *Harvard Business Review,* May 1996.

6. Larry Donnithorne, *The West Point Way of Leadership* (New York: Currency Doubleday, 1993).

7. See *The Leadership Challenge* by James Kouzes and Barry Posner (San Francisco: Jossey Bass, 1987).

8. See *The Leadership Factor* by John Kotter (New York: Free Press, 1988) for a discussion of the "little 'l' leadership" needed everywhere in organizations.

9. See Charles Manz, "Self Leadership," *Academy of Management Review* 11, no. 3 (July 1986): 585.

CHAPTER

Levels of Leadership

3

Chapter Outline

- Body, Head, and Heart

- Connecting Three Levels to Scholarly Views

- Learning Level Three Leadership

- The Strong History of Level One Leadership

- The Focus of Level Three Leadership

- The Dark Side Potential of Level Three Leadership and Engagement

- Organizational Implications

- Applying Level Three Leadership at Both the Individual and Organizational Levels

> *For every thousand hacking away at the leaves*
> *of evil, there is one striking at the root.*
> —Henry David Thoreau

Before we begin to address the various aspects of the general model, there is an important set of ideas we need to consider. These ideas have to do with the difference between focusing on the superficial and focusing on the deeper, more powerful aspects of leadership. Leadership is about affecting human activity. Human activity can be thought of as occurring at three levels: observable behavior, conscious thought, and basic values and assumptions. Behavior is simply that which others do, that which

TABLE 3-1 Basic Levels of Human Activity	
Level One:	Behaviors
	(Observable)
	(Not observable)
Level Two:	Conscious thoughts
Level Three:	Values, assumptions,
	beliefs, and expectations

we can observe with a camera with sound equipment. People speak and act. They make gestures and movements that we can see and hear. This behavior is what I call Level One activity.

At Level Two, people have conscious thoughts that they may or may not reveal to us. Although we may not be aware of these thoughts, the person very much is. Our attempts to lead others may or may not pay attention to what others are thinking.

At a deeper level—I call it Level Three—people hold a set of values, assumptions, beliefs, and expectations. These values and beliefs have developed over time and have become so much a part of the person that they may be only partially visible or available to the person. These **VABEs (values, assumptions, beliefs, and expectations)** are therefore semiconscious or partially conscious collections of what we have come to think of as the way the world should be. These three levels are shown in Table 3–1; the heavy line denotes a separation between what we can see and what we cannot.

Of these three levels, behavior is the most readily available because it is visible to us. Levels Two and Three are available to us only through two means: (1) when people decide to reveal themselves to us, and (2) through our observations of their behavior—through which we can infer what those VABEs might be. Both of these methods are imprecise. We cannot always be sure that what someone says is an accurate reflection of what they are thinking. They may be hesitant to tell us the truth, or they may not be very clear in their own minds about their thinking. If we are careful when we observe people, we may get some good clues about why people behave the way they do. In fact, sometimes our observations may give us a clearer picture than if we just listened to what they said. People do not always behave consistently with their stated beliefs.

Because it is seemingly difficult to understand Levels Two and Three, we often deal with people only at the level of their behavior; it is simpler and seemingly more accurate. In fact, many theorists and observers argue strongly that leaders can only deal with Level One and that attempts to influence Levels Two and Three are unethical and an invasion of privacy. This argument is a Skinnerian view. B. F. Skinner, the famous psychologist, conducted research and wrote extensively, arguing that we could condition animals and people to behave in certain ways by managing the mechanisms by which they were rewarded.[1] You may recall learning about one of his many experiments: He put a chicken in a box with a button, and when the chicken pecked on the button, it was rewarded with a kernel of corn. By reinforcing the pecking behavior with the corn, Skinner was able to teach the chicken to peck in a certain way. Skinnerians, then, tend to argue that leadership should focus on behavior and not think about nor worry about what goes inside a person.

The model presented in this book is decidedly not Skinnerian. Rather, recognizing the levels of conscious thought and of somewhat vague but strongly held values, I assert that effective leadership must take into account Levels Two and Three. Unless we do, we have little hope of understanding why people behave the way they do and of influencing them in profound ways, ways that move beyond monitoring and constraining behavior.

BODY, HEAD, AND HEART

Because behavior is decidedly physical and observable, we can liken Level One to the body. Some companies and managers have explicitly stated their wish that employees would check their thoughts and emotions at the door and just do their jobs. In essence, this philosophy is focused on Level One and attempts to manage behavior in isolation. A commonly quoted joke is that companies are frustrated because they hire workers and people keep coming to work. I assert that most managerial systems since the beginning of the Industrial Revolution have focused on Level One, on behavior, with much less attention on Levels Two and Three. Frederick Taylor's work on time-motion studies around the turn of the century, for instance, focused largely on managing the behavior of employees and devoted little attention to their inner thinking and feeling.[2] The underlying assumption here is that people are like machines and that the goal of the managerial systems is to minimize variance from work objectives by managing people to behave in the most efficient manner.

Increasingly, in a changing world with enormous volumes of information available to employees at every rank, the centralized control mentality is outdated and unworkable. People keep bringing their heads and their hearts to work, and these influence their behavior constantly. Further, as competition increases, corporations are concerned about building high performance workplaces in which employees at all levels are committed and engaged in serving customers. The present approach argues that unless management can tap into the potentials at Levels Two and Three, the company will be unable to compete with the best of their competitors. Unless the whole employee is engaged in the work, the work will not be as high quality as it otherwise would be. Focusing on Level One is insufficient for obtaining commitment and engagement.

Effective leadership also needs to influence Level Two. Level Two, or thought, is that of which *we* are immediately aware in ourselves, our conscious processes. We think thoughts and choose whether to communicate them, and if we do, whether to communicate them accurately. We are aware of Level Two activity within ourselves, and we presume it in others. We can liken Level Two to the mind because that is where Level Two action takes place.

Level Three, VABEs, refers to the deep-seated beliefs that we hold about what, for us, has become so true in life that we take it for granted and no longer need to think about or reflect on it. Level Three includes our hierarchy of priorities, our list of what we value most. It includes our summary of the "shoulds" and "oughts" in the world, the way the world and the people in it should behave.

Our VABEs are by nature highly cultural and family specific. The circumstances of where we were born and grew up, the quality of our relationships with our parents and what they taught us, in fact, all our life's experiences, have contributed to the set of VABEs we hold as adults.

In a sense, our VABEs are like limestone caverns. The interior of these caverns is dark and wet. Over time, tiny drops of limestone-laden water drip from the ceilings and land on the floors. As they do, evaporating partially each time, a small deposit is left.

After millions of repetitions, these deposits form into stalactites and stalagmites. Some of these structures are thin and easily broken. Others are thick and may even have formed into solid columns extending from ceiling to floor. Our VABEs are like these limestone structures. Some are pretty weak; others are central pillars to our personality and views of the world. Some have become so familiar to us that we no longer notice them.

To see our own Level Three VABEs, we often need assistance. Like fish swimming in water, or birds flying in air, we have come to take for granted these fundamental VABEs and to assume their verity. Thoughtful, honest conversations with others, particularly people who are skilled in recognizing VABEs when they see them, can be very helpful for both parties in clarifying what a person's—or an organization's—VABEs are. This does *not* mean that you have to be a psychologist to be a Level Three Leader. Psychology is the study of where a person's VABEs come from. Management and leadership has to do with *recognizing* what the VABEs are and then working with that person or organization to accomplish some goals with those VABEs.

VABEs come in a variety of forms. They are usually most clear when stated as sentences, statements of fact, or normative declarations (X should Y), for instance, "People should tell the truth," "The early bird gets the worm," "Be respectful to your elders," "Don't spit in public," and so on. Many VABEs are weak, but others are quite strong and central to our way of living. Whenever you hear a person say "should" or "really oughta wanna," or "Good Xs do it this way," your personal VABE radar should go "beep beep beep" because that person has just revealed to you a portion of their VABEs. If you watch and listen, you can pick up a lot about a person's VABEs.

Level Three, then, is a gray area between conscious thought and the subconscious, an area that may be available to us, but about which we seldom think and into which we seldom delve. Yet Level Three controls our lives, our thinking, and clearly our judgments about what we view to be "right" or "wrong." We can liken Level Three to the heart although there is no physiological evidence that our values, assumptions, beliefs, and expectations in any way reside there.

These three levels of human activity are closely intertwined. Clearly our VABEs affect our thinking, and clearly our thinking affects our behavior. The Skinnerians, on the other hand, argue that our behavior affects our thoughts and feelings. The effective Level Three Leader will be aware of these flowing influences and will strive to influence all three levels, not just one. A singular focus on behavior ignores two-thirds of what makes people do what they do.

CONNECTING THREE LEVELS TO SCHOLARLY VIEWS

This three-level view of human activity is straightforward and is well understood by scholars and many practicing leaders. In discussing the development of leadership in ethnic and organizational cultures, for instance, Ed Schein, arguably the world's leading authority on the subject, introduces what he calls three levels of cultural manifestations: (1) artifacts, the visible structures and processes of a culture; (2) espoused values, the espoused justifications for behavior; and (3) basic underlying assumptions, the "unconscious, taken-for-granted beliefs, perceptions, thoughts, and feelings" that drive culture.[3]

If you are interested in further exploration of Schein's work, his book contains an excellent description of how these underlying basic assumptions are formed and how they shape individual and organizational behavior.

LEARNING LEVEL THREE LEADERSHIP

If you accept the assertion that human activity occurs at three levels and that leaders should pay attention to all three levels, the next question you ask is "How do I learn Level Three Leadership?" The first step is to unlearn many things you have come to believe about how to lead. The present definition of leadership—the ability and willingness to influence people to do willingly what you want them to do—might have read, "influencing people to do what you want them to do." The target of this definition is Level One, or behavior.

This approach would approximate much of the bureaucratic or "traditional" approach to leadership taken over the last two hundred years of the industrial era. In bureaucracies, the fitting of individuals into jobs and the attempt to control variance from job descriptions are Level One approaches to leadership. When we use this bureaucratic approach to lead, we are not concerned with what people think or personally care about; rather, we only want them to do as we ask, and in return we give them some reward. In essence, this relationship is a mercenary one, an exchange of time and some effort for money. Often, in a traditional leadership situation focused on Level One, the employees' minds and hearts are not engaged in the work even though their bodies may be going through the motions.

Many people in leadership positions subscribe to a Level One definition of leadership. They are uncomfortable with tinkering with a person's mind or personality, and they believe that an ethical approach is to focus only on behavior. For such leaders, the carrot and stick method is tried-and-true: Entice employees with carrots, and if they do not respond, beat them with sticks. This distinctly Skinnerian view puts human thought and value as the indiscernible content of a hidden box, irrelevant to the goals of a leader. I agree that people should be rewarded for desirable behavior and that it is folly to hope for one behavior while intentionally or unintentionally rewarding another.[4] However, I also believe that, although people will work for rewards and thus their behavior may be adjusted in order to get those rewards, people also value different rewards. To one person, extra pay is an incentive, whereas to another, job fulfillment is a stronger incentive. People will indeed exchange time and some effort for financial return, in some cases, for a pitifully small financial return. Much of the research about operant conditioning in psychology and about its cousin, expectancy theory in management, has attempted to clarify the connections between reward and behavior.[5] Even expectancy theory—which asserts that motivation to effort, in general, is a function of people's belief that they can do a task times their belief that they will be rewarded for doing that task times the value of that reward to them—begins to question the strictly Skinnerian view. If a person does not value the reward, expectancy theorists note, the motivation of the individual declines rapidly.

The other side of the carrot and stick approach is that workers are not motivated naturally, that they need to be "managed," watched carefully, given minute instructions, and told what to do moment by moment. If the kernel of corn or the paycheck is the carrot, the stick is to threaten people with punishment if they do not perform correctly. Clearly this Level One approach is time consuming and is not likely to produce world-class performance.

The often overlooked implication of the carrot and stick approach (which, by the way, implies that the object of attention in the middle is a mule) is that leaders have to take into account what is happening inside the workers in addition to observing their external behavior. Expectancy theorists, therefore, want to know what rewards people value and why. This decidedly non-Skinnerian viewpoint leads to the concept that leaders must understand and work with more than behavior, that effective leaders must work at Levels Two and Three.

People are different from machines and animals in many ways, although leaders for at least one hundred years have taken a mechanistic view of organizations.[6] Our abilities to think and to value one thing above another set us apart. We also believe that human behavior is so closely connected to both thought and to values and basic assumptions that if we hope to understand why people behave the way they do, we must understand something about their thought processes and their hierarchies of values and basic assumptions about the way the world *ought* to be.

Further, our very definition of leadership implies that in true leadership-followership situations, the *willingness* of the followers is essential to effective leadership. If so, we must be concerned with what people think and feel. Otherwise, we cannot tell if we are leaving the realm of leadership and are beginning to wander into strong-over-weak power relationships in which the durability of the employees' willingness to comply with the leader's wishes comes into question. If the leader retreats or goes away, what do the followers do and why? If the rewards offered by the leader go away, what do the followers do and why? If followers choose to continue performing as they were asked, perhaps leadership is truly occurring. If not, perhaps what was happening was not leadership but some kind of power relationship.

THE STRONG HISTORY OF LEVEL ONE LEADERSHIP

Level One Leadership is not very powerful; indeed, it may not even be leadership. When we focus only on the behavior of workers and ignore and downplay an understanding of what they are thinking and believing and feeling, we retreat from leadership as influencing others to respond willingly and move toward an exchange or coercion-based relationship. In this kind of relationship, employees are aware that management, the self-proclaimed "leaders," are not interested in them as people, only as cogs in the bureaucratic machinery or as means to a goal. Consequently, their level of engagement in the work and their commitment to fulfill it will decline. If and when this kind of relationship is tested by events or situations that hit at or question what the employees think or believe, their loyalty to the Level One Leader will be severely threatened. Their stamina for continuing the requested activity will seep away. Their willingness to contribute creative thought and passionate effort will be drained off. Employees who are subjected to Level One Leadership for long periods of time will become what the system has systematically encouraged them to become, mentally and emotionally disengaged from their work. They bring their bodies to the job, but leave their minds and hearts at the entrance, out of gear and idling in neutral.

Level One Leadership, the traditional approach, worked remarkably well for a long time. Worldwide economies were expanding, labor was relatively inexpensive and easy to find, and the relative stability of domestic markets allowed managements to view labor as a commodity, like plants and equipment. In this light, the formation of the labor unions can been seen as a reaction to this impersonal approach. Nevertheless, the system worked and companies grew and were profitable.

Today, however, the environment has changed so dramatically, and continues to do so, and competition has become so fierce that management teams can no longer successfully compete by using that kind of mercenary, Level One relationship with their employees. Everywhere now, leaders are looking for ways to create high-performance workplaces. Unfortunately, many managers retain their old management principles while attempting to apply the new, emerging leadership techniques superficially, at Level One. This half-hearted attempt can be observed when a company applies the latest management fad—be it TQM, empowerment, or self-directed work teams—without making concomitant changes in the other aspects of the organizational reality, like reward systems, promotion systems, training, structures, operating cultures, and leadership approach. Many of these new systems are targeted at Levels Two and Three. If they are applied in a Level One way, they often fail, and those who tried say, "See, I told you. This won't work." This gap between a new program and the old, persistent style of managing breeds alienation in the workforce. It also inhibits the trust and respect necessary to begin developing a Level Three kind of leadership that recognizes, relates to, and deals with employees' thoughts and values.

THE FOCUS OF LEVEL THREE LEADERSHIP

Level Two and Level Three Leadership recognize the importance of the thoughts and values of potential followers. Level Three Leadership assumes that effective leadership speaks to people's hearts and is able to engage them in profound ways, almost regardless of compensation. Whereas Level One Leadership focuses on getting movement out of people, Level Three Leadership seeks engagement. Level Three Leadership recognizes that today's generation of workers, at least in the industrialized world where poverty and famine are for the most part peripheral issues, are looking for more than a monthly paycheck; they are looking for meaningful work that is worthy of not only their time and talent but also of their creativity and heartfelt commitment.

Level Three Leadership recognizes that in a service-oriented economy, workers who are not engaged at Level Three will not deliver customer satisfaction. In a Level One leadership organization, the myriad "moments of truth," that is, when the service or product is delivered to the customer, will be found by the customer to be unsatisfying and irritating.[7] The fast-food drive-in window employee operating at Level One delivers the sack of food with a fake smile and, when questioned about the four missing items, says, "I put them in there, you must not be seeing them," and then gives you an impatient look because you are holding up the line. Level One employees are going through the motions. In a world in which competition is growing, some companies are learning how to organize large numbers of employees to care about what the customer thinks and feels; those companies offer alternatives that are more attractive to customers tired of dealing with Level One employees.

Level Three Leadership seeks to understand the basic assumptions and values of people and to lead employees toward harmony with the goals and strategic directions of the firm. Level Three Leadership recognizes the importance of dealing with people at this level and rejects the basic assumption that leaders do not need to know what people are thinking and feeling. Level Three Leadership assumes that employees' behavior is closely intertwined with their thoughts and feelings.

Clearly, Level Three Leadership is more work for the individual leader, especially on the front end. As I said at the outset, it is not easy, without practice and skill development, to infer what people are thinking and believing. The real questions in this book, though, are "Are you willing to work at Levels Two and Three, or are you going to continue working at Level One? Are you willing to learn how to engage people not only in their behavior, but also in their hearts and minds?" If you are whispering to yourself, "I don't care what they think or feel, I just want a good day's work for a good day's wages," I invite you to pause and reflect on the consequences of your approach. Will you be able to organize a high-performance workplace with a series of exchange-based mercenary relationships? Will you be able to develop an organizational culture of excellence and quality if your management team is constantly worried about controlling and guiding employees' behavior when they are not there? Can you expect to create an organization characterized by extraordinary performance if you work only at Level One? What does it take to get extraordinary performance?

You may be thinking that there are lots of people out there who do not *want* to be engaged in their work, who want only to work a day, collect their paycheck, and go home. That is Level One thinking. A Level Two or Level Three question might be to ask yourself, "Go home to what? What is it that motivates these people? Do they drudge through work and then go home and begin yelling enthusiastically during the match at their local bowling or softball league?" If you followed them around before and after work, would you ever find them working hard, even passionately, to accomplish some goal? What would that goal be? If you can imagine them doing *something* with passion, you might ask yourself, "How can I get some of that passion here at work?" Maybe there are some people who go home to nothing. Maybe their level of activity at home is even lower than at work in a Level One organization. If so, you are not going to make a significant change in their lives. Perhaps then you need to reexamine and redesign the recruiting system that invited these people to work in your organization.

THE DARK SIDE POTENTIAL OF LEVEL THREE LEADERSHIP AND ENGAGEMENT

If you accept the thesis that effective leadership works at Levels Two and Three, there is a danger of which you should be aware. When people work on something that they believe in and value, they often work very hard. When they work on something that they believe in and are focused on the goals of the effort, they can work so hard that they begin to do damage to themselves, working excessively and burning out. This burnout can extend to others, to coworkers and subordinates who are asked to do more than they can or should.

More and more literature is appearing that describes this phenomenon, and my guess is that it will continue to grow as the pace of the world, the volume of information available to us, and the pressures of stiffened competition continue. If you are interested in this topic, you might read *Workaholics* by Marilyn Machlowitz, *Working Ourselves to Death* by Diane Fassel, or *The Addictive Organization* by Anne Wilson Schaef and Diane Fassel. Although Level Three Leadership can lead to extraordinary results and deeply committed relationships between individuals and their companies, it can lead to the dark side of burnout and exhaustion.

Working with people at Levels Two and Three initially requires more effort and more involvement on the leader's part, but it promises a more committed group of followers and higher quality of production. The need for management involvement begins to dissipate when the work group reaches the point at which they can function without the boss's oversight and can function at a high level of productivity with high levels of quality. Level Three Leadership is front-end loaded; you make a significant investment up front learning and focusing on coworkers' Level Three values, but once you understand those values and can align them with the work, your need to monitor and manage drops significantly.

Because it targets coworkers' VABEs, Level Three Leadership also brings to the fore several ethical issues. These issues are important enough to be introduced separately in the next chapter.

ORGANIZATIONAL IMPLICATIONS

So far, we have discussed Level Three Leadership primarily from individual and interpersonal perspectives. We can also speak of three levels of activity in a broader, organizational sense. A Level One, behavioral or superficial, focus in organizational leadership is reflected in the application of the latest fads or techniques. Level One Leaders read about the latest technique in the literature and try to apply these techniques over the top of their existing organizations. I see this behavior a lot in managements that attempt to apply the current hot topic to their organizations without a consideration of how these new techniques affect all the other interrelated systems and structures and cultures of the organization. Sometimes this tendency manifests itself by managements that commission expensive educational programs—but never attend personally.

Level Two at the organization includes the organizational design of its structure, its key systems, and the formal design of the firm. These consciously, historically designed aspects of the organization are the result of conscious thought; hence we can align them with Level Two.

The way in which an organization's design factors combine with the people who work in it—including the managerial or leadership style of the people in charge—to create a set of values, assumptions, beliefs, and expectations about how people in the organization should behave is the organizational culture (and subcultures). Level Three in the organization is the organizational culture, the set of commonly held values and operating principles that people have come to take for granted as the "way we do things around here." These cultural realities may or may not line up with the formal organization and its subordinate designs. When they do not, the designers have experienced "unintended consequences."

Level Three in the organization, like in the individual, is semiconscious. Some employees may be able to talk about aspects of the extant culture, others may not be clear enough about it to articulate it—although they behave it. Using Chris Argyris's terms,

TABLE 3-2 Levels of Organizational Activity	
Level One:	Managerial fad (short-term programs)
Level Two:	Intentional organizational design (structure and systems)
Level Three:	Organizational culture and operating values

Level Two is the espoused theory of the organization, whereas Level Three is the theory-in-action.[8] These elements are shown in Table 3–2. They differ somewhat from Ed Schein's characterization, yet for our purposes here they illustrate the potential differences among what managers do (trying to apply the latest fad in the literature), what they think about the organization (its structure and processes), and what they believe deeply about how to manage and organize.

APPLYING LEVEL THREE LEADERSHIP AT BOTH THE INDIVIDUAL AND ORGANIZATIONAL LEVELS

Level Three Leadership works at Level Three in both individual relationships and in the management of the organization. In both instances, Level Three Leadership assumes that high performance only comes when the central features of Levels One, Two, and Three are all aligned. When there are variations between the directions and main thrusts across these three levels, between what people or organizations do, think, and feel, inefficiencies are introduced and leadership becomes diffused and ineffective.

Increasingly in today's turbulent world, leaders who want to be effective must learn to influence people at Level Three. The titular power bases of bureaucracies continue to melt. Personal influence is increasingly more important. Although Level One is seemingly faster and there are two centuries of momentum for dealing with people at Level One, the increasing importance of customer service moments of truth and the explosion in worldwide competition demand that employees participate in a world-class effort—often an effort based on high levels of engagement at all levels of an organization—if an organization is going to survive and thrive. Although the up-front costs of learning to influence people at Level Three may be more time consuming than the costs of operating at Level One, the long-term benefits include more deeply committed employees and coworkers, higher quality work, more satisfied customers, and a higher probability of surviving. The downside is that Level Three Leaders must learn to recognize and manage in themselves and others the dangers of overworking and burnout. This observation leads to a consideration of the moral aspects of Level Three Leadership, which is addressed in the next chapter.

Principles of Level Three Leadership

1. Level One Leadership, which focuses only on behavior, ignores two major sources of motivation for most people: What they think and what they believe and feel.

2. Level Three Leadership, which is aware of and influences people's values and basic assumptions, has the potential of being far more powerful than Level One Leadership.

3. Level Three Leadership does not imply that managers must be psychologists (who study the origins of values and assumptions), but it does imply that effective leaders will be skilled in recognizing and clarifying VABEs in the people they work with.

4. VABEs affect thoughts and thoughts affect behavior, and probably the reverse is true also. Consequently, effective leaders will pay attention to all three levels.

5. Historically, most leaders in the Industrial Age have targeted Level One. In the new Information Age, effective leaders must be aware of and understand and target Levels Two and Three.

6. Levels One, Two, and Three apply to organizations as well as to individuals. Most organizational leaders focus on Level One and ignore the realities of Levels Two and Three.

Questions for Reflection

1. What are your boss's VABEs? Your coworkers'? Can you write these VABEs down? If you listened more carefully, could you figure them out?

2. What are your basic values and assumptions about the way your organization should be working? Can you write these down? In other words, can you see the Level Three culture of your organization clearly enough to write it down?

3. Identify the ways during the past week that you have behaved as a Level One Leader. At home? At work? In your avocation? What was the impact of these behaviors?

4. How could you have behaved as a Level Three Leader during the episodes you identified in question 3?

Notes

1. See for example, B. F. Skinner, *Walden Two* (New York: Macmillan, 1976) or *Beyond Freedom and Dignity* (New York: Bantam, 1971).

2. See Frederick Winslow Taylor, *The Principles of Scientific Management* (New York: Harper & Brothers, 1911).

3. Ed Schein, *Organizational Culture and Leadership* (San Francisco: Jossey-Bass, 1992), 17.

4. See Steven Kerr's classic article, "On the Folly of Rewarding A while Hoping for B," *Academy of Management Journal* 18 (1975): 769–783.

5. See, for example, Robert Merton, *Social Theory and Social Structure* (New York: Free Press, 1957) and Edward E. Lawler III, *The Ultimate Advantage: Creating the High-Involvement Organization* (San Francisco: Jossey-Bass, 1992).

6. For a good summary of this phenomenon, see chapter 2 in Gareth Morgan, *Images of Organizations* (Newbury Park, CA: Sage, 1986).

7. For a nice discussion of the importance of moments of truth in service industries, see Jan Carlzon, *Moments of Truth* (New York: HarperCollins, 1987).

8. See, for example, Chris Argyris, *Reasoning, Learning, and Action: Individual and Organizational* (San Francisco: Jossey-Bass, 1992).

C H A P T E R

The Moral Foundation
of Extraordinary Leadership

Chapter Outline

■ Morality, Ethics, and Legality

■ Morality and Leadership

■ Universality of the Moral Rock of Level Three Leadership

What you do thunders so loudly in my ears, I cannot hear what you say.
— RALPH WALDO EMERSON

All leadership has a moral dimension, and Level Three Leadership must give consideration to morality. Because leadership is about influencing others, it begs the questions of whether it is right to do so and what means should be employed. Some people feel very strongly that they have no right or desire to influence others and prefer that others be left alone to determine the path of their lives without external pressures. In an increasingly crowded, an electronically, economically, and environmentally connected, and a potentially hostile world, the freedom to determine one's own life path is becoming difficult. Decisions made by strangers minutes or miles or continents away affect our daily lives in many ways. Yet there is this dilemma that within our sphere of contacts and acquaintances, we choose whether to try to get others to change the way they behave, and if you accept the premise of the previous chapter, think and believe.

MORALITY, ETHICS, AND LEGALITY

Let us make a distinction for the moment between morals, ethics, and legalities. **Morality** is the individual determination of what is right and wrong. An act may be immoral to a person but is not viewed as unethical or illegal by other authorities. At the same time, what may be moral to one person may be immoral or unethical or illegal to others. Groups of people may or may not share views of what is moral or what is right and wrong, and they may attach judgments of others to those determinations. Typically, if a group judges the behavior of a person to be immoral or wrong, the group will ostracize that individual.

Ethics are the established and accepted guidelines of behavior for groups or institutions. To be a physician, for instance, you must accept the code of ethics set down by the licensing board of the medical profession. If you violate that code, you can lose your membership in that professional group. Ethical behavior varies from professional group to group. Ethical considerations have to do with right and wrong, as does morality, but in the context of a professional group's standards. If the criteria for membership in the professional group are fuzzy—as in business management, for example, which has no comprehensive governing body like medicine or law does—the definition of ethical behavior becomes more problematic. As with morality, violation of the ethics established by a group usually results in expulsion from that group.

Legality has to do with obeying the established laws of a society. Violations of the laws are illegal, but they may or may not be viewed by members of that society as immoral or unethical. For instance, many people violate the posted speed limits on major highways almost with impunity, obviously not believing that to do so is wrong or immoral or professionally unethical.

As we strive to clarify the moral dimension of leadership, we can use these definitions of morality, ethics, and legality, but we can also use a stakeholder perspective that speaks of harms and benefits to others.[1] If we can first identify all those people who would be influenced by an act, that is, the stakeholders in a situation, we could then assess whether the act is harming or benefiting those people. Does the attempt to influence another person harm or benefit him or her? If the act harms another, the act may be immoral.

MORALITY AND LEADERSHIP

Leadership creates many moral questions. We can begin, as I have already noted, with the question of a person's right to influence another person. Is there such a right? Does that influence in any way abridge the "unalienable rights" that Thomas Jefferson and America's other founders declared accrued to all humankind? Does everyone have a right to "life, liberty, the pursuit of happiness," and freedom from influence? We live in a social world. Unless we live as hermits (and even then), we are unable to escape the influence of others' decisions. Whether we intend it or not, our choices are having influence on others. The routes we take in traffic, the way we manage our garbage, the purchases we make, at one level, all have influence. Some people, perhaps including those who have been victimized, resent the very notion of leadership, of one person's intention to influence and guide another's behavior. Anyone who chooses to lead is choosing to influence others and should, I think, be aware of the moral responsibilities of that role. Leaders have an impact, and if that impact is negative, the leaders must bear at least part of the responsibility for the outcomes. Bearing this responsibility is another reason why, as I mentioned earlier, some talented people shrink from leadership situations.

The three-part definition of leadership that was presented in chapter 2 has several moral positions in it. First, I said that individuals have the right to choose whether they wish to influence others. Many are not willing to do so and yet are thrust into positions of leadership. These people often wrestle with the emotional and moral burden of their roles, but because of their desire to be "successful," they may continue in the leadership position. Others choose to take on leadership positions, but they are seemingly unaware and uncaring about the consequences of their leadership decisions. Leaders should be aware of the impact of leadership and should assess whether that impact is harmful or beneficial.

Second, I said that not all people have the same ability to influence should they choose to try. Leadership ability varies, and a person may choose to develop that ability or not. Leadership ability usually includes finding a vision, a goal toward which the community should, in the eyes of the leader, work. The leader exercises his or her skills to obtain that goal and, in galvanizing the efforts of others, engages them in this cause. Some people with strong leadership abilities may choose, as did Hitler and Stalin, goals that we would say are immoral, are wrong. Others may choose more worthy goals, as Gandhi did. Using our leadership skills forces us to consider the value of our objectives.

Third, I said that leadership involves influence, not coercion, that true followers follow *willingly.* Leaders have, I believe, a moral obligation to use influence, not force. I differentiate between the two actions; people who use force, I argue, are no longer practicing leadership. They may be using power, but they are not leading.

In summary, leadership has a very strong moral dimension, and many moral questions are embedded in it. Level Three Leadership purports to influence not only what people do and think, but also what they believe and feel. This level of leadership is, in some sense, an invasion of privacy, an exploration into the basic assumptions and values of another person. Whether we should engage in this level of leadership and how we would implement this level of influence are also moral issues. At this point, our discussion requires a few additional definitions.

> **Manipulation** is getting people to do what you want them to do without them agreeing to or knowing what you are doing.

Some managers view values-based leadership as manipulation. I see two kinds of manipulation: deceptive manipulation and coercive manipulation. Deceptive manipulation is when we maneuver people to do certain things but they are not aware of the forces influencing them. Coercive manipulation is when we maneuver people into choosing what we want them to instead of what they would have freely chosen.

Both kinds of manipulation are, I say, immoral or wrong in the sense that they violate our definition of leadership—the followers are not following willingly. Only when people have full information and freedom to choose can they be enabled as followers. Further, manipulations involve violations of several moral principles, which I will outline later in this chapter and which also undermine our ability to lead. When people discover at some point, as they always do, that they have been manipulated or been "had" or been treated unfairly, their motivation and interest in following the so-called leader drops precipitously. Manipulation is not leadership. Manipulation is a leadership counterfeit used by some people who believe that they are getting what they want out of a situation by

TABLE 4-1 The Four Cornerstones of the Moral Foundation of Effective Leadership
Truth telling
Promise keeping
Fairness
Respect for the individual

"leading," but the net result is distrust, lack of respect, and weak relationships that will not produce quality over the long run. Manipulation is a short-term fix used by people who lack leadership to cover up their own inadequacies.

The Moral Foundation of Effective Leadership

Because Level Three Leadership involves moral issues, we need to find a moral foundation for exercising this kind of leadership. I believe that there are four cornerstones to what I call *the moral foundation of leadership.* Without these four cornerstones, I do not believe that leadership will be effective or long lasting. These four pillars of leadership are truth telling, promise keeping, fairness, and respect for the individual (see Table 4–1).[2] We could actually distill these four ideas down to the last principle, respect for the individual, because people who have respect for other people would not lie, break promises, or be unfair. In a sense, then, these four principles are different windows onto the same core moral concept of integrity in relationships. However, I find it useful to look at respect for the individual in greater detail by breaking out the other three dimensions. In the end, though, how we answer the question, "Are you showing respect for the individual?" is a good indicator of how we apply the other three principles.

Truth Telling

Truth telling in leadership means telling the other person the truth as you see it when it will have an impact on the other person. Although it may seem trite to say that truth telling is a moral foundation for effective leadership, I find that not all managers or would-be leaders believe in truth telling. During one seminar in which senior managers of a major firm were gathered together to discuss leadership and influence, they were considering the question, "Should one tell the truth in business?" As the discussion progressed, the group became violently divided on this question, so much so that at one point individuals were literally standing on chairs and pounding the table and pointing and shouting at their "colleagues" across the room. Those managers who argued in favor of truth telling, whether it be to employees or customers or suppliers or the press or the parent company or whatever stakeholder, said that business is based on trust and that if the ability to trust another (either to behave consistently or to behave with our best interests at heart) erodes, the ability to do business disappears. People may do one deal, but they will not do two. Those managers who argued against truth telling said that if businesses told people the truth (e.g., how much money the company is making on a deal, the quality of the product, etc.), they would not be able to do any business, in part because deals are based on margins, margins are a product of people's perceptions, and truth telling destroys perceptions.

> The truth, as you see it and communicate it to others, is a great crucible that burns out would-be leaders and hardens effective and true leaders.

I believe that truth telling is essential to effective leadership. If you are unwilling to tell people the truth, you will not be able to lead them, if for no other reason than they will be unable to respond to your ultimate goals *willingly*. The truth, as you see it and communicate it to others, is a great crucible. It refines relationships by cleaning out hidden goals, ulterior motives, suppressed resentments, manufactured conclusions, and uncertainties about the values of the other person. Exchanging the truth as you see it is an essential part of the mutual, fair exchange that must occur for business to function.

People feel that they need to withhold the truth for a variety of reasons. Sometimes people feel pressured to withhold or distort the truth when there is bad news—bad news either from an objective viewpoint, from a personal viewpoint, or from an imagined viewpoint of the other person. This need to withhold is true in part because we sometimes give data more evaluative power than exists inherently in it. In another view, though, data is just data. Some of it may be disconfirming to our present style of behavior, some may be confirming, but in the end, whether we accept the data or reject it is entirely up to us. People are constantly accepting, rejecting, discounting, distorting, or ignoring the information that they receive. When we imagine that others will attribute to our data a negative, evaluative overtone, or when we fear that the receiver will punish us for telling the truth as we see it, we are under influence to not tell the truth. On the other side of the relationship, if potential leaders cannot create an atmosphere around them in which others are encouraged to tell the truth and find it safe to do so, the business will be making decisions based on late or faulty or incomplete information far too often.

In relationships, feedback from others is data, neither moral nor immoral, neither right nor wrong until we respond to it, either accepting it or rejecting it or doing something about it. The challenge for the person listening to another person's truth telling is to remain nondefensive with ears and heart open, listening carefully to what is being communicated. Too often people begin to get defensive immediately and miss the main message or its meaning. If you can also view the information you give to others in this light, you can learn to tell your truth more effectively.

Promise Keeping

Promises today often seem made to be broken. Management leaks to the press information from confidential meetings, executives in offices of public trust are indicted for insider trading and other forms of fraud, and commitments to employees seem to be routinely changed or broken outright. Worse, executives seem willing to make whatever promises are necessary to "keep the lid" on a management situation and all too ready to abandon those promises a few short months later. Broken promises are destructive to trust and respect and ultimately to leadership. They are also characteristic of addictive behavior in which people promise without intention of following through in order to get what they want in the short run. To the extent that willing followership is a function of trust, promise keeping is an essential leadership skill and a part of the moral foundation of effective leadership. People who make promises or commitments and then break them are like the shepherd who cried wolf too many times; before long the community did not believe anymore. Potential leaders need to be careful of making commitments—and then careful of keeping the ones they make. Broken promises quickly undermine leader-follower relationships.

Fairness

Fairness is part of the moral foundation of effective leadership because it ensures that the followers will get their share of the rewards of the enterprise. When employees begin to perceive that they are not being treated fairly, their motivation to follow declines drastically. Much has been made recently about the gaps between the salaries of first line employees and chief executive officers. Most reports indicate that in Japan CEO salaries average about 9 to 10 times that of production employees. In Europe, the figure ranges from 9 to 15 times, while in the United States, the figure is closer to 25 times.[3] You may believe that this gap is fair in that the senior managers are more experienced, better trained, more valuable to the firm, brighter, and . . . any number of other reasons. Whether these reasons are valid does not matter, however, because if the workers perceive an imbalance between their compensation and that of the managers in the organization, distrust will set in and productivity and performance will suffer. Why should we follow someone who has been proven to withhold fair compensation for value added and who is likely, therefore, to be exploiting the organization and its members for personal gain?

Fairness was less of an issue in traditional organizations than it will be in the new organizations because information about the health of the firm will be much more broadly distributed. If the employees do not know the financial picture of the firm, they might be managed or manipulated to accept lower wages and still work hard. In the new organizations, though, with large and readily available information networks, employees will have better information about the health of the firm and its industry, so that data about a firm and its distribution of resources will be increasingly difficult to manipulate.

Respect for the Individual

The first three moral cornerstones of effective leadership can be distilled into the last: respect for the individual. When we tell the truth, we respect the other person well enough to be honest. When we keep our promises, we show respect for the other person. When we treat other people fairly, we are being respectful. Respect for the individual means viewing and treating others as human beings with dignity who have value and who are adding value to the mission of the enterprise. Respect for the individual means believing that all individuals have some intrinsic worth and should be treated with courtesy and kindness. I am reminded of the common Buddhist greeting in Southeastern Asia in which the greeter brings palms together in front, gives a slight bow, and says *Namaste,* "I respect the part of god that is within you." Every person has something divine in him or her; Level Three Leaders show respect for that.

Respect does not mean that all individuals should have equal influence on self or others, only that all should be treated with basic human courtesy. The assumption is that because they live, people deserve to be treated with dignity. Paradoxically, treating people with respect accrues respect to the leader and enhances a leader's circle of influence, because all who observe this display of courtesy will grow in respect for the leader. Yet many "leaders," people in positions of influence, begin to lose sight of and respect for workers in the lower ranks of the organization. Those managers begin to judge the relative contributions of employees to the firm's outcomes according to their rank and to treat people based on that judgment. Those workers that the managers judge to be in the lower end of the distribution of contributors are treated with some disdain and perhaps even outright disrespect. This lack of respect can have disastrous results.

The Normal Distribution of Employees' Value Added

Any given group of people will be distributed from high performers to moderate performers to weaker performers when compared with the other members of that group. This distribution is true of any organization. Also, regardless of the organization, members will vary in their contributions to the organization's mission. This distribution of performance will likely approximate the normal distribution that is shown in Figure 4–1, which contains a small group of extraordinary performers, a large group of good enough performers, and a small group of subpar performers. One of the challenges for the effective leader is to move the good enough group toward the extraordinary tail. How can a leader encourage good enough workers to work extraordinarily? In other words, how can a leader shift the performance distribution to the right? Recognizing and using the moral foundation of leadership is key to this movement. Unless you are able to engage good enough people and motivate them to perform as 4s and 5s, your organization will continue to perform at the good enough, but not great, level. Unless you have a moral foundation in your leadership attempts, you will be unable to lead more people to perform at the 4 and 5 level.

Let us test that assertion. Ask yourself, "If I tell my people, or if we tell each other, the truth half of the time, can we become an extraordinary team? If we keep our promises to each other half of the time, can we become world-class performers? If we treat each other fairly half of the time, can we become the competitor to beat in our business? If we show respect for each other half of the time, can we be world-class leaders?" My guess is that you answered "no" to each of these questions. If so, then you agree that the moral rock, or foundation, is essential to effective leadership.

I agree that an established moral foundation does not guarantee that you will be able to shift the performance curve to the right, but I believe that the moral foundation enables that shift. Leadership has two main foci: first, the moral foundation and, second,

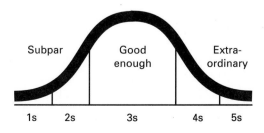

FIGURE 4–1 A Normal Distribution of Performance

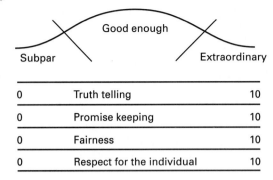

FIGURE 4–2 The Moral Rock
of Effective Leadership

leadership skills. If the four cornerstones are not in place, you will not have the basis for a shift to the right. I assert that without that foundation, you can practice leadership skills (like strategic thinking, effective speaking, and good organizational design work) until you are blue in the face and still have no chance of moving the group's performance to the right. On the other hand, if you have already established the moral foundation, you must still exercise all your leadership skills in order to improve performance. In this view, the moral foundation is a necessary precondition for an improvement in performance, and leadership skills are the motive force that gets the performance to shift; the more leadership skills you pile on top of the moral foundation, the more efficiently you can get the distribution to shift.

You may think that the 2s and 3s in an organization are not motivated. As soon as you begin believing and operating on this principle, you begin to lose respect for the individual, and your communications and actions will belie your beliefs. It may be that these people simply are not motivated by what is happening at work or the way in which that work is presented and organized. What if you were to follow these people home? You might find that many of them perform in nonwork activities with extraordinary quality, performing well in activities that engage them deeply. These people may be rescue squad volunteers, cloggers, softball players, bowlers, church administrators, or little league coaches. The challenge to the effective leader is to find ways to engage the extraordinary capabilities of the employees and to channel that energy in part toward the goals of the enterprise.

One of the most direct ways of engaging people's best efforts, and therefore of developing Level Three Leadership skills, is to build your leadership attempts on the moral rock described earlier, that is, consistently telling the truth, keeping promises, and treating people fairly and with respect. I have diagrammed this relationship in Figure 4–2 and have placed the four dimensions of the moral rock below the normal curve of performance. My observation is that the more that leaders believe in and behave in accordance with the moral rock dimensions, the more powerful their relationships with their employees and the more extraordinary the performance of those employees will be. You can see in Figure 4–2 that each of the four cornerstones has been put on a 10–point scale. You might do a little self-assessment of your work group and rate your team as a group on each of these four dimensions. A score of 10 means that you practice that dimension all, or 100 percent, of the time. A score of 5 would mean that you practice that dimension half, or 50 percent, of the time and so on.

UNIVERSALITY OF THE MORAL ROCK
OF LEVEL THREE LEADERSHIP

Is the moral rock of Level Three Leadership possible for all? Does respect for the individual mean that we have to like all our employees or strive to have them like us? Is this general approach reasonable? What do you think?

My answer is "yes." Moral leadership is possible for all, and it does not require necessarily that you like each individual on your team. It does require that you recognize the potential of every individual and find it a worthy challenge to bring that potential to the fore. Sterling Livingston's classic article, *Pygmalion in Management,* cites the *My Fair Lady* story as a powerful example.[4] Dr. Higgins was able to bring out of Eliza that which others could not see and did not work to bring forth. The challenge of effective leadership is to bring out the best in others.

I acknowledge that many people choose not to treat others with respect. Many managers do not show respect for others but at the same time claim to be leaders of integrity. I believe that effective leadership is Level Three Leadership and that Level Three Leadership is built on the moral rock that has been described. This moral rock is what integrity means to me. People often claim integrity and defend their own possession of it vigorously, yet never stop to examine what it is and how it plays out in dealings with suppliers, employees, and customers. Integrity means to be whole, to be unified. How can we not tell the truth and have integrity? How can we not tell the truth and yet expect employees to respond willingly to our attempts to influence them? How can we break promises and claim integrity? How can we treat people unfairly and claim to be leaders with integrity?

This line of reasoning does not necessarily mean that everyone will like the leader or that the leader will like all the employees. This framework allows plenty of room for disagreements and, at the same time, for mutual respect for each other and the basic beliefs on which the relationship is built. Even though disagreements may occur, the moral rock in place ensures that those disagreements are clear, on the table, and well understood. All participants have invested time in showing respect for the other persons, in understanding all the aspects of the disagreements, and in clarifying the issues for everyone. Obviously, if the topic of disagreement is major, it may lead to a parting of the ways, but the parting will be based on mutual understanding rather than manipulation, deceit, jealousies, or contempt.

Commitment to the moral rock dimensions is evident in an effective leader's behavior. It emanates from a person's center so that in speeches, conversations, meetings, plans, and programs, the four basic principles are evident. A good exercise is to have senior groups pause and assess themselves on these four dimensions; when they do, the insight of the group jumps another level. In one senior management meeting, it was evident that the people in the room were not using the moral rock principles and that their company was suffering from ordinary performance. One of my colleagues, although at a first meeting with the group, interrupted and introduced the moral rock dimensions and then asked the group to rate privately its past and present behavior on each of the four dimensions on a scale of 1 to 10 as described in Figure 4–2. A few minutes later, the senior executives in the room reported average scores between 3 and 5 for each of the four dimensions. A lively discussion then ensued as to whether the group would be able to manage itself, much less the company, unless dramatic changes were made in the ways that they dealt with each other. This senior group began working immediately on improving their abilities to use the moral rock dimensions. They discovered that making that kind of Level Three change was not easy, yet each agreed that it was necessary if the executives hoped to move the company from ordinary to extraordinary performance.

This point is portrayed powerfully by survey results reported in *Industry Week* magazine. Two independent national polling firms conducted surveys of American middle managers over a 10–year span, from 1973 to 1983. (When contacted, the publisher revealed that a 1993 study had also been held and was used privately in consultation.) In these controlled samples of middle managers from many industries across America, two basic questions were asked: "Do you trust senior management?" and "Do you respect senior management?" In the 1973 results, the "yes" answers averaged about two-thirds. By 1983, the "yes" answers had fallen to about one-third. This survey makes me wonder how they can manage, much less lead, their businesses if two-thirds of the middle managers do not trust or respect senior management.[5]

Another indicator of the universal applicability and impact of morally founded leadership comes from my own research in which surveys and interviews were given to more than 100 matched pairs of superiors and subordinates in a large insurance company. Both individuals in the relationships rated how much the subordinate had learned in the relationship, which is a measure of the superior's influence on the subordinate at Levels Two and Three. In addition, measures of more than 50 characteristics of the individuals and their relationship were included in the survey. The results indicated that the combined levels of *trust* and *respect* accounted for about three-quarters, yes, 75 percent, of the variance in the amount of learning in the relationship.[6] Both these studies suggest that trust and respect are key factors in successful management and leadership relationships.

Conclusion

Effective leadership is built on a foundation of moral principles. If you ignore these principles, your attempts to lead will be undermined. On the other hand, if you can establish trust and respect among your colleagues by practicing the four cornerstones of moral leadership—truth telling, promise keeping, fairness, and respect for the individual—then you will have a foundation from which your attempts to lead can spring. Leading morally will not ensure dramatic results, but it will enable your other leadership skills to have influence.

Principles of Level Three Leadership

1. All effective leadership has a moral foundation.
2. Effective leaders tell the truth.
3. Effective leaders keep their promises.
4. Effective leaders treat people fairly.
5. Effective leaders have and show respect for the individual.

Questions for Reflection

1. Could you be an effective leader if you told your people the truth half of the time? If you kept your promises to them half of the time?

2. Rate your current work group on the four cornerstones of the moral foundation on scales from 0 to 10. (See the Self-Assessment Exercise that follows.)
3. What could you do to strengthen the moral foundation of your leadership base and of the leadership base of your organization?
4. How does the moral foundation of leadership relate to the concept of Level Three Leadership?

Self-Assessment Exercise: The Moral Foundation for Extraordinary Performance of My Work Group

Rate your current work group on the following dimensions. Zero means "none of the time" and 100 means "all of the time." After you have made your rating, ask all members of your work group to give their ratings, anonymously if necessary; then calculate the averages and discuss the results.

Truth Telling

0	50	100

Promise Keeping

0	50	100

Fairness

0	50	100

Respect for the Individual

0	50	100

WORK GROUP AVERAGES:

TT = _____   PK = _____   F = _____   RFI = _____

Implications of these scores?

Notes

1. See Ed Freeman, *Strategic Management: A Stakeholder Approach* (Marshfield, MA: Pitman, 1984).

2. This concept was first introduced to me by my colleague Alex Horniman, who developed it while head of the Olsson Center for Business Ethics at the Darden School. The ideas are also apparently used by Rich Teerlink, CEO of Harley Davidson, as noted in Tom Peters, *The Tom Peters Seminar* (New York: Vintage Books, 1994), 81.

3. See the Towers Perrin salary study reported in *Industry Week* (June 15, 1992): 29.

4. Sterling Livingston, "Pygmalion in Management," *Harvard Business Review* (September 1988).

5. Bruce Jacobs and William Miller, "The Verdict on Corporate Management," *Industry Week* (July 25, 1983): 58.

6. James G. Clawson, "The Role of Interpersonal Respect and Trust in Developmental Relationships," *International Journal of Mentoring,* Spring, 1990.

Part II: The Individual Leader

CHAPTER

Six Steps to Effective Leadership

Chapter Outline

- Clarifying Your Center

- Clarifying What Is Possible

- Clarifying What Others Can Contribute

- Supporting Others So They Can Contribute

- Being Relentless

- Measuring and Celebrating Progress

The northern, or top, element in the diamond general model of leadership introduced in chapter 2 is *leader* and refers to characteristics of you as a potential
leader. My assertion throughout this book is that "you can make a difference."
Whether you want to or choose to is up to you. How large a difference over how large a
circle of influence is also up to you. You can choose whether to influence one other, ten
others, or millions of others and in what way.

Of course, each choice carries with it demands and consequences. If you choose to
influence millions, your choice will require that you spend your time among the millions
constantly working to gain their followership. This lifestyle is very different from the one
chosen by a person who wishes only to influence a few or none. Whatever lifestyle you
choose will have consequences for you and those around you. It is important to remember, though, that the choice is yours.

Adapted from "Six Steps to Effective Leadership," (UVA-OB-617), copyright © 1996 by the University of Virginia
Darden School Foundation, Charlottesville, VA. All rights reserved. Written by James G. Clawson. Reprinted with
permission.

Let us assume for the moment that you want to influence others, to be a leader. That is the wrong start. You have put the cart before the horse, so to speak, and your results are likely to be mixed or inconsequential. Effective leaders do not start out wishing to be leaders. The title, the position, the stature, the power, the accoutrements of leadership do not wear well on those who seek them as the primary goal.

Rather, ask yourself, "what value do I want to add to society (my community)?" or "what changes do I believe deep down are necessary to improve my organization, my world (my community)?" Truly effective leaders begin with a cause, a purpose, a goal that serves fellow citizens—not with the goal of being the "leader" because the position appears attractive, powerful, respected, and well paid. In my experience, those people who seek leadership positions mostly for the position's sake ultimately end up being caretakers who do little and are not long remembered.

Think about leadership. Reflect on people you know who have set goals to "be" some title and made it. What did they do once they became leaders? My guess is that their administrations were confused, ill directed, diffuse in policy and results, and not particularly powerful in accomplishing good for the society. Behaving as and becoming an effective leader is a by-product of an intense commitment to a purpose.

> Behaving as and becoming an effective leader is a by-product of an intense commitment to a purpose.

The effective leader is one who has a powerful purpose. In the relentless desire to accomplish that purpose, a person becomes a leader, influencing others voluntarily to join in that purpose. Without this purposeful base, so-called leaders are little more than caretakers, maintainers, and perhaps even self-aggrandizers. They seek title and prestige for their own gratification rather than to serve or improve the world around them.

The question in this chapter is, "if you want to develop your leadership skills, how can you proceed?" I recommend six steps (see Figure 5–1) that can, if you pursue them vigorously, make you a more effective, powerful leader. Notice that these steps all use the present participle form of the verb, the "-ing" form. I use this verb form intentionally to communicate the idea that none of these steps are binary processes; that is, you do not choose to either do the step or not do the step, nor do you do the step once and then are done with it. Rather, each step is a process that involves a lifelong commitment to continuous improvement and constant polishing, revisiting, and adjusting. These six steps become a way of life; you do not just put them on for a few moments to impress others, nor are they a goal that, once achieved, is fixed forever. Such a simple approach to these steps will surely not make you an effective leader.

1. Clarifying Your Center
2. Clarifying What Is Possible
3. Clarifying What Others Can Contribute
4. Supporting Others So They Can Contribute
5. Being Relentless
6. Measuring and Celebrating Progress

FIGURE 5–1 Six Steps to Effective Leadership

Let me make one more point. Although I name six steps here, I do not think of them as a recipe for becoming a leader. If these principles become a part of your life, you will be an effective leader; on the other hand, these principles cannot be faked or be effective if used in a half-hearted way. If you reflect on these principles and think about how they are connected, they can guide your efforts toward making things happen.

CLARIFYING YOUR CENTER

James Allen once noted, "as a man thinketh, so he is."[1] This perspective begs the question, "What is at a person's core, or center?" The answer is that our core, or center, contains our basic assumptions about the way the world ought to be and about what is most important to us in the world. In other words, at our center are our VABEs, which we discussed in chapter 3.

Your center and its contents are crucial to your ability to lead. When your center is clear and focused, you are more likely to have a powerful influence on others. When your center is foggy and diffuse, you are less able to move others. Physically, emotionally, socially, and organizationally, you will be off balance and unable to provide dependable anchor points to others.

A clear and focused center can be demonstrated physically. Students of the martial arts, for instance, learn to stand in a stable manner and in balance. They focus on their physical center of gravity, which in aikido is called the *one-point*, a physical metaphor for the VABE concept of center. A physically centered person is very difficult to move. You can push and shove, and this person stands stably without wavering. The same stability is true of people who are centered socially and in life. As a former mentor once commented, such people have "mass."

When you are centered, you cannot be unsettled or dissuaded or knocked off balance by opposing forces, shifting currents of approval or disapproval, unstable foundations, or even censure by those you love. Once you understand the strength of this concept, you will begin to develop a desire to clarify your center. As you do so, you will become more calm, more purposeful, more stable in the midst of turbulence around you. Although you can practice some physical techniques to develop this capacity, clarifying your emotional center is about clarifying what you believe in and value. Centering, therefore, is often a reflective, meditative exercise.

We can never fully clarify our center. The reason is that we can never fully experience all of life, and life will constantly impact and force us to revisit and polish, perhaps remold, our core values. We may think we know how we would react in a given situation, we may hope we know, but the truth is we will never really know how we would react in a given situation until we have encountered that situation at least once—probably several times.

Here is an extreme but poignant example. Although I did not serve in the military during the Vietnam War, many of my classmates did. Since then, I have felt compelled to read about their experiences. Mark Baker's book *Nam* is a compilation of firsthand, eyewitness accounts of what it was like to prepare for, go to, fight in, and return from Vietnam.[2] One account tells of a platoon of young Americans who had been days on patrol in a free-fire zone; they were tired, hungry, scared, and, pumped full of adrenaline, on a keen edge. At one point, they spotted an elderly Vietnamese man and a young woman on a motor scooter. They stopped the two, searched their bags, and found American canned fruit. They accused the man of stealing the fruit from American soldiers. The old man protested. As he did, two of the soldiers took the young woman, his granddaughter he said, out into the rice paddy and raped her. The rest of the platoon lined up. When the old man protested, someone shot him almost in half with automatic weapons fire. When they were all done with the girl, they killed her.

Most of us find this story appalling and disgusting. Most of us would like to think that our reactions would have been different if we had been members of that platoon. We can imagine ourselves, at 19, standing up to our platoon mates, saying, "Don't do this!" or "This won't happen here!" Perhaps we can imagine ourselves even being willing to lose our lives to not participate in or silently support the episode.

Yet, truthfully, we do not really know what we would do if threatened with death by our "friends," people with whom we had trained, ate, and slept, people we had saved and been saved by. If we had previously been attacked by young women and children with rifles and grenades or if we were hungry and not thinking clearly or if we for any reason were unable to see a grandfather and his granddaughter as individuals worthy of respect, our actual reactions might be different from those we conjured up while we contemplated the situation from the comfort of our living rooms or classrooms. We need to be constantly clarifying our center, to be thinking about, practicing, and behaving in accord with our basic values.

We can explore and polish our center, and we can resolve and reinforce our core values from time to time. If we wish to change our approach to life's situations, it behooves us to explore, examine, and refine our center. We need constantly to be as clear as we can about what we carry in our center and how we will implement its content as we live.

I once visited *Matsushita Seikei Juku,* a leadership institute established in Kanagawa, Japan, by the founder of Matsushita Electric Company, Konosuke Matsushita. A truly remarkable individual, Matsushita and his leadership style have been the subject of several books.[3] His school of leadership was no less remarkable. In 1993, the school received more than 250 completed applications, yet only 5 applicants were admitted to study, an application-to-admit ratio of 50:1. The program of study is five years. The first year of study has no faculty and no courses. At the end of the first year, students are given a one-question examination. If they fail, they are out. The question is, "What is your life's purpose?" First-year students are given the year to determine their life's mission. The underlying assumption is that to qualify for leadership, people must know their life's mission; otherwise, how could they purport to lead others? It is a simple but powerful tenet.

Are you clear on what your life's mission is? Are you clear about what is at your center? Do you know what you stand for? If not, you will find it difficult to lead. Are you willing to spend some time wrestling with this issue? If you were at the Matsushita Leadership Institute, you would have an entire year, with no other distractions, to explore the single question of life's purpose. Are you willing to devote a month, a semester, something less than a year, to answering that question? Chapter 7, "Resonance, Leadership, and the Purpose of Life," was designed in large part to help you think about the fundamental question of life's purpose. Following are some additional suggestions for how you can begin to clarify your center.

Clarifying What You Stand For/Engagement

Many people go through life never clarifying their center. They live and die having never tested their inner beliefs to see if and how they hold up under fire. Many people avoid leadership roles that would call their center into activity and hence never become leaders. One way to begin clarifying your center is to identify what *engages* you. I mean here more than what interests you or, as Stephen Covey would say, what "concerns" you.[4] I mean, what is it that captures your imagination, your leisure thinking moments, and your dreams? What is it that causes you to smile spontaneously, to increase your pulse, and to speak animatedly with others? What is it that motivates you into expending tremendous energy, mental and physical?

Leadership is an act of engagement.

—ALEX HORNIMAN

The answers to these questions are the beginnings of a description of your core, your center. My colleague Alex Horniman is fond of saying that leadership is an act of engagement. When we are truly engaged in something, we begin to influence others without even trying. They begin to notice the energy and excellence with which we pursue our engagement, they begin to hear the animation in our voices, they begin to see our motivation, and this energy rubs off on them and they want to be a part of it. In effect, we have begun to lead without even trying. When we are truly engaged, leadership just begins to happen. Engagement is contagious; it spreads spontaneously so that others begin to feel it and to be swept into it.

Identifying and examining your central engagements can help clarify the content of your center. The process, again, can even help you refine and redirect the content of your engagements. This centering process will be critical to your becoming more influential. Such introspection is not something you can do in an afternoon, and it is certainly not a simple task. Clarifying your center by reviewing and refining your engagements will cause you to be constantly polishing your definition of who you are. The next step in that process is looking at the process values that you hold, that is, looking at the *how* of getting to the realization of your core engagements.

Developing Character/End versus Means

People's character is the sum of their choices of goals and choices about how to achieve those goals. This definition implies a moral dimension to leadership. One way to check the moral level of your leadership, that is, your respect for the follower, is to ask yourself if, given your behavior toward the other person, you would be willing to trade places with that person immediately. If not, you might ask yourself if you are behaving with respect for the individual.

A common second method is to imagine that your dealings with this person were suddenly made into headlines on the front page of the national newspaper you read. Would you be proud to have the story out in public for all to see? Or would you find yourself leaving out certain conversations, side deals, or actions in hopes of being better thought of? If you hesitate with either of these tests, I suggest that you rethink your attempts to influence the other person and that you reflect on what this hesitation might mean in terms of clarifying your center.

Various Forms of Meditation

A third method for clarifying your center is more metaphysical and involves various forms of meditation. People often find increasing clarity on their centers by praying, meditating, or practicing stress-reducing exercises. The physical centering that is done in martial arts training can also help. And interestingly, the physical practice of centering can help you strengthen your center and manage your life. My experience studying aikido, for instance, helped me see new ways of thinking about my life and about my relationships. You can achieve a remarkable sense of calm and peace if you learn to sit or stand quietly for several moments, to focus your mind on your breathing (breathing in through your nose and out through your mouth), and to let all other thoughts leave your mind. This physical/mental exercise puts you in touch more clearly with what you believe and feel.

As I have already said, we are never finished clarifying our center. It does not make sense then to wait to influence others until the center is completely clear. We still have to carry on with our lives even if we have not reached a final realization or even if life is not crystal clear at the moment.

The strategic corollary to clarifying your center is clarifying what is possible for you and your work group, organization, or society. If you clarify your center but have no view of what the future holds for those around you, not much will happen. The second step to effective leadership is clarifying what is possible.

CLARIFYING WHAT IS POSSIBLE

Clarifying your center involves looking inward to the core, whereas clarifying what is possible involves looking outward to the extreme. For most of us, this exercise stretches our horizons beyond what we usually see and apprehend. To clarify what is possible is to imagine in sharp detail what can and should happen for an individual or an institution in the future. In essence, this step is strategic thinking. Chapter 8 is devoted to that topic, but I can make some general comments now.

Stan Davis, in his excellent book *Future Perfect,* claims that leaders think in the future perfect tense; that is, leaders have seen what they want to accomplish so clearly and understand the steps to that dream so carefully that they literally speak in the future perfect tense. A leaders will say, for instance, that "when we have achieved our dream, we will have done A, B, and C."[5] It is as if the leader is working backward having *seen,* as Martin Luther King Jr. put it, the promised land. Most of us do not see the promised land or even the quadrant of the future in which it lies. Effective leaders have seen this future and therefore know where they are trying to go. You can call it strategic thinking or visioning or whatever you want, but effective leaders have an idea in their minds about what they are trying to do.

Clarifying Mental Images of What Can Be

Clarifying your mental images of what you or your organization can become is not easy. It requires getting out of present mental boxes, relaxing present mental constraints (assumptions), and vigorously pursuing a mental mural painstakingly put together with thousands of mosaic thought tiles. Some of us may find this clarification easy when imagining a romantic liaison or playing a major league baseball game or driving to the world championship on the Formula One circuit. With these exciting pursuits in mind, we can imagine tiny details of how we would behave in those situations. Effective leaders have this same energy about their personal and organizational dreams and visions. To become an effective leader, you must develop this skill.

One of the biggest difficulties in developing mental pictures of the future is allocating time to the process. Most of us do not turn off the phone, close the door, put our feet up and simply think, think hard about where we are going and how we are going to get there. In the rush to respond to the daily press of mail, phone messages, meetings, and emergencies, we spend our working lives, as Covey puts it, in Quadrant I,[6] working on high-priority items that have become urgent. In so doing, we lose sight of, and even lose the desire to gain sight of, the long view. Of course, I am not saying that strategic thinking and visioning is just a result of putting your feet up and thinking; I offer more about strategic thinking in chapter 8.

Another difficulty we face is keeping these future-oriented images current in our minds. We often glimpse the future and then lose sight of it in our daily routines. For instance, can you state from memory your organization's mission statement? Pulling the card out from your wallet does not count. If you cannot keep your future clearly in mind, that image cannot influence your thinking, much less the thinking of the people you interact with daily.

Furthermore, can you see clearly where your organization should be in 5, 10, 20, 50, or 100 years? You may find this question silly. Many participants in my executive education classes do. They wrestle, they say, with 30- and 90-day horizons, maybe a 360-day horizon, but argue that they cannot see what is going to happen months down the road, much less years, especially in this increasingly turbulent world.

Konosuke Matsushita, again, provides an interesting counterpoint. Asked in the late 1980s if he was concerned about the recent losses his firm, Matsushita Denki, was sustaining, he said, "No, everything was on schedule." When asked how long his schedule extended, he replied, "250 years"! He had a vision of his firm, the firm he founded, that extended through ten 25-year periods. Each period had a set of goals and objectives that had to be accomplished in order to reach his view of what could be, of what was possible, $2\frac{1}{2}$ centuries into the dark curtain of the future. Although his firm was experiencing some short-term losses, the basic elements of that first 25-year period were on schedule and moving as planned. Certainly Matsushita was interested in a profitable company; yet his primary focus was not on quarterly monotonically increasing profits, but rather on the underlying elements and strategic pillars that would generate those profits over the long haul. In the meantime, Matsushita Denki has moved into the second 25-year period having completed the goals for the first period.

I urge you to begin now developing the habit of allocating time regularly to discipline your mind to think into the future, to imagine what could be, to play with the details, to follow the thin threads of reasoning that describe how those images could be brought to pass. This mental exercise will not come to you in a flash; like physical tone, your mental imagining tone will come from repeated and vigorous effort. Chapter 8, "Strategic Thinking," will give you additional guidance on visioning.

Reading is a great way to increase your stockpile of ideas. If you read widely, not just in your field, you will begin to see connections between and among different disciplines and industries. Be willing to read in other fields so you can begin to identify trends and events that will impact yours. I recently had a participant in an executive program who reported that he read two books a night. Yes, two books a night! He began to develop this skill many years ago when, in the desire to take a class from a favorite high school instructor, he signed up for remedial reading because it was the only class this instructor was offering that term. Although our friend was a normal reader, he learned techniques and insights into the reading process that now, after years of practice, leave him able to consume and understand close to 600 books a year. Can you imagine how this kind of input would inform and stimulate your mind into seeing the future?

Scenario Building

I also encourage you to begin developing scenarios that will inform the paths you might take to your dreams. Peter Schwartz, in his book *The Art of the Long View,* describes this process very well. Scenario building is different from strategic planning and corporate planning. I will describe scenario building in more detail in chapter 8.

CLARIFYING WHAT OTHERS CAN CONTRIBUTE

One of the fundamental issues that a potential leader faces is clarifying his or her own view of what the others, the potential followers, can do. Unless you can develop a view of what others can do and how they can contribute to your objectives and vision, you will not be able to get their commitment. The breadth of your view of what others can contribute can make a big difference in your effectiveness as a leader. Some managers take a very narrow view of what others can add, whereas others see a wide range of possibilities. Two factors are critical in clarifying what others can contribute: first, your basic underlying assumptions about others, and second, clarity in identifying the critical skills you will need to reach your vision.

Basic Assumptions about Others

One common and dangerous outcome of the bureaucratic, industrial era has been that many of us think of our people in terms of the job descriptions they have. The corollary to this approach is thinking of people in terms of the job descriptions we would like them to fill. This perspective constrains us from thinking about the talents of individuals and imagining what they might contribute to a particular goal or agenda. This kind of bureaucratic thinking—based on the assumptions that we need to find people to fit into particular job descriptions and that the management task is to minimize variance from the performance of that task—can be devastating to highly talented individuals. This perspective is a Level One way of thinking about what people could contribute to an effort.

I argued in chapter 1 that this approach assumes management knows exactly what needs to be done, that people can behave in that robotic way, and that the environment will be stable enough to avoid the need for quick response time and creative employees. Clearly, these conditions are not found in today's world.

A more powerful leadership approach is to assume that people have talents, can learn new ones, and have a basic desire to do well. Of course, these skills vary from person to person, and behavior will always need to be monitored. However, if we view, hire, train, and manage people with an eye to developing their skills and judgment, we are increasingly able to rely on their abilities at work rather than on their job descriptions. Further, their insights on the job may, especially in turbulent times, be more informed and accurate than management's, several layers up the organization. This whole process of working with people's talents and willingness to accept responsibilities for outcomes has been termed *empowering* and has become something of a trite phrase, in part because many managements give it lip service but do not really believe its underlying assumptions.

In a sense, clarifying what others could contribute by examining your own deep assumptions about the value that others bring to work is a part of clarifying your center. If your basic assumptions about what others can do are limited, then your ability to clarify what others can contribute will be limited as well. If you are able to imagine and perceive people as growing, learning, developing beings and are willing to invest in that growth, you elicit a very different kind of response. What you see about people certainly helps to determine how they will respond. If you treat people like robots, they will begin to behave like robots. If you treat people with expectations of higher contributions, they will begin to make higher contributions.

Identifying the Critical Skills

Another challenge to reframing how we look at people and conceive of what they have to offer is knowing what we need to accomplish our purposes. Most people look primarily at technical skills when assessing fit between a job and a candidate. Again, this view is Level One thinking. Consider a different approach.

The FMC plant in Aberdeen, South Dakota, builds missile launching canisters for the U.S. Navy. This facility was organized by an unusual and very effective leader, Bob Lancaster, who worked hard to develop a different kind of working environment in the facility. When the facility needed a new welder, management used the basic assumptions of their new organization rather than a traditional approach to find the next new employee. The traditional approach, the Level One approach, would be that a company would advertise for a welder, accept applications with resumes summarizing experience, and then pick the most qualified welder based on experience, references, and maybe an interview.

FMC Aberdeen, though, applied a different set of underlying assumptions and, correspondingly, a different set of identified critical skills.[7] The first basic new assumption was that the process of the organization is more important than the technical skills in the organization. According to this logic, if you had a collection of highly qualified people who could not work together, your organization would be less effective than if you had a group of moderately talented people who could work together well. The second assumption was that social skills are harder to teach than technical skills are, that is, that it is easier to teach welding than it is to teach teamwork, a desire to learn, self-esteem, and other related interpersonal talents. The third assumption was that people trained in one technical way of doing things, and perhaps reinforced by a union experience that encouraged focusing on a narrow range of skills, would have difficulty learning new ways of organizing their work.

With these three assumptions in mind, the management of FMC Aberdeen realized that the critical skills they needed were self-esteem (so the new worker would be able to receive feedback without getting defensive), a learning attitude (so the new worker would be interested and even eager to learn new skills and techniques), team spirit (so the new worker would be willing to share in the work and responsibility for results), and a pride in quality (so the new worker would be eager to find ways to improve results). Consequently, management developed a recruiting/screening process that lasted four hours and focused on these principles *rather than on the technical skills of welding*.

After using this process, FMC Aberdeen screened *out* virtually all the experienced welders who had applied for the job and ended up hiring a woman who had never welded before in her life! They chose her because she was bright, interested in learning, socially well adjusted, willing to take feedback, and clearly a team player. As it turned out, she became a master welder within a short period of time and then went on to learn a wide variety of the rest of the technical skills listed in the plant's pay-for-skill compensation system. Management was convinced that if they had hired a skilled welder, maybe with union experience, they would have had difficulty teaching the person new, now more important, social skills and a wider range of technical skills. Although it took several weeks before the new welder could weld well, within the first year the value added to the firm was far beyond what it would have been had they hired a "welder."

How could such a recruitment come about? One part of the answer was in the philosophy that was central in the founding of the plant. Another part lay in the innovative ways that FMC Aberdeen organized its critical human resources. And a big part had to do with its leadership: first, Bob Lancaster, then Jeff Bust, and later, Roger Campbell. These managers understood the importance of building an organization that supported people so that those people could do their best. A central part of that organization was determining the critical skills that were needed to create the kind of workplace managers wanted to have. In this case, many of those skills were the so-called softer skills of giving and receiving feedback, of learning, of team play, of flexibility, and of interpersonal relationships.

SUPPORTING OTHERS SO THEY CAN CONTRIBUTE

The traditional assumption mentioned earlier, that people should fit into job descriptions, limits what management expects from job incumbents. This same assumption also limits the structure, systems, and culture of organizations. Increasingly, in changing environments, organizations are having to find new, nontraditional ways of organizing and managing their people.

> Forces at play in the modern world—such as the explosion in information technology and the ever-burgeoning demand of people to be free—increasingly require that managements design all elements of their organizations to respect and respond to those forces.

Two forces are shaping this redesign: the explosion of information technology and the constantly burgeoning press of people to be in control of their lives. Both forces are empowering the workforce whether management wants it to or not. Both forces demand that effective leaders find ways of supporting their people by designing new organizational forms that no longer hinder people's creativity and sense of responsibility for results but rather encourage it.

Information Age Organizational Structures

Perhaps nothing has been as influential in the organizational redesign wave that has hit the world as has the explosion in new information technologies. As I mentioned in chapter 1, the growing, widespread availability of accurate, voluminous, and timely data about business activity has begun to literally transform the shape of modern organizations. Co-locating becomes less of an issue as simultaneous databases, video conferencing, net-based meetings, and e-mail become more prevalent and inexpensive. Cheap, distributed computer power for analysis and communications means that people at all levels of organizations can gather, analyze, decide, and communicate with people at all levels of other organizations. The need for vertical hierarchies to make good decisions is rapidly evaporating. In fact, in many cases, better decisions are being made by people who are closer to the data and the customer than by people several layers up. And the layers are disappearing.

> The need for vertical hierarchies to make good decisions is rapidly evaporating.

The new, emerging organizations are looking more and more like what we used to call the informal, or organic, organization. In older cities like Boston, streets eventually grew out of meandering cow paths; likewise in organizations, new lines of authority and influence are developing out of informal lines of communication in which the data is fast and accurate. In some cases, organizational control is being swiftly shifted away from vertical hierarchies toward information-based networks. Take, for instance, the case of rapidly expanding BancOne in the Midwest.

BancOne was a large and growing regional bank that had taken a different and exciting tack to managing its growth. Unlike some other growing regional banks, who acquired a new subsidiary and then not only repainted the buildings and added new signs but also delivered volumes of new operating procedures in the attempt to get the new affiliates to do things "our way," BancOne used information technology to manage its new partners.

First, being clear on their goals, BancOne management identified 47 key indicators of the kind of performance they wanted to see. Second, they developed an information network that allowed them to tie new affiliates in quickly. Third, the information system was designed to give almost instantaneous feedback on results from data collected. Fourth, management decided to share the results with the managers of the more than 50 banks in their system rather than keep it to themselves. All these features are dramatic departures from the traditional methods of planning, organizing, motivating, and controlling that grew out of the bureaucratic mind-set.[8]

With this system, a newly acquired bank president in the BancOne system suddenly began receiving on a weekly basis a listing of all the banks in the system ranked on each of the 47 key indicators. What do you suppose happened next? If you assume that people do not care about their performance (a commonly held bureaucratic assumption that limits thinking), then you might think not much would happen. On the other hand, if you believe that people want to think well of themselves and want to do well among their peers, then you might expect something major to happen.

What happened was that bank presidents looked quickly to see how their bank was doing compared with the others in the system. When they saw that they were not doing so well on a particular indicator, they looked to see who was doing well. And this discovery led the acquired bank president to a critical point. If the bank president was proud and lacking in the learning spirit, he or she might stonewall for a while and avoid learning from others in the system.

What happened more often, and in the process created a new and emerging culture, was that the bank presidents began to call one another, completely bypassing corporate management, to find out how they got such good results. Quickly, much more quickly than corporate training or quarterly review meetings could hope to accomplish it, the best practices of the organization were not filtering, but *flowing* from one part of the system to the next, week by week, as each of the decision makers, the small "l" leaders throughout the organization, got timely data, compared their results with others, and sought to improve their standing. Each implemented the suggestions of others in ways that fit their organizations and people; each adjusted, modified, and recast the suggestions they received to match what they thought they could do and what their current priorities were.

The following week, all the presidents received another current listing of what was happening with their bank and with the other banks in the system, and they were confronted again with the consequences, the results of whatever management steps they had taken. All these improvements were done without negative organizational politics and without the time delays caused by waiting for senior management analysis, decision making, training programs, and coordination. This progress would have been impossible without superb information technology *and* a senior management philosophy that utilized it efficiently.

BancOne is an example of how effective leadership can redesign organizational systems to support others/followers and make it easier rather than more difficult to release those systems' potential contributions to the organization. Effective leaders are able to clarify, where others cannot, not only what potential followers have to contribute, but also to clarify how the work systems in which they operate could be reorganized to realize their potential.

Empowering Systems Design

The BancOne system is also an example of a system that empowers people. Its tacit assumption was that the bank presidents all wanted to do well, that they all knew their banks better than anyone else, that they all would do what they could within their historical tradition and operating environment to improve performance on the key indicators. Very little was said to them about what they had to do or not do. Senior management assumed that these managers would know what to do if they had the right information and could see the direction the company wanted to go. (To be fair to Skinnerians, given our earlier discussion, this system is fundamentally behavioral in that it focused on inputs and outputs and gave little attention to Levels Two and Three.)

Often, our organizational structures, systems, and cultures inhibit rather than encourage people to use their full talents. Too many workers have heard, "That's on a need-to-know basis only" or "Don't ask questions, just do it!" or "You're not paid to think, you're paid to do what you're told" or "My job is to think, your job is to do" or some other, similar comment.[9] This kind of language and the assumptions on which this language was based form the foundation of the bureaucratic mind-set, but the new, emerging, postbureaucratic organizations, or infocracies, will be characterized by different kinds of language based on different sets of assumptions.

One change occurring in infocracies is a movement away from the assumption that people should fit into the organization ("Here's my organization chart, now let's figure out who fits into it and where") and toward the assumption that we give talented people current information and let them organize their work to fit the need ("Here are my people, let's figure out how to organize for the moment to meet the customer's needs"). What this shift means is that, as Peter Senge has written, leaders more and more are becoming designers of new kinds of organizational forms.[10] Many of these forms are built around circles and/or networks rather than pyramidal bureaucracies. The organizing principle is no longer based on who has what authority; instead, the forms for the new organizations are based on who has the right information and insight.

Effective leadership means, in part, casting away bureaucratic assumptions that we have taught in business schools for decades, assumptions often based on Weber's principles of the bureaucratic organization, and searching for and creating new organizing principles that allow for and encourage the rapid use of good information and the multiple talents of the people employed.

BEING RELENTLESS

Effective leaders are relentless. They exhibit stamina often in enormous volumes. People who have purpose and vision and a drive to achieve cannot be pushed off their chosen track. If their commitment to their purpose and vision is weak, they can be diverted, which makes them less effective with others and more confused even to themselves. I asserted earlier that it is difficult to know what values we truly hold until they are tested, tested among our peers and in high-stakes situations in which our true (operating) basic assumptions and priorities will be manifest. The same is true of our commitment to our purpose. We often learn how committed we are to an endeavor by watching ourselves in our commitment to that endeavor. Like the other steps introduced in this chapter, this principle is both a reflection of our center and a means of clarifying our center. We learn how much stamina we have by watching our own commitments to our goals. We clarify our center by learning from that observation.

Life as a Motorboat or a Wood Chip

One way to think of the commitment-building or stamina-building process is to compare life and business to an ocean—vast, constantly changing, open, available, and inviting to the skilled sailor. At the same time, life's sea has currents, winds, storms, denizens of the deep, and the possibility of total destruction. Some people launch on life without a purpose or direction, seeking in their naïveté to experience life as quickly as they can. Not thinking beyond their prows, they push off from shore with no motor, no sail, and no rudder and become a chip upon the tide, floating to and fro without destination. Sometimes such chips find themselves, by luck and the wind, ashore on favorable beaches and enjoying the finer things of life. Most however, never get anywhere and sink before they realize that the trip could have been different.

Leaders have a purpose to which they are committed. This purpose provides the charts by which they sail. Their stamina becomes the large sails and their center the compass to help them move ahead. When the winds of fate blow, leaders adjust the trim and the rudder to utilize whatever facets they still have under control to keep heading toward their destination. Leaders also have internal motors that keep them moving when the external winds are calm or blowing against them. Leaders have fuel to burn and reserve bunkers to feed their motors when the going gets tough and the waves mount. Leaders are not easily blown off course.[11]

This relentlessness, this drive to get up when you are knocked down, to right yourself when capsized, is essential to achieving important goals. Without it, leaders-to-be will become followers. This attitude may seem to be stubbornness, but there is a distinct difference between stubbornness and relentlessness. The relentless leader can still be willing to listen, willing to understand and utilize any fact, truth, or valuable information or alliance that will move toward or polish the visioned goal. Stubborn people stick to the original vision or strategic means selected without modification. This premise leads to the question, "So how do we develop leaderlike relentlessness?"

Developing Commitment

Easily chosen goals do not engender deep commitment. Constancy of commitment is a function of careful thought, sometimes painful scrutiny of the purpose and vision—often stimulated by other people's criticisms and by an ever-clarifying sense of center. Commitment grows out of knowing yourself. If you know what you want and why you operate the way you do, and are willing to change your ways of operating in order to get what you want, you will develop commitment. The more commitment you develop, the more relentless you will become.

Relentlessness is also born of self-confidence. If you do not believe in your goals or in your ability to achieve them, you will be easily pushed aside. Perhaps the most dramatic example of relentlessness is that of Thomas Edison, the inventor of the lightbulb. He tried more than a thousand configurations before he found the one that produced light from electricity. Can you imagine how you would feel, working on your goal and having just failed the 200th time? The 600th time? The 900th time? This kind of relentlessness requires a high level of confidence in the value of your purpose and in your contribution to achieving it.

MEASURING AND CELEBRATING PROGRESS

Few of us can carry on without some positive feedback. We all need some data that says to us, one way or another, "Okay, you're getting there! You're making progress!" Without a measure, our sense of forward movement, our sense of value added, our sense of the possibilities and hence our motivation and hope begin to wither. Effective leaders recognize this principle in the way they deal with themselves and with others. Two points are important to make.

Focusing on the Right Measures

As the BancOne example demonstrates, a key leadership skill is focusing on the right measures. Steve Kerr once wrote an article entitled "On the Folly of Hoping for A while Rewarding B."[12] His point, a strong one, was that we cannot realistically expect to get results A while we model and reward behavior that leads people to an entirely different outcome, B. Yet, he notes, many managers and management systems get caught up in that very misconception. Bureaucratic organizations, operating on the basic principle that "the boss knows best," too often make decisions that actually worsen the problem they are trying to solve. We often refer to these results as unintended consequences.

Unintended consequences occur when we cannot see ahead clearly and we do not understand the people with whom we are dealing. A good example of an unintended consequence is seen in the air pollution problem of Mexico City, one of the largest cities in the world. Lying as it does in a geographical bowl, Mexico City often has intense air pollution, caused mostly by the huge number of automobiles being used there. In an attempt to alleviate this problem, city officials came up with a plan to reduce the number of cars on the roads and hence, they hoped, to reduce the air pollution.

City officials decided that every person should be barred from using his or her car at least one day a week. They viewed this regulation as a way to stimulate car pooling and reduce the number of cars on the roads. They assigned a day of the week to the last digit of all license plates: Drivers whose license plate numbers ended in 1 could not drive their cars on Monday, and so on. City officials expected to reduce air pollution by 15 percent immediately. Instead, most people bought an older, used car with a less efficient engine and exhaust system and drove that car on the restricted day. Rather than reducing the air pollution problem, the law actually *worsened* the problem; in fact, it almost doubled the air pollution! Unintended consequences.

The ability to focus on the right measures is a key leadership skill. If the workers begin to believe that the results they are creating are trivial and/or diversionary from the basic goal or purpose, they will lose heart and become weak followers. On the other hand, if the leader can hone in on a small set of key indicators and show the people how those indicators relate to the purpose and the vision, the people will be focused and clear on what they are working for.

Monthly or quarterly profit figures are a good example of a focus on a diversionary goal. Everyone, especially investors, wants to have stable, monotonically increasing profits (meaning steady increases without any dips). Stable profits as the primary focus, however, can have unintended consequences among followers. I know of one facility at which employees regularly shipped the next month's orders in the current month to make up any shortfall in the current month's shipping goals and in so doing eventually built up an enormous surplus in customers' warehouses. Finally, customer orders fell precipitously when customers said, "We can't take any more!" The short-term goal of monthly shipments diverted attention from the long-term goal of financial health and stability and ultimately caused some severe repercussions throughout the company.

Focusing on the Half-Full Glass

Another common measurement-related residue of the bureaucratic mind-set is variance management. Variance management is the willingness to let things go until there is a variance from the organization's plan, at which time management's job is to step in and get things back on track. Fundamentally, this approach is a negative one and ultimately demotivating to the people involved.

First, who knows if the plan was accurate and right for the current business conditions? Because business conditions change rapidly, business plans can grow obsolete and out of touch. More and more companies are developing flexible plans that respond more quickly than the traditional semi-annual or annual reporting and management cycles. Second, if management's primary communication with the employees revolves around criticism when things are not going well, how can employees be expected to be enthusiastic followers and coordinate their efforts smoothly with management? This formula manages the downside, not the upside. Determining the right measures and developing a positive philosophy about how to administer them makes the difference between an average organization and a vibrant, leading one.

Effective leaders watch for progress on key indicators and celebrate the positive with their people. Rather than looking for the half-empty glass, that is, finding the mistakes and faults of the organization, they look for the half-full glass and ways to fill it further. They build on the successes rather than rail on the failures. Sure, yelling at employees may bring about short-term, Level One results, but if the leader leaves for a while, have the employees learned how to carry on? Probably not. Rather, employees have learned an insidious, unintended dependence on that manager on matters of performance and quality. Employees who have worked with a Level Three Leader know when they are doing the work right because they are acknowledged and celebrated. They begin to look for other ways to earn positive feedback. Celebrations of forward progress bring the work up out of the mundane and the routine and present it as a contribution to the organization's purpose and vision.

Conclusion

Personal leadership characteristics are not all that is necessary for effective leadership to occur. Nevertheless, who you are and what you do as an individual is a major part of a positive leadership outcome. This chapter presents six suggestions for improving your personal leadership effectiveness. Each step is an ongoing process, not something that can be done once and discarded. Leadership requires a long-term commitment to personal exploration and to personal visions. Without that level of engagement, leadership is not likely to happen.

Principles of Level Three Leadership

1. Effective leaders are centered; that is, they know who they are, what they believe in, and what they want to accomplish with their lives.

2. Effective leaders have a clear view of what's possible for the organization; they have created a vision of where the organization should go.

3. Effective leaders are able to see what others, in their unique ways and with their unique talents, can contribute to the accomplishment of the vision.

4. Effective leaders are good organizational designers; they reshape the organization to support talented people as they work toward the vision, trying to position the organization as a help rather than a hindrance to people working in it.

5. Effective leaders are relentless. They do not give up, although they are flexible enough to take different routes to their goals.

6. Effective leaders recognize progress and praise those who contribute to it.

Questions for Reflection

1. What are your core leadership principles? That is, if you were asked to take charge of an organization, what have you learned thus far in life about how you would lead?

2. What is the purpose of your organization? Can you write it succinctly and immediately? Are you engaged in that purpose? Why or why not?

3. What do your coworkers contribute to this purpose? Can you identify contributions that each makes?

4. How would you reorganize your organization to make it more effective? How could you make your ideas happen?

5. What in life are you relentlessly committed to? What, if anything, are you willing to spend 10 years working on? How does this relate to your ability to lead?

Notes

1. James Allen, *As a Man Thinketh* (Santa Monica, CA: DeVorss & Co., 1913). This passage is also contained in the Bible (Prov. 23:7).

2. Mark Baker, *Nam* (New York: Morrow, 1981).

3. See, for example, Konosuke Matsushita, *As I See It* (Tokyo: PHP Institute, 1989).

4. Steve, who was my first instructor in business school, speaks of Circles of Concern and Circles of Influence in his best-selling book *The Seven Habits of Highly Effective People* (New York: Simon & Schuster, 1989).

5. See Stan Davis, *Future Perfect* (Reading, MA: Addison-Wesley, 1987).

6. Covey's four-quadrant model depicts our attention to things important or not and things urgent or not. Quadrant I refers to things both urgent and important, the so-called Crisis Zone.

7. See *FMC Aberdeen* (UVA-OB-385), available through Darden Educational Materials Services, Charlottesville, Virginia.

8. See *Banc One Diversified Services* (UVA-BP-335), available through Darden Educational Materials Services, Charlottesville, Virginia.

9. Comments like the ones listed in the text are what Chic Thompson in his book *What a Great Idea!* (New York: Harper Perennial, 1992) calls "killer phrases," phrases that kill motivation and creativity.

10. See Peter Senge, *The Fifth Discipline* (New York: Doubleday Currency, 1990).

11. If you find the sailing analogy interesting, you may enjoy reading *First You Have to Row a Small Boat* by Richard Bode (New York: Warner, 1993), which describes learning life's lessons through sailing.

12. *Academy of Management Journal* (August 15, 1988): 298.

CHAPTER

Leadership 6 and Intelligence

Chapter Outline

- ■ Not One Intelligence, But Many: Gardner's Research
- ■ Intellectual Intelligence
- ■ Emotional Quotient
- ■ Social Quotient
- ■ Change Quotient

Most observers believe that intelligence is an important precursor to effective leadership. Smart people are generally considered to have the best potential for being the leaders of industry, nations, and institutions. Interestingly, however, a study of valedictorians—people who graduate at the top of their high school classes—described in Daniel Goleman's book *Emotional Intelligence* indicates that after 20 years, most of them are working for their classmates.[1] This counterintuitive result causes us to rethink our beliefs about intelligence and its relationship to effective leadership.

For more than a century, business leaders have, for the most part, tried to manage down and to avoid emotions as being unprofessional, undisciplined, and unrelated to good decision making. This reserve stems in part from the philosophy of the Age of Enlightenment in western civilization. Knowledge, said Sir Francis Bacon, is power. Like the other philosophers of the Enlightenment, Bacon saw knowledge as the pathway to universal liberation and saw emotions and passions as obstacles to knowledge. Many of the leadership models taught in business schools have focused on rational decision making in which emotions are viewed as detriments or obstacles to making good decisions.

Prepared by Greg Bevan and James G. Clawson. Copyright © 1996 by the Darden Graduate Business School Foundation, Charlottesville, VA. (Adapted from UVA-OB-652.) All rights reserved. Reprinted with permission.

Further, American school systems have focused on the notion of rational intelligence in striving to educate millions of children. The concept of intelligence quotient (or IQ) was the most prominent measure of intelligence and shaped the design of curricula with the intent of utilizing more of students' IQs if not adding to them. Although the validity of IQ tests and their general intelligence or aptitude substitutes have come into question in recent years,[2] tests of purely rational thinking—the Scholastic Aptitude Test (SAT) and the General Management Aptitude Test (GMAT), for example—still wield a great deal of influence over our individual fortunes and those of our children.

Recently, however, some startling conclusions about the nature of intelligence— many of them directly at odds with old assumptions—have begun to emerge. Daniel Goleman points out three important inferences we can draw from recent studies:

1. Existing standardized intelligence tests fail to predict success in life or in business because they do not tell the whole story. Intelligence is not singular; rather, it comes in a number of forms. There are, current thinking goes, *multiple intelligences,* and intellectual intelligence, the kind measured by IQ tests, is only one kind.

2. Emotion, even though it can sometimes sabotage clearheaded thought, has been scientifically shown to be an indispensable contributor to rational thinking and decision making. As oxymoronic as it would have seemed to Sir Francis Bacon, there is a range of intelligences that can be called "emotional"—and they are important for aspiring business leaders to understand better.

3. Despite traditional views that IQ is inherited and that not much can be done to change it, the newly recognized various intelligences seem to be, to a large extent, learned.

NOT ONE INTELLIGENCE, BUT MANY: GARDNER'S RESEARCH

Goleman draws on the work of several researchers to demonstrate the existence of multiple intelligences. Howard Gardner, a psychologist at the Harvard School of Education, found the long-standing notion of a single kind of intelligence both wrongheaded and injurious. He blamed this belief largely on the IQ test itself—calling it, in fact, the "IQ way of thinking:" "that people are either smart or not, are born that way, that there's nothing much you can do about it, and that tests can tell you if you are one of the smart ones. The SAT test for college admissions is based on the same notion of a single kind of aptitude that determines your future. This way of thinking permeates society."[3] Statistically speaking, though, IQ measurements, SAT scores, and grades turn out to be poor predictors of who will succeed in life and who will not (Goleman puts the contribution of IQ to a person's success at about 20 percent.).

Gardner's groundbreaking 1993 book *Frames of Mind* repudiated the idea of one kind of intelligence and the IQ way of thinking by positing a wide array of intelligences. Gardner identified seven: verbal, mathematical-logical, spatial (as demonstrated by painters or pilots), kinesthetic (as seen in the physical grace of a dancer or athlete), musical, interpersonal (on which a therapist or a diplomat might rely), and intrapersonal intelligence (something akin to self-awareness). Gardner's perspective explained why traditional tests had been ineffective in predicting success: They measured only one or two of many necessary and important kinds of intelligence.

Goleman took Gardner's "personal" kinds of intelligences—the interpersonal and the intrapersonal—and cited hundreds of studies to create a story that described something called *emotional intelligence*, or EQ. Goleman asserted that EQ was just as important as IQ in helping people become effective leaders. As Gardner pointed out, "Many people with IQs of 160 work for people with IQs of 100, if the former have poor intrapersonal intelligence and the latter have a high one. And in the day-to-day world no intelligence is more important than the interpersonal. If you don't have it, you'll make poor choices about who to marry, what job to take, and so on. We need to train children in the personal intelligences in school." Let us examine IQ and EQ and some related concepts in more detail.

INTELLECTUAL INTELLIGENCE

IQ (which we will use as a substitute for mental capacity in general) is largely genetic but can be honed or made more manifest by curiosity, by discipline in studying, and by adding a range of experiences to a person's life (see Table 6–1). Your IQ depends in large part on the mental machinery you inherited from your parents, but if you are curious, if you learn to discipline yourself in your study habits and to seek out new experiences, you can bring your mental capacity to the fore. You may not be able to change your IQ score on IQ tests, but you can learn to do more with what you have been given. If you do not know your IQ, do not worry about it, because, broadly speaking, although standardized tests have some predictive power (people with low IQs often end up making little money, and people with high IQs frequently take demanding, high-powered, better-paying jobs), IQ tests reflect only one kind of intelligence. Other kinds are equal if not more important to developing leadership influence.

EMOTIONAL QUOTIENT

Emotional intelligence, as introduced by Goleman, is the ability to manage your own emotions. The first step of emotional intelligence is the ability to recognize your emotions, the second step is to understand them, and the last step is to manage yourself out of what Goleman calls "emotional hijackings." In this view, IQ is your brain power, whereas EQ is your emotional control power.

To develop your EQ, you must first learn to recognize your emotions. Many people are not very aware of their emotions—although they often say they are. Have you ever talked with someone who seemed visibly upset, whose neck veins were bulging, whose

TABLE 6-1 Characteristics of Intelligence Quotient

Genetic
Revealed in curiosity
Honed by discipline in study
Supported by range of experiences

face was red, whose voice was raised, and yet, when you asked this person to calm down, he or she screamed, "I *am* calm!" This person is not in touch with his or her own emotional reality or experiences. Further, when you ask people how they are feeling, they often will describe behaviors or thoughts. Many are not skilled in recognizing and paying attention to their own emotional state. Many of these people have learned that the emotional world is not legitimate, and after years of practicing to suppress or subdue their emotions, they have lost touch with how they feel. I am repeatedly surprised how few talented, practicing managers and leaders are able to identify and talk about their emotions.

Aware of them or not, people can often become prisoners of their emotions. In Goleman's terms, people get "hijacked" by their emotions and lose control of their rational processes. In an emotional hijacking, a person begins with a little emotion, and then it builds and builds until the person is not thinking clearly and is overwhelmed by the emotion. The most common emotional hijackings are related to anger, fear, and depression. A person hijacked by anger, for instance, may start out being a little irritated, but as time passes, they get more and more angry until they are bursting at the seams and acting openly hostile whether the situation calls for such behavior or not. People with a low EQ who become angry, afraid, or depressed find themselves in an ever-widening spiral of emotions in which they are unable to think clearly or to make good decisions.

Let us look closely at a hijacking by fear. Modern equipment has given us much greater insight into how this hijacking occurs, because we can trace with increasing accuracy the electrical impulses that course through the brain during different events. We used to think that when you saw something dangerous, like a snake, the eye would send a signal to the thinking part of the brain, the brain would consciously register "danger" and send signals to the muscles to move quickly—and you would jump. We have since learned, however, of a "short circuit" that bypasses the thinking part of the brain and transmits danger signals directly to a small, peanut-sized structure, called the amygdala, that sits atop the human brain stem.

The amygdala is an old structure in terms of the development of the human brain; it evolved earlier than the neocortex above it—the area that handles conscious thought—and its functioning is largely beyond the control of the thinking brain. When it receives a short circuit signal from the optic nerve that you have seen a snake, the amygdala immediately begins a complex chemical process that pumps muscle stimulants into the bloodstream and you literally jump *without* thinking. If your ability to manage these chemical outbursts is underdeveloped, your body can create a growing whirlpool of fear so strong that it could cause you to jump when you should hold still or be paralyzed by fear when you should jump. When you are so enraged that you cannot think straight or so blue that you cannot function, blame your amygdala.

Dr. Antonio Damasio, a neurologist at the University of Iowa, studied patients with damage to the circuits between the amygdala and the brain's memory center. These patients showed no IQ deterioration at all, and yet their decision-making skills were amazingly poor. They made disastrous choices in their careers and personal lives, and the most mundane decisions—white bread or wheat?—often left them paralyzed with confusion. Damasio concluded that their decision making was impaired because they had no access to their *emotional* learning. These patients, searching their memories for the last time they were in a similar situation, did not remember how they *felt* about the outcome because the emotional lessons, stored in or regulated by the amygdala, apparently were out of reach.

TABLE 6-2 Components of Emotional Intelligence
1. Recognizing your own emotions
2. Managing your emotions appropriately
3. Productive self-talk out of emotional hijackings

If Damasio was right, the conventional wisdom imparted to us by the Age of Reason philosophers and the intervening years of scientific and business experience was, at least part of the time, wrong: Emotions are in fact *essential* for rational decisions. Memories of ecstatic successes and painful failures help steer the decisions we make every day.

By contrast, people who have a strong connection between the amygdala and the neocortex seem to be better equipped to make good decisions, decisions that are based on a balance between rational and emotional input rather than on one without the other. Applying this insight to business and organizational life, we can conclude that people who have learned over the years to manage their emotions have learned to manage their behavior better and their relationships better—and that this better management translates to more success in the social world of business.

To a certain extent, just like with our IQ, we are stuck with the emotional cards that we were dealt at birth: Depression, for instance, has been shown to have a hereditary component. But the good news is that EQ seems to be more responsive to learning activities than IQ is. You can develop emotional skills that will help enrich both your personal and professional life. Following the outline in Table 6–2, let us explore some ways we can improve our EQ.

Recognizing Your Own Emotions

The first step toward building your EQ, of course, is recognizing or being aware of your emotions. This step may seem to you a simple task: Your feelings are self-evident, and so this point is hardly worth making, but closer examination reveals otherwise.

We all sometimes lose sight of our emotions. Goleman offers examples of situations that we all recognize, for instance, getting up on the wrong side of the bed and being grouchy all day long. What we would call "getting up on the wrong side of the bed" might actually have stemmed from kicking your toe on the bathroom door, a curt exchange with your significant other, bad news on the radio, a bad night's sleep stemming from a heavy dinner, or some modest chemical imbalance. Perhaps your bad day was really related to the rainy weather. Whatever the source of this initial emotional set, many people are unaware that they are behaving crossly, are seemingly depressed, or are "down" throughout their work day.

Being aware of emotions requires reflection. If you learn to pause, to focus inward, and to seek your emotions, you can become more aware of them. You might begin by asking yourself several times during a normal day, "What am I feeling now?" If you do this exercise for a week, you will probably be able to notice your feelings more readily. The challenge, one accepted by people with high EQs, is to manage those emotions in a more positive way. People who have developed a high EQ do not yield to their emotions easily; instead, they seek to manage them.

Managing Your Emotions

Maybe the thought of managing your emotions is too rational for you, or too contrived. Perhaps you prefer to allow your emotions to ebb and flow; you like the spontaneity of them. You are still okay. The point here is that the data seem to suggest that if you manage your emotions—if you do not just suppress them and ignore them, but instead become more aware of them and deal with them—you are more likely to have a positive impact on yourself and the people around you at work or elsewhere. This positive impact is particularly true for the potentially debilitating emotions of anger, fear, and depression.

To a person with low EQ, an emotional hijacking may seem like an irresistible call to action: Anger leads to shouting, fear leads to fleeing, depression leads to crying or withdrawal. But with practice, the urgings of the amygdala can be overcome through what Goleman, borrowing from Albert Ellis and others, calls productive self-talk.[4] When someone cuts you off on the highway, in other words, you do not have to respond by yelling, pounding on the steering wheel, and clenching your jaw and arm muscles.

To manage your emotions, you must decide that you want to be in control of them. You cannot manage emotions by willpower alone; unless you make the decision to manage them, you are not likely to increase your EQ. Start by saying to yourself, "I want to learn to not be angry so often, or to not be depressed so often, or to be more courageous."

Eventually you will start to ask, "Why do people behave the way they do?" Consider the rude driver again. If you imagine that the driver who cut you off is in a hurry to get to the hospital, suddenly you do not have much to get angry about.

The analytical thought process of anxiety, on the other hand, is itself often the source of trouble: Some people can worry about anything. If you choose, however, to look at your pessimistic assumptions critically ("Is this outcome really inevitable? What other possible outcomes are there? Is there something constructive I can do?"), you may be able gradually to break them down. People with a high EQ have learned over the years how to quell their anxiety. Sometimes they use productive self-talk and at other times they might even use physical relaxation methods such as meditation or prayer to help to stem the onset of anxiety once the emotion has been recognized.[5]

Managing your emotions is a personal challenge. Do you think you can do it? Would you like to be able to do so? Are you willing to test your abilities to do so? If you can, I think, not only will you feel better about your life, you will be better able to manage your relationships. Goleman lumped the personal and interpersonal aspects of EQ into one concept, but in the following sections, I separate them for clarity's sake.

SOCIAL QUOTIENT

Goleman asserts that a high EQ has a positive impact on relationships. If EQ is the ability to manage emotions, then social quotient, or SQ, has to do with recognizing and managing the emotions in interpersonal relationships. SQ skills are similar to those used in EQ but are directed toward others. Hence, the SQ skills include recognizing emotions in others, developing a concern or caring about the emotional state of others, and being able to help them manage their emotional states as outlined in Table 6–3.

TABLE 6-3 Components of Social Intelligence

1. Recognizing emotions in others
2. Listening
3. Caring about the emotional state of others
4. Helping others manage their emotions

Like EQ, SQ can in large part be learned. And in an organizational world that places a premium on interpersonal skills—in which you cannot, as they say, fax a handshake—a well-developed SQ can take you places that IQ, by itself, cannot.

Recognizing the Emotions of Others

Recognizing the emotions of others is the interpersonal corollary to the EQ skill of recognizing your own emotions. The better you are at understanding your own emotions, the more adept you will be at picking up on the feelings of others. The difficulty with "tuning in" on the emotional state of other people, of course, is that people do not usually put their emotions into words. More often, they express their emotions nonverbally—through cues like tone of voice, facial expression, gesture, and other forms of body language. Some research suggests that, in general, women are better than men at this kind of attunement; however, with attention and effort anyone can learn the ability to see emotions in others.

In the organizational environment, opportunities for this kind of learning are plentiful. In meetings, sales presentations, and chance exchanges with subordinates and superiors, attention to nonverbal cues can yield sharp insights into what another person is experiencing *emotionally.* Knowing how to read the signs is a valuable interpersonal skill. Practice in your conversations, in your meetings, and in group settings. While you listen, see if you can identify the emotions of the people you are talking with. At first, this exercise may be confusing to you; however, if you practice, it will become second nature. You will learn to listen more completely.

Listening

Lots of people give lip service to the concept of listening as an important leadership skill. Yet many people do not listen well because they focus only on content. Listening as it applies to SQ means more than just letting someone else speak. It means listening attentively, with an ear—and an eye—toward recognizing emotion in addition to content. Listening means putting out of your mind, for a moment at least, what you plan to say when it is your turn to respond. It means trying to register what other people are saying with their heart, not just their mouth. Then, if you are able to see what the other person is feeling, the question is, "Do you care?"

Empathy and Caring

When you become open to and aware of the feelings of others, you become able to empathize—to tune into their emotional experience. Empathy—and the caring for another's well-being that usually results—is a Level Three connection that binds us in our personal lives and strengthens our attempts at leadership. When we can see what others feel, and when we care about that, we have a major opportunity to influence—and to be influenced. If you are able to help others manage their emotions, you can be a Level Three Leader.

Helping Others Manage Their Emotions

If you see the emotions of others, if you care about that emotional reality for them, and if you have the skills to help them manage their emotions, you will have the opportunity to influence others. This is leadership.

In some cases, you may help others manage their internal emotions, help them out of emotional hijackings. A personal example relates to my youngest child, an eight-year-old girl. Although she is very talented and energetic, she also has a tendency to become overwhelmed by daily events. When she is feeling this way, she can talk herself into a dither until she collapses in a sobbing heap on the couch or in her bed. As parents, we can see this emotional storm developing almost as clearly as the rain clouds gathering on the horizon. Armed with Goleman's insights, we try now to help her manage her emotions by talking with her and showing her that (1) she can get control of her feelings and stop the downward spiral, (2) she can focus on only one thing that needs to be done and do it without worrying about the others, and (3) she can begin to feel good about herself not only for doing that one thing but also for managing her feelings.

Coworkers in business are susceptible to the same emotional hijackings. You can help some of your coworkers learn to manage their emotions more effectively. Start by finding out why they are feeling their emotions. Often, emotions are based on a comparison between an event and an underlying value, assumption, or belief. If you ask yourself, "Why are they feeling that way?" you can gain insight into their basic values and assumptions. If you can understand those values, you can see more clearly how these people respond to the world around them. Then you may begin to help these coworkers reexamine their assumptions. Although many managers feel ill at ease with this approach, those with some skill at it are able to have profound impact on colleagues.

SQ also can come into play in helping others manage emotions related to their relationships. One of the most valuable skills in the organizational environment—and one of the most striking examples of SQ in action—lies in resolving conflicts and disputes. Conflicts arise frequently in the business world, sometimes accompanied by heated feelings and accusations. All too often, "solutions" are handed down from above—and emotionally speaking, these are solutions in name only: Business goes on, but someone inevitably comes away feeling wronged and resentful. In the long run, as morale and cohesiveness break down, the organization as a whole will suffer.

Consequently, skill in conflict resolution is a valuable asset. People with low EQs and SQs can let their emotions get the better of them. If you are skilled in recognizing emotions and in managing emotions, both in yourself and in your relationships, you can balance the rational content and the emotional content—and you can influence people to make better decisions. Good mediators are not only smart, they have strong EQ and SQ skills.

Here is a simple example. An employee reacts to a coworker's criticism, gets hijacked, and launches a volley of defensive remarks that make matters more volatile and charged. A person with high EQ skills would have instead turned to self-talk, interpreting the criticism judiciously in order to keep destructive emotions in check. In much the same way, a high-SQ mediator can explain to the injured party that the remarks may not have been intended to wound; that, at any rate, the comments are only opinion and not necessarily fact; and that the comments do not need to be internalized. The mediator can also explain to the critic the importance of tact and diplomacy in influencing others.

Common sense, you say? Yes, common for people with high SQ, maybe not so common for people with lower SQ. One person gifted in SQ can help offset the EQ deficiencies of many others—and in so doing, is likely to be seen by coworkers as an extraordinary kind of person, a person worthy of leadership. Needless to say, organizations find such mediators extremely valuable. And conflict-resolution skills, as any diplomat or marriage counselor will tell you, can be learned.

CHANGE QUOTIENT

I want to introduce here another kind of intelligence, not one that Gardner or Goleman identified explicitly, but one that has a big impact on leadership and the ability to lead. I call it CQ, or change quotient. People seem to vary in their change intelligence, that is, their ability to recognize the need for change, their comfort in managing change, and their understanding of and mastery of the change process. Table 6–4 outlines this intelligence, which parallels the other intelligences introduced in this chapter.

High-CQ people are the so-called lifelong learners who adapt to rapidly changing business environments much better than do their more stubborn counterparts. When high-CQ people look at challenges, they see opportunities rather than threats. They are willing to learn whatever new skills are called for in a situation rather than look for ways to reapply what they already know. Here are a few ideas for managing your development in CQ.

Recognizing the Need to Change

Many people find it difficult to recognize signals of change that surround them in the environment. Maybe the signals are coming from customers, from significant others, from employees, from financial indicators, or from colleagues and peers. E. C. Zeeman, an English researcher, made an interesting observation in this regard. He noted the dangerous behavior of drunk drivers: They begin to steer off the road, see a tree, overcorrect, see oncoming headlights, and overcorrect again, perhaps plowing into the next set of trees.

Zeeman then noted paradoxically that sober drivers drive the same way. That is, sober drivers never drive perfectly straight; instead, they see disconfirming data coming

---

TABLE 6-4 Components of Change Intelligence

1. Recognizing the need for change
2. Understanding the change process
3. Mastering and implementing the change process
4. Comfort in managing the change process

in and make a small midcourse correction. The difference is that the drunk driver's ability to see the disconfirming data is impaired and he or she waits until too late to make the appropriate correction. Of course, the opposite is equally dangerous: People who are hypersensitive to incoming data may get so overloaded they become paralyzed.[6]

We can apply the same reasoning to business leaders. Effective leaders will have a high CQ; that is, they will be able to recognize the need for change before it is too late. In fact, one of the six core leadership maxims of Jack Welch, CEO of General Electric, is change before you have to.[7] Potential leaders must possess the ability to sift from among a multitude of signals and pick out the ones that are important; they must combine that ability with a willingness to change, to consider new ways of doing things, and to implement changes.

Understanding and Mastering the Change Process

Many people are afraid of things they do not understand. The more we understand and become competent with something, the less frightening it becomes. Change is no different. There are some predictable patterns and reactions to change that can be described and understood. People can practice managing small change efforts and in so doing become more adept at managing larger ones. A general change process and ways of managing it are presented in chapter 12, "Leading Change."

Emotional Comfort with Change

For many of us, change in and of itself does not offer much that is comforting: By definition change means getting out of our comfort zone and experiencing different things. Although some people enjoy and seek out "out of the comfort zone" experiences, most of us seek comfort and solace in the things we know well. But one sign of a high CQ is a positive emotional attitude toward constant change: the feeling that change will be for the better and ought to be embraced. One participant in a management seminar described one of his core leadership principles as "Pain is your friend." What he meant by that principle was that learning is almost always the result of something that is uncomfortable or even, in a small way, painful and that learning is good because it helps enhance your competitive advantage.

This idea is consistent with the theme of the best-selling book *The Road Less Traveled* by Scott Peck.[8] Peck argues that most people take the comfortable road, the one they know, but that the person who learns and grows and contributes more takes the road less traveled, the one with a little discomfort, a little pain, a little learning in it. Peck notes that taking this path usually means a little extra effort but that the person who takes this path is better adapted to the surrounding world and is more influential in it.

Conclusion

In his book, Goleman uses the metaphor of a journey to underscore the idea that emotional learning is not a single lesson but a course of study: "In this book I serve as a guide in a journey through these scientific insights into the emotions, a voyage aimed at bringing greater understanding to some of the most perplexing moments in our own lives and in the world around us." As with most journeys, a guide can take us only so far. In the end, each traveler must make the effort to get from one place to another. This chapter challenges each of us to assess our emotional preparedness for leadership and to invest in our abilities to improve that kind of intelligence. We must view intelligence in a broader context, one that includes not only IQ, but also EQ, SQ, and CQ.

Principles of Level Three Leadership

1. Although intelligence is often associated with good leaders, recent research suggests that effective leaders have many kinds of intelligence.
2. Effective leaders have a high EQ; they are able to manage their emotions appropriately.
3. Effective leaders have a high SQ; they are able to recognize and help manage emotions in others.
4. Effective leaders have a high CQ; they can recognize the need for change, and they possess some comfort and skill in understanding and managing the change process.

Questions for Reflection

1. How well do you manage your emotions? If you would like a little help in assessing your EQ, this Internet site, http://www.utne.com/cgi-bin/eq, offers a preliminary self-assessment instrument that Goleman is using to gather data on EQ. A more comprehensive and carefully validated instrument is "The Emotional IQ Test," developed by Jack Mayer, Peter Salovey, and David Caruso and is available on CD-ROM from Virtual Knowledge, 200 Highland Avenue, Needham, MA 02194, 1-800-301-9545, http://www.virtualknowledge.com.
2. How well can you discern the emotional states of the people you work with on a daily basis? Do you ever check with your coworkers to confirm or disconfirm your views? What emotions did you observe at work this past week?
3. When did you last help someone else manage his or her emotions? What did you do? How did it go? What could you have done better?
4. How is a person with high EQ different from a person who subverts or ignores emotion? What are the consequences of both approaches?
5. List the major changes that you have made in your life. How well did you navigate them? What did you learn from them? What feelings were associated with those changes?
6. What signals for change do you see around you today? What kinds of changes are these signals asking you make? How do you feel about those changes?

Notes

1. Daniel Goleman, *Emotional Intelligence* (New York: Bantam, 1995). Many of the concepts in this chapter come from this excellent book.
2. Harvard Business School, for instance, discontinued use of the GMAT in making admissions decisions after concluding that the test scores were not highly correlated with graduate success.
3. Howard Gardner, *Frames of Mind* (New York: Basic Books, 1993).
4. Much of Goleman's approach here is similar to Rational-Emotive-Therapy, developed by Albert Ellis, in which you learn to talk yourself out of dysfunctional conclusions and thoughts. See, for example, Albert Ellis, *A New Guide to Rational Living* (Los Angeles: Wilshire Book Company, 1975) or Gerald Kranzler, *You Can Change How You Feel* (Eugene, OR: University of Oregon, 1974).

5. Relaxation techniques are a central part of many religious and health perspectives. See, for instance, Dr. Dean Ornish's well-known techniques for reducing risk of heart disease in *Dr. Dean Ornish's Program for Reversing Heart Disease* (New York: Ballantine Books, 1990).

6. See E. C. Zeeman, "Catastrophe Theory," *Scientific American* 234 (April 1976): 65–83.

7. See Noel Tichy and Stratford Sherman, *Control Your Destiny or Someone Else Will* (New York: Harper Business, 1993).

8. Scott Peck, *The Road Less Traveled* (New York: Touchstone, 1978).

C H A P T E R

Resonance, Leadership, and the Purpose of Life

7

Chapter Outline

■ Freedoms and Responsibilities

■ Ideas

■ Dreams

■ Resonance

■ The Purpose of Life

I've always been interested in the mountains. The first time I went to Switzerland, I saw the mountains, and I said, "This is where I've got to be." I dropped everything and found a mountain-climbing school and spent a couple of weeks in Switzerland and learned some basics of climbing, how to cut ice steps in glaciers and basic mountaineering. I really liked that. Clearly, in technical climbing you get in situations where, if you slip, you are dead. You don't consciously seek those situations, but you reach dicey points where you basically can only go forward rather than back. And the level of concentration and thrill of operating at that level is just . . . you are alive *then, and it's almost like your sense of . . . your visual acuity and sensual acuity dial up tenfold, and you can see things and you are aware of things that you are not aware of in everyday life. That is the part of rock climbing that I really enjoy.*

—TOM CURREN, FORMER SENIOR VICE PRESIDENT
OF STRATEGIC PLANNING, MARRIOTT CORPORATION

Prepared by James G. Clawson and Doug Newburg. Copyright © 1997 by the University of Virginia Darden School Foundation, Charlottesville, VA. All rights reserved. Adapted from UVA-OB-626. Reprinted with permission.

A world-renowned musician performs in concerts all over the globe.

The world record holder in a swimming event wins the gold medal at the Olympics.

The CEO of a consumer electronics firm reports annualized growth of 40 percent per year for the last 10 years.

The head of thoracic surgery at a major teaching hospital performs a coronary bypass operation on his 400th patient.

What do all these people have in common? First, and most obviously, they are performing at the peak of their professions and probably at the peak of their abilities. Second, surprisingly, although they come from radically different backgrounds and are performing in very different careers, they seem to be following a consistent pattern. Interestingly, what works in music also seems to work in surgery; what works in business also seems to work in athletics. Each of the people described here and almost 200 others like them—all participants in a study of world-class performers (WCPs) conducted by Doug Newburg[1]—seem to be following a pattern of thinking and behaving that is remarkably consistent. From interviews with these WCPs in various professions, Newburg has developed a powerful model of world-class performance. The concepts in this model could help you learn how to perform better, to be happier in your work, whatever it may be, even to engage a simple but powerful definition of the meaning of life.

The term *world-class performers* as used in this text refers to people who are performing at the pinnacle of their professions. The people in Newburg's study include, for example, world record holder and Olympic gold medal athletes, internationally known jazz musicians, nationally recognized thoracic surgeons, and chief executive officers of remarkable, fast-growing businesses.

Newburg's world-class performance model highlights several similarities in these people. High performers, for example, all seem to have a strong dream that has become the driving force of their efforts. Their efforts begin with intense periods of preparation that are often lengthy, demanding, and depressing. These performers continually try to use the preparation to realize their dreams, but in doing so often run into barriers, setbacks, obstacles, and interestingly, diverting minor successes. We can call these hazards the *SOS barrier*.

The common response to setbacks is to retreat into preparation, which can create a nonproductive ping-pong-like effect in which people bounce back and forth between preparation and setbacks and in the process become more and more stressed and less and less able to perform. This cycle can be vicious and debilitating. Performers who overcome it must break though the SOS barrier, which the WCPs do by revisiting their dreams. By revisiting and rethinking their dreams, WCPs are able to manage their performance to a higher level, which in turn produces a euphoric experience that Newburg calls *resonance*. Resonance is intensely rewarding, fulfilling, and enriching.

An associated "energy cycle" accompanies the model and feeds into each part of it. This energy cycle is composed of an understanding of the relationship between freedoms and responsibilities, which feeds an intense desire for new ideas. In other words, the WCPs have a strong sense that if they are to perform well, if they are to be free to perform well, they bear the responsibility. Responsibility will not be given to them. The

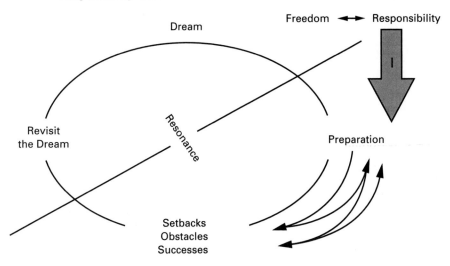

WORLD CLASS PERFORMANCE
Doug Newburg, UVA

FIGURE 7–1 The Resonance Model

search for new ideas at each stage of the model helps the WCPs continuously find ways to improve. One way to depict Newburg's world class performance model is shown in Figure 7–1.

FREEDOMS AND RESPONSIBILITIES

Freedom is very important to world-class performers. Those in Newburg's sample, in their various ways, talked about the need to feel free, to be free, and to behave freely. They talked about freedoms *of,* freedoms *to,* and freedoms *from.* These distinctions can help us explore the relationship of the concept of freedom to world-class performance.

Freedom *of* has to do with a developed capacity for performing or with release from the inability to perform. Freedom of expression for an artist or musician, for example, is the developed capacity to put on canvas or into notes an accurate representation of what that person sees, feels, and experiences inside. Freedom of performance resides in an athlete who can jump high enough to stuff a basketball in the hoop or who can swish the ball consistently from 30 feet. Freedom *of* performance resides with a surgeon who has done repeatedly and successfully what the body on the operating table needs to have done. Those of us who wrestle with our abilities to perform, whether at work, in conversation, in writing, in conducting a meeting, in coordinating a complex project, are still developing our freedoms *of.*

Freedom *to,* on the other hand, has to do with overcoming and moving beyond the parameters and constraints that inhibit us from performing what we know how to do. We may have the ability internal to us, that is, the freedom *of* performing, but if we are not invited to the key meeting or if we are restricted from the big tournament or if we are unable to see patients, we may not have the freedom *to* do what we know we can do. Organizational regulations, customs, traditions, expectations of others, financial constraints, legal guidelines, and other external factors can prevent us from doing what we are able. Unless we have developed a set of freedoms *to* related to managing our external environment, we may not have the freedoms *to* be in situations where our freedom *of*s can be exercised. One famous musician in a well-known touring group, for instance, says that he puts up with the hassles of traveling from city to city, wrestling with agents, airlines, motels, and difficult schedules just so he can be free to perform when the lights go down and the spots come up on stage.[2]

overcoming obstacles

Freedoms *from* relate to conditions or states of mind that keep someone from performing at his or her highest level. These conditions include lack of confidence, depression, a sense of mediocrity or anonymity, ignorance, and lack of motivation. Freedoms *from* are in one sense enablers of freedoms *of*. In sum, freedom is a key concept for WCPs. They seek to have freedom of expression, to be in situations in which they are free to express themselves, and to free themselves from internal constraints that might inhibit the realization of their dreams.

More important to the world-class performers, though, than the nuances among the different kinds of freedom is the strong relationship between freedoms and responsibilities. WCPs understand that they must exert themselves, they must explore and make their dreams come true if they are to realize them. This understanding expresses itself as a strong determination to make their dreams happen. WCPs know that the freedoms mentioned here do not come gratis, they require advance payment and continuing fees. WCPs understand that and are willing to pay those dues and to bear the burden of responsibility for gaining their freedom.

Most of us dream about the various freedoms. We think, "Wouldn't it be nice if I had Tiger Woods's huge commercial contracts and golfing skill!" or "If I could only sing like Bette Midler!" or "If I could manage a business like Jack Welch!" In truth, though, most of us, compared with the WCPs, have lesser degrees of understanding about the personal connection between freedoms and responsibilities. We may be envious or even frustrated because someone else has won freedom and we have not. What we lose sight of is that WCPs have worked years, maybe decades, to win their freedom—usually with no guarantee that they will achieve a goal.

Maybe we recognize the connection between freedom and responsibility and have made a conscious choice that we are not willing to pay the price for developing those freedoms. In this case, we may not be frustrated, we may have just chosen a simpler, gentler, easier path. If we are congruent with ourselves, we will admit that we are content with the consequences—not performing at the further reaches of our potential. WCPs are willing to pay the price to find that potential.

My colleague Alex Horniman[3] often notes that "excellence is a neurotic lifestyle." Many people find this statement irritating and uncomfortable, but those people may have lost an understanding of the connection between freedoms and responsibilities. What Horniman means by this statement is that to perform at your highest level, you must dedicate a significant portion of your life to developing that freedom *of*. Michael Jordan, for instance, was cut from his school's basketball team in his early high school years, but became so dedicated to improving himself that he began cutting school classes in order to play basketball. Surgeons spend years and years at rigorous schedules, developing almost obsessive study habits to get through medical school and then surgery residencies to be able to perform in the operating room. Successful chief executives in the private sector often work longer hours than do most of their colleagues. Because these executives work evenings and weekends, some people think that they are obsessed with their work. To the extent that a neurosis is a fixation on a particular aspect of life, there is a striking similarity between what "normals" might call neurotic behavior and the focused existence that world-class performers live.

In many respects this level of commitment is similar to that of effective leaders regardless of their profession or career. One simple, powerful definition of leadership, again from Horniman, is that leadership is an act of engagement. That is, when a person becomes really, deeply engaged in a cause, an issue, an activity, or a theme, people begin to notice and to respond. The commitment becomes infectious and "leadership" happens. Likewise, when a WCP becomes committed to developing a freedom, he or she begins to work diligently on the responsibilities associated with achieving that freedom.

IDEAS

Once WCPs identify freedoms that they want to achieve and accept the responsibilities that come with winning that freedom, they begin exploring. Exploring may mean reading, taking courses, creating new experiences, building new relationships, or going different places. WCPs understand that, as Alcoholics Anonymous says, "insanity is expecting different results while continuing to do the same thing." To get from where they are to where they want to be, WCPs need to find and do something different. They realize the connection between freedoms and responsibilities. This exploration leads to lots of new ideas.

The new ideas may come from conversations, films, readings, research, or taking classes, from delving into new experiences in new places or reshaping old experiences in familiar places. The point is that WCPs keep their minds open to and search for new ways of framing who they are, what they want to do, and how they can go about doing what they enjoy. In a sense, this search for new ideas helps them develop a freedom from ignorance.

We all, to some degree, engage in this search. In fact, we can think of career development as a series of explorations down blind alleys in which we try things, dislike them, and back out until we find a path that suits our interests, talents, and preferences. WCPs explore these various possibilities with a passion in their search for answers that will help them reach their dreams.

DREAMS

Not everyone has a life's dream. Many people float along, responding to the events around them rather than pursuing a dream. Thomas Jefferson's famous characterization of "life, liberty, and the pursuit of happiness" as unalienable rights inherent in all humankind does not elaborate on what constitutes happiness for any given individual. In a profound sense, discovering and defining our happiness is a major challenge for each of us. If I ask you what your goal in life is and you say, to be happy, I can reasonably infer that you have not thought about what would make you happy and therefore are in grave danger of never finding it.

The identification of a dream that can and would shape a person's life is available to everyone. Some people live their whole life and never form a dream. Some have a dream and lose it. Others have a dream, lose it, and then regain it later in life. WCPs are clear about what their dream is and are able to focus their efforts on achieving it.

I see that there are three kinds of dreams: natural dreams, given dreams, and discovered or built dreams. Natural dreams occur early in life and seem to just be there. One Olympic gold medalist in swimming began waking his parents at age six to take him to the pool for early morning workouts. Although he was a gifted athlete in several sports, he said he only got a deep, resonant feeling from swimming, something he called "easy speed." He enjoyed this experience so much that he wanted to go do it even when most kids his age were stuck to the mattress. This feeling and desire came to him naturally.

Given dreams, by contrast, are couched in someone else's experience. Strong religious orders, parents with an intense desire and focus for their children, and some schools can all impart dreams to other people. Some religions, for example, offer explanations for where you came from, what you should do at each stage in life, where you are going, and what will happen after death. The purpose and central focus of life is all laid out, and if you accept that construction, it can become your life's dream. These religions characterize such a life as "praising God" or "glorifying God" or "assisting God in his work." Given dreams can also be imparted by parents who are determined to raise a doctor, a lawyer, an NBA star, or a miner "like your father." From well before the age at which children are able to psychologically defend themselves and to explore life on their own, parental visions of who they are and what they will do are inculcated into them. Given dreams come from outside and are "given" to people who accept them. For some people, given dreams can dominate life entirely.

Many people do not have a dream, or their dream seems to change from time to time. These people may have to discover or build a dream—if they want to improve their performance and influence as the WCPs do. This discovery process may entail years of exploration, self-reflection, and determination.

The WCPs in Newburg's study were able to identify and specify their life's dreams. This vision of what they wanted to do became their central motivation and sustaining power. For the swimmer mentioned earlier, it was "easy speed" in the water. For a famous touring musician, it was to play like Elton John, whom he heard one day on the car radio.

Dreams and Goals

There is an important distinction to be made here. Dreams are not goals. A goal is a momentary manifestation of concerted effort; it is not the effort itself. A dream is what sustains us through the effort, the feeling we get that allows us to continue. A goal is like a balance sheet for a corporation, merely a snapshot at one point in time of how the activities of the organism are doing. For one Olympic gold medalist, winning the gold medal was the goal, but the dream was "to play to win at the highest level for as long as I could." For this person, daily practice with the best players in the world was a partial fulfillment of her dream. Mountaineers, too, often say that summiting is an anticlimax. Usually their first thought after summiting is, "Get me down off this damn mountain." Rather, many feel the euphoria and sense of harmony with the world during the climb. Maurice Herzog, a French climber usually attributed with the accomplishment of being the first to climb an 8,000–meter peak, Annapurna, wrote,

> We were now above the whole area of alternate ice walls and snow slopes. Lifting my head and looking upwards I saw an even snow slope in the middle of which I could pick out Terray's tracks. On the left was the great central couloir, very steep and looking as if it was waiting to swallow up anything and everything that fell from the upper slopes. The air was luminous, and the light was tinged with the most delicate blue. On the other side of the couloir, ridges of bare ice refracted the light—like prisms and sparkled with rainbow hues. The weather was still set fine—not a single cloud—and the air was dry. I felt in splendid form and as if, somehow, I had found a perfect balance within myself—was this, I wondered, the essence of happiness.[4]

Dreams are a remarkable complementarity between activities and feelings. Some people say that a dream results in certain feelings, as Herzog described. Others suggest that those feelings are the result of certain activities. I believe that this dichotomy is like the common Chinese symbol for yin and yang, in which the one flows into the other and the seeds of one lie in the other. For the swimmer, "easy speed" was a feeling he got when swimming, but not elsewhere. For the basketball player, the feeling of "playing to win at the highest level" was a part of, and in part a result of, that playing.

So, your dream may be stated so simply—"to feel in harmony with myself and the world"—and you may search for ways to make that harmony happen. Clearly, it often does not. Newburg says WCPs can and do realize their dreams frequently, even daily. The power of Newburg's research is that it helps identify a process through which we can identify life's purpose and then work to re-create our dream frequently rather than wait helplessly for it to come and go—or not to come at all.

Preparation

People who eventually perform at the world-class level advance from the formation of a life's dream to intense, sometimes extended periods of preparation. Preparation is an operationalization of their understanding of the relationship between freedoms and responsibilities. The creation of a dream may be freeing, but it is the preparation for living that dream that carries the weight of the responsibility. Preparation may include schooling, training, practice, study, scheduling different experiences, travel, making appointments with experts, reading, and changing their life structure. Each of these activities builds on the central goal of gaining mental, emotional, physical, and even cosmological mastery in their chosen dream arena. The dedication and commitment needed to plan, execute, and grow from all these experiences comes out of the understanding of—something more than the intellectual knowledge of—the relationship between freedoms and responsibilities. Preparation can take months, years, even decades. One well-known musician told of renting a remote farm with a small barn behind the house. For more than a year, he would spend 8 to 10 hours a day in the "shed," as he called it, playing scales on a baby grand piano. His wife says that it was not a very pleasant time. The musician seldom bathed, changed his clothes, or got a haircut, but when he emerged from the shed, he had developed freedom *of.* He could express his every thought and feeling through his fingers on the keyboard. In fact, he became so proficient during his preparation period that he could play the same music with either hand and would practice by simply crossing his hands and playing on—something that most musicians assert is simply astounding.

If the preparation is on target and in line with the realization of a life's dream, time becomes irrelevant. The preparation becomes a part of the resonance experienced when the dream, for periods of time, becomes a reality. In that sense, the time at which the fingers and the keyboard or the fingers and the surgeon's scalpel are working in smooth harmony becomes a realization of the dream. Additional preparation, then, is the work required to lengthen those experiences and to make them more frequent, to increase the glimpses of resonance that come from momentary realizations of the dream.

Setbacks, Obstacles, and Successes

Unfortunately, lengthy preparation does not guarantee realization of the dream. Many people prepare hard and then encounter setbacks. The preparation and training, for example, does not produce the result hoped for by the athlete, but produces an injury instead. The scientist's study does not yield new insight, but instead yields an unexpected result. The traveling creates fatigue rather than energy. The "experts" do not lend much insight. The workouts do not produce more speed or better accuracy.

At this stage, Newburg's subjects began to bounce back and forth between preparation and setbacks. When they ran into an obstacle, they redoubled their efforts and worked harder. Sometimes the WCPs fell into a vicious cycle: work harder, setback, work harder, setback. In the course of cycling this energy, this commitment, they became overprepared. Their practice became mechanical, the study became drudgery, the exploration became a task, a chore; WCPs lost their energy.

Many people, it seems, become trapped in this preparation-setback cycle, lose heart, and begin exploring other ways of making ends meet. The aspiring actor becomes a waiter, then a maître d', buys a car, and becomes, slowly, a prisoner of obligations and, paradoxically, of the ancillary and diverting small successes in areas other than the dream. When we experience some positive feedback in another area, the temptation to put more energy there and less into the dream preparation grows insidiously. Then one day, in a moment of clarity, we wonder how we got where we are and how we had let go of our dream. The WCPs in Newburg's study reported a common means of breaking through the setback/obstacle/success barrier.

Revisiting the Dream

When WCPs lost sight of their dreams, their efforts became mechanical and less than world class. When they remembered and focused on their dream, they were able to move ahead with a sense of clarity, purpose, and commitment. Distractions became less enervating, obstacles became less formidable, and setbacks became less depressing. The establishment and maintenance of a life's dream form a core, essential piece to the pattern developed by the subjects in Newburg's study.

When the preparation did not seem to be working and the setbacks and obstacles seemed insurmountable, WCPs were able to break through the barrier consistently by one method: revisiting the dream. The WCPs paused, got out of the vicious cycle, rethought why they chose the dream, revisited their definition of the dream, relived the experiences leading up to the dream's birth, and refocused their mind and attention on the joy that the dream brought even in its ethereal visionary form. They remembered the glimpses of dream realization that occurred earlier in preparation, and they immersed themselves in that memory. This process is a recharging process, a renewal, a refreshing of the vision.

Preparation is essential, *and* it can be like a well-used battery in that eventually it runs down. Unless you have a way of reenergizing your view of the dream, the obstacles begin to have more power than the dream, and they win. Take, for example, the heart surgeon who has his 403rd operation scheduled one afternoon. That morning, perhaps, he lost a patient. Does patient 403 understand the frame of mind that the surgeon is in just before her operation? If the surgeon cannot get past the setback experienced earlier in the day, he may not be able to perform at the world-class level that afternoon, something that you or I as patient 403 would be concerned about. If the surgeon has a means, external or internal, of revisiting his dream, he may be able to revitalize his emotional, mental, and physical self before the 403rd operation. Newburg, in a situation similar to this one, interviewed the surgeon and asked him why he was in surgery. Eventually, the surgeon recalled his original dream: As a six-year-old boy, he stood in his family living room and watched his grandfather die of a heart attack. The boy felt helpless, and he vowed to prepare himself so that such an event would never happen again. Then the two, Newburg and the surgeon, went to visit patient 403. After several minutes of inquiry about why the 65-year-old woman wanted to live longer, she paused, got a tear in her eye, and said that she had two grandchildren that she wanted to go swimming with. The surgeon at this point was able to revisit his dream and reconnect with his best abilities. Patient 403 survived the operation and was able to swim with her grandchildren.

By revisiting the dream, WCPs can approach preparation with a renewed vigor, with a sense of purpose, and, more important, with enjoyment. By developing the internal capacity to reconnect with the joy of fulfilling their life's dream, the WCPs can bring energy, enthusiasm, and freedom *of* together in ways that allow them to perform at their best.

This same revitalization is possible for those of us who work in the work-a-day world in which we might not often think about world-class performance. Whenever we begin to think that our work is a drudgery and that our energy is lost, we can revitalize our efforts by pausing and revisiting the choices we made that got us to where we are. If we allow ourselves to stay in the drudgery mode, we will not do our best efforts and our opportunities will shrink. If, on the other hand, we are able to reenergize each day by remembering that, of all the choices we had before us, we chose this path and this work and that we have some specific goals in mind to work on, then we can invigorate ourselves and our work. When we do that revisiting, when we remember how we are working toward a dream, something special happens.

RESONANCE

The key to the whole cycle of world-class performance, or superior performance in any field, is something called *resonance*. Resonance is a special kind of experience that high-level performance in a chosen, valued field brings to an individual. People who perform at their best report a common kind of experience.

First, they are performing at the limit of their abilities and beyond, yet it seems effortless; second, time seems to warp, either speeding up or slowing down so that they lose track of time or time seems to be moving in slow motion; third, they become utterly focused on what they are doing; fourth, they lose a sense of self and begin to merge as if in some kind of cosmic harmony with events and things around them; and fifth and most of all, they find this entire experience intensely and intrinsically rewarding and enjoyable. This phenomenon is resonance. Mihalyi Cziksentmihalyi, the best-selling author and former chair of the psychology department at the University of Chicago, refers to it as *flow*.[5] Basketball players refer to it as "being in the zone." Eastern religions and languages refer to it as *wa*,[6] or being in harmony with your surroundings. Resonance is feeling your being vibrate in harmony with the situation and events in which you are performing to such an extent that you are able to influence those events masterfully, effortlessly, and with great psychic reward.

In a broader sense, much of human activity is directed at the search for resonance. WCPs have recognized it, have found a field in which they can experience it, and have invested heavily in re-creating it as much as they can in their lives.

CHARACTERISTICS OF FLOW
1. Time warp (either fast or slow)
2. Loss of sense of self
3. Intense focus on activity at hand
4. Performance that is at peak of abilities
5. Performance that seems effortless (flow)
6. Performance that is very satisfying
7. Larger sense of self that is gained afterward

Most of you have probably experienced flow at one time or another in your lives. Perhaps you thought that this feeling is fleeting, that it comes and goes without much advance warning or notice. WCPs have learned that this feeling can be re-created, perhaps not every time they want it, but they can significantly raise the probabilities of experiencing it on demand. Newburg's model describes the process they use to re-create resonance. Resonance can accompany an individual who, after preparing, is ready to perform, is offered the opportunity to perform, and then is able to perform at the highest level. This experience, the journey if you will, not the arrival—produces resonance.

Consider a time in your life during which you experienced resonance. What were you doing? What led up to this event? What was it like? What would it take to re-create it? How, if at all, are you able to re-create that resonance in various aspects of your life today? If you can identify the feeling and the circumstances that led up to resonance, perhaps you can create it again and again in your life.

I said earlier that leadership is an act of engagement. People who have not identified their life's dream and have not begun work to achieve it are less engaged than those who have. Do not underestimate the power of this engagement to influence others. In some sense, we all admire and respect the kind of deep engagement that leads to world-class performance. And if the engagement overlaps with our own dreams in some way, we are likely to be very influenced by the people who demonstrate it. This power, in fact, is an underlying premise of the Matsushita Leadership Institute in Kanagawa, Japan. I described this institute in chapter 5, but I will recap it here. In a three-year program, the five admitted students (chosen from hundreds throughout the country) are given no class work or instruction the first year. Their whole assignment is to do whatever they need to do in order to answer one question: "What is the purpose of your life?" The underlying premise is that unless you can speak articulately about the purpose of your own life, how could you presume to lead 150 million fellow citizens? The clarity of this purpose, of this center in your life, and of the engagement that it produces when melded with the energy cycle outlined earlier can produce enormous influence on others. The power of this purpose is at the core of what it means to be an effective Level Three Leader.

> All people dream; but not equally. Those who dream by night in the dusty recesses of their minds wake in the day to find that it was vanity. But the dreamers of the day are dangerous people, for they may act their dream with open eyes to make it possible.
>
> —T. E. LAWRENCE

THE PURPOSE OF LIFE

The resonance model presented in Figure 7–1 yields a very powerful answer to an age-old question: "What is the purpose of life?" Although many people have argued that this question is meaningless, millions seem to search for the answer daily. People search for purpose, not necessarily to satisfy curiosity or to answer philosophers, but rather to make meaning in their own lives. While I do not intend to seem presumptuous, I suggest that one powerful answer to this question is the following four-part statement: The purpose of life is, first, to identify what resonates for you; second, to invest in your capacity to re-create that resonance; third, to perform and enjoy the resonance; and fourth, to help others find their resonance.

While serving as a lay clergyman responsible for 2,800 people in eight different units for more than seven years, I presided over marriages and funerals and counseled hundreds of people. This environment was one in which a given dream was very applicable to people, but I often met people who never became clear about what their life's dream was. Some seemed to drift from job to job and from place to place, never finding any purpose in their existence. By contrast, those people who had a natural dream, or who had incorporated the given dream into their lives, or who had found their own dream, were focused, purposeful, and generally successful in their endeavors. Sometimes they felt resonance from their activities.

I think it is a great tragedy in life that people live and die and never find a dream around which they can feel resonance, a tragedy in part because a dream is available to people who seek it and a tragedy in part because of the lost and unrealized potential of individuals. Whether you are born by chance in the outback of Australia, the back streets of Calcutta, the privileged classes of England, or a middle-class suburban home in America, *the* challenge in life, I say, is to find what resonates for you before you die. Some people argue that the poverty-stricken masses have no such thoughts, that their lives revolve around finding food; these arguers often quote Maslow's famous hierarchy of human needs as support for their argument. I agree and say that if the masses are to get out of that cycle, how is it to be done? If they find a dream, then and only then, it seems, will they begin to work toward it.

Investing in your dream involves the preparation I have outlined in this chapter. If you have found your dream, your challenge is to invest in it as much as you can as early as you can. Read, study, practice, emulate, borrow, travel, observe, and do whatever you can daily in your life to learn how to create that dream. If you do not invest this preparation time, you may still have a dream, but your energy cycle will be out of gas.

Once you have developed the freedom of expression, what more in life is there than to perform at your absolute best and to enjoy that performance to your core? This realization of your dream through your investments seems to be the pinnacle of life. What else is there? Well, you may say, "The purpose of life is to live a good life" or "The purpose of life is to glorify god" or "The purpose of life is to make others' lives easier." If you find resonance in these activities, then I say, "Carry on!" The resonance model does not inhibit your choice of activity. If raising children is where you resonate, then I hope you will invest in your capacity to parent ever more effectively and experience ever more frequently the resonance that comes from your parenting. If you resonate in religious work, then invest in your capacity to do it well and enjoy the resonance it brings. If you resonate in building organizations, then organization building can be the purpose of your life. Enjoying the resonance of doing what you dream of, at your highest level, effortlessly, is the pinnacle of experience in this life.

Finally, if you can help others find their resonance, you can extend your dream beyond your own experience to influence others in a positive way. The challenge in this step is to help others find *their* dream and not try to induce in them your own. If you can help others find their dream, if you can teach them how to invest in it and how to connect it to your organization's work, then you can begin to develop world-class performers. Understanding resonance and how it motivates people can help you open the door to world-class performance for yourself and for your organization. Without this understanding, you face the danger of continuing in "good enough," in a kind of mediocrity that allows you to continue, but not to achieve what you could.

Conclusion

World-class performers in many different professions exhibit a common pattern of thinking and behavior. They not only *know* but *understand* the relationship between freedom and responsibility. They seek and generate new ideas about how they might develop these freedoms, and from these ideas, they form, sometimes epiphanously, a life's dream. They work hard to prepare to realize that dream, and when they encounter the setbacks, obstacles, and alternative successes that lie along the road, they devise personal methods for mentally and emotionally revisiting the dream for renewal and refueling. As they become more and more competent and skilled in the demands of their dreams, they experience resonance, in tiny drops at first and then with increasing regularity and of longer duration.

This process suggests an answer to one of life's most difficult questions: What is the purpose of life? The resonance answer to this question is fourfold: (1) to identify the area in life that resonates for the self, (2) to invest in the ability to create and reproduce that resonance, (3) to experience and enjoy the resonance by performing at the highest potential, and (4) to help others find their source of resonance. This approach allows for religious experience as well as scientific focus, for fine arts expression as well as business achievement. Too many people go through life and never identify what resonates for them, never find the endeavor that engages them and calls on their best efforts, never experience in more than fleeting ways the deeply satisfying experience of resonance. What more positive cause could there be for aspiring leaders than to find resonance, to invest in re-creating it, to enjoy it, and to help others find theirs?

What about people who have a dream but seem destined never to achieve it? Take, for instance, basketball players who never make the NBA, students who never get to medical school, or managers who never become CEOs. In some cases, we observe almost pitiful attempts to carry on in spite of clear evidence that the dream will not happen. Well, who can say that the former collegiate basketball star playing in Italy is not enjoying his work? Who can say that the pharmacist who wanted to be a doctor is not engaged in helping others improve their health? Who can say that the middle manager, frustrated in her attempts to be promoted, cannot enjoy her work with her present subordinates or seek a larger job in another company?

Sometimes we do have to revise our dreams to deal with reality. Clinging to an unrealistic dream is, in a way, its own loss of freedom and an avoidance of the responsibilities that come with seeking freedom. Finding resonance is also about finding what it is that we can do and doing that activity to the best of our abilities. When we achieve that goal, life is enormously rewarding. If we have felt that resonance ourselves and are investing to re-create it more voluminously in our lives, perhaps we can understand why some people who seem to be at the end of their careers hang on for a little longer, seeking out of their lives that last ounce of resonance.

Principles of Level Three Leadership

1. In an increasingly global market, world-class performance is more and more required to survive and compete.

2. Research shows that people perform at their best under a remarkably similar set of conditions and that when they do, they experience a similar phenomenon—flow.

3. Flow, or resonance, can be characterized by a time warp, intense focus, loss of sense of self, peak performance that seems effortless, deep internal satisfaction, and renewed larger sense of self.

4. Resonance experiences can be re-created; we do not need to wait for them. In fact, many professions have to re-create them regularly.

5. Resonance begins with a life's dream. This dream may be natural, given, or discovered and built. Dreams are often a relationship between activities and feelings, a way of being.

6. A goal is not a dream; rather, it is a short-term marker experienced in the midst of realizing a dream. Goals are like corporate balance sheets—snapshots in time but not where the resonance is experienced.

7. Dreams lead to intense preparation.

8. World-class performers fuel their efforts with a strong understanding of the connection between freedoms and responsibilities; they realize they must make their dreams come true. This realization leads to a constant search for new ideas. The freedoms/responsibilities/ideas energy cycle feeds all aspects of the resonance experience.

9. World-class performers often encounter obstacles that prevent them from realizing their dreams.

10. World-class performers break through obstacles by finding or creating mental, physical, and emotional ways of revisiting their dreams. This exercise releases tension and helps these people become more able to perform and to experience resonance.

11. The resonance model provides a powerful answer to one of life's key questions: What is the meaning of life? The resonance model's answer is in four parts: (1) find your resonance;

(2) invest in your capacity to re-create the resonance; (3) enjoy your resonance; and (4) help others find their resonance (dreams).

12. People in positions of leadership without a life's dream will be at a disadvantage compared to those people who have one.

Questions for Reflection

1. What is your life's dream?
2. Identify a time during which you felt flow, or resonance. What were you doing? What happened? How did you feel? How could you re-create this experience more often?
3. How could you bring resonance to your work?
4. If you cannot bring resonance to your work, how will you compete against those who do?
5. What are the life's dreams of the people you work with?
6. How can you tap into the life dreams of others to realize resonance as an organization?

Notes

1. Mr. Newburg received his Ph.D. in sports psychology from the University of Virginia, where he studied under Bob Rotella. As of this writing he is employed by the UVA medical school, where he works with thoracic surgery residents to improve their performance. He is also the founder and president of his own consulting firm, Resonance Inc.
2. The names of many WCPs are omitted here because a condition of participation in the study included relative anonymity. Many of these people are careful about who uses their names and for what and wish to minimize their public exposure as they see fit.
3. Alex Horniman is a tenured, full professor at the Darden Graduate School of Business Administration and teaches a variety of programs at the school and worldwide. Trained at Harvard University, he works in the areas of organizational behavior, leadership, managing change, and creating high-performance workplaces.
4. Maurice Herzog, *Annapurna* (New York: Dutton, 1953), 166.
5. See Mihalyi Csikszentmihalyi, *Flow: The Psychology of Optimal Experience* (New York: Harper and Row, 1990).
6. In Japanese, this word is pronounced *wah*. *Wa* is the *on,* or Chinese reading, for a character meaning harmony and is depicted as a sheaf of rice next to a mouth.

Part III: Strategic Thinking (The Northeast Axis)

CHAPTER

Strategic Thinking

8

Chapter Outline

■ Definitions

■ Fundamentals of Strategic Thinking

■ Developing Strategic Thinking

■ Essential Elements of Strategic Thinking

In part II, we explored various principles and concepts related to the northern element in our general leadership model: the individual LEADER. Part III explores concepts related to the eastern element, TASK, and to the north-east connection between LEADER and TASK. This connection is about strategic thinking, about a way of viewing the world that can see past, present, and future aspects of time, that can appreciate current competitive and market realities, and that can envision the development of key capabilities, even over long periods of time.

Although I made this argument in chapter 2, I reassert it here: Leadership is nothing without strategy. If there is no strategic thinking, leaders have nowhere to go, nowhere to point. Effective leaders, by definition, have a strategic view and direction. To become effective leaders, we need to become strategic thinkers. This need is even stronger at the end of the twentieth century, because we live in a time during which the Information Revolution is transforming the nature of our lives, our organizations, and our societies. Unless potential leaders can begin to make some sense of our present world and can see what kind of world they would like, their attempts to lead will be impotent.

Prepared by James G. Clawson. Copyright © 1997 by the Darden Graduate Business School Foundation, Charlottesville, VA. All rights reserved. BP-391.

Great leaders have great strategic dreams, visions of what could be and what they think should be. Robert Greenleaf, in his seminal book *Servant Leadership,* made this comment, "Not much happens without a dream. And for something great to happen, there must be a great dream. Behind every great achievement is a dreamer of great dreams. Much more than a dreamer is required to bring it to reality; but the dream must be there first."[1] Although you may not have thought of yourself as a dreamer or a strategist, I assert that unless you are able to develop powerful strategic dreams, your abilities as a leader will be greatly undermined. To be a powerful leader, you must first have a dream, a strategic dream that defines and describes what could be or, rather, what you believe should be. Before we explore this concept in detail, let us establish some common language.

DEFINITIONS

When people begin thinking and talking about strategy and strategic thinking, they often get confused with meanings. Some simple definitions and concepts can help us move forward. A *strategic issue* is any issue that affects your ability to develop and maintain a competitive advantage. Without a competitive advantage, you do not have much of a strategic future. Eventually, the organizations that have a competitive advantage will exercise that advantage and put those who are at disadvantage out of business or existence. Strategic thinking is about conceiving ways to build and sustain competitive advantages.

> A strategic issue is any issue that affects your ability to develop and maintain a competitive advantage.

A *competitive advantage* in turn has three components (see Table 8–1).[2] First, it means that we can offer superior value to customers. If we cannot offer superior value to those who use our goods and services, we have no advantage over others who would fill those customers' needs—and eventually they will do so. Superior value may be defined by the customer in terms of quality of the product or service, convenience of access to it, cost, or unique features or in many other ways. Unless we know what our customers value, we will have difficulty identifying how, if at all, we can offer them something of superior value.

Second, competitive advantage means that our ability to offer superior goods and services is hard to imitate. If it is not, others will quickly copy what we do and our advantage will disappear. Difficulty in imitation can come from several sources. Patent protection is a common one, although it expires after a set period of time. Quality of service based on careful employee hiring practices, intensive and consistent training, and advanced human resource management policies can also be a source of competitive advantage that can take years or decades to imitate. Installed equipment base, superior hiring practices, brand recognition and reputation, geographic dominance, and government subsidy and support are also examples of sources of difficulty in imitation.

Third, our ability to offer superior goods and services must paradoxically be hard to imitate and yet enhance our own flexibility. If we learn to do things in a superior way

TABLE 8-1 Components of a Sustainable Competitive Advantage
Add superior value
Inhibit imitation
Enhance flexibility

but then the market environment changes quickly and we are unable to respond or adapt, our advantage vanishes. The very systems that made us hard to imitate can also make us inflexible in our ability to adapt. The paradox and management challenge here is that we want our delivery capabilities to be hard for others to imitate yet not hard for us to modify or adapt. Unless our management style and organizational realities include the capacity to learn and grow quickly, we will, in this rapidly changing world, become obsolete.

Our definition of strategy said, "*your* competitive advantage." My next point is, who is "you"? Strategic issues and thinking do not just apply to large organizations. Every organism faces strategic challenges, and if that organism is not able to meet and surmount those challenges, it will lose its competitive advantage and begin to die out. In the biological world, if rabbits are unable to figure out how to live in the presence of wolves, they begin to die out. If the wolves are unable to learn how to hunt better than cougars or to live among humans, they begin to die out. In the business world, units that cannot meet their competitive challenges begin to disappear.

> Strategic challenges and issues occur in three immediately relevant domains: the organization, the work group, and the individual.

The concept of strategic challenge applies to at least three levels: the organization, the work group, and the individual. If our organizations cannot compete successfully against other companies, they eventually die. If our work group (accounting or computing or telemarketing, for instance) cannot compete successfully against other, for-hire accounting units or systems consultants or telemarketing companies, for instance, our group will lose competitive advantage and eventually be sold off or outsourced. This has happened a lot during the downsizing and right sizing activities of the 1980s and 1990s. If we as individuals are not adding superior value to our employers, they find others to do the work we used to do.

As you read through this chapter on the basics of strategic thinking, I urge you to remember that there are strategic issues to be considered at the organizational level, the work group level, and the individual level. Perhaps you have not previously pictured yourself as facing strategic challenges. Picture that scenario now and you will see that unless you can provide hard-to-imitate superior value that leaves you more flexible for adapting to changes in the future, you are growing more obsolete day by day and your personal strategic competitive advantage is shrinking. Let us now look at some concepts that will help you build your strategic thinking capacity.

FUNDAMENTALS OF STRATEGIC THINKING

Bruce Henderson, founder of one of the world's great consulting firms, the Boston Consulting Group, summarizes strategy succinctly this way: "Strategy is the management of natural competition."[3] Henderson points out five basic elements of strategic competition: (1) the ability to understand the interaction dynamics of competitors in an arena, (2) the ability to predict how action will affect those dynamics, (3) the ability to commit resources to future outcomes, (4) the ability to predict risk and return on those commitments, and (5) the courage to act. These principles relate directly to your skills and abilities at strategic thinking. Several different and related approaches taken in the last 50 years build on this foundation and seek to strengthen our understanding of strategic competition. Each of these approaches can add to your ability to think strategically.

Fit Model

Ken Andrews was one of the earliest modern strategy observers and commentators.[4] Andrews popularized the separation of strategy formulation and implementation in which he argued that corporate leaders had to first create strategy and then lead and manage so as to implement it. He proposed nine criteria for evaluating the strength of corporate strategies:

1. Has the strategy been made clear and identifiable?
2. Does the strategy fully exploit domestic and international opportunities?
3. Is the strategy consistent with current and future corporate capabilities?
4. Is the strategy internally consistent?
5. Does the strategy present a manageable risk level?
6. Does the strategy match the personal values and goals of senior management?
7. Does the strategy match the company's societal contribution goals?
8. Does the strategy stimulate to action?
9. Does the marketplace seem to be responding to the strategy?

Although these questions can be answered just "yes" or "no," you will want to consider them carefully as you assess the clarity and appropriateness of your own strategic thinking.

Andrews's approach was a *fit model* in that it encouraged management to find appropriate niches in the world of opportunities and to use strengths to exploit those opportunities. Andrews's views led to a widely used model of strategic analysis commonly referred to as the SWOT model. SWOT stands for Strengths, Weaknesses, Opportunities, and Threats. Managers were to examine all four items carefully and find areas in which their particular strengths and weaknesses could be brought to bear most effectively. Figure 8–1 illustrates how the SWOT model was usually presented and conceived. The SWOT model was also often used to discuss four additional, related, action-oriented questions that corresponded with the SWOT analysis. These related questions are shown in Figure 8–2.

During the 1980s, Michael Porter from the Harvard Business School introduced what became a very popular strategic model, what he called a five forces model. Porter's

FIGURE 8–1 Four Questions That Guide Strategic Choices

economics background led him to focus more on industries than did Andrews with his corporate perspective. In Porter's model, you assess your advantages compared with other firms in an industry.[5] The five forces that shape an industry are (1) new entrants (held at bay by barriers to entry), (2) the power of suppliers, (3) the power of customers, (4) the threat of substitution, and (5) your company's core capabilities to compete amid the other companies in your industry and the other four forces.

Barriers to entry make it difficult for new entrants to compete in your industry. Barriers to entry may include patent protection, geographic proximity, established share of

FIGURE 8–2 Four More Questions That Guide Strategic Choices

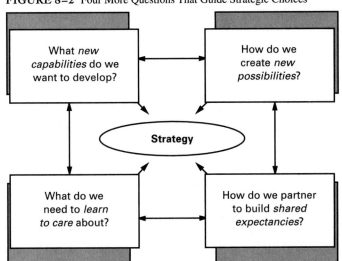

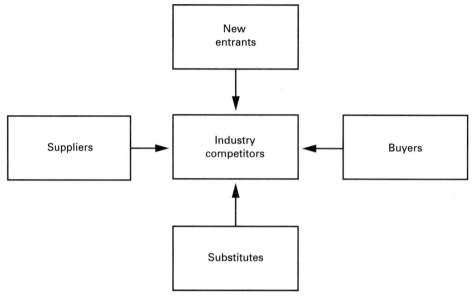

FIGURE 8–3 Porter's Five Forces Model

market, and huge but necessary initial investment costs in plant and equipment. Customers have power over your company to the extent that they want additional products or services that your company may not offer. Suppliers can influence your ability to compete to the extent that you are dependent on them for their outputs in order to meet your customers' demands. Industry innovations that leapfrog your products and services by providing substitutions for them can be a major threat to your firm's survival. Finally, if your firm's internal skills and abilities do not compare favorably with those of your competitors in an industry, your position in that industry will erode. Porter's work seemed to build well on Andrews's model, and managers accepted the "five forces model" as a natural extension of SWOT analysis. Figure 8–3 depicts Porter's five forces model.

Value Chain

Porter also clarified another important strategic concept, the value chain. In Porter's model, each company had a value chain that enabled it to compete against other companies. A value chain is a stream of activities that add value to inputs and make them desirable to others. You can examine the strength of your ability to compete by understanding the economics of each link in the value chain. Porter identified a generic value chain that consisted of nine basic elements: five primary links and four supporting structures. The five primary links were inbound logistics, operations, outbound logistics, marketing and sales, and service. Porter asserted that every organization followed this pattern of taking something in, manipulating it, delivering it to others through marketing and sales groups, and finally, servicing it if necessary. The quality of the value added at each of those steps collectively defined the strategic competitive advantage that a company had. If value was lacking at each step or was easy to imitate, the organization had little competitive advantage.

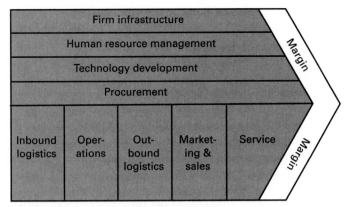

FIGURE 8–4 Porter's Generic Value Chain

Reprinted with the permission of The Free Press, a Division of Simon & Schuster from *COMPETITIVE ADVANTAGE: Creating and Sustaining Superior Performance* by Michael E. Porter. Copyright © 1985 by Michael E. Porter.

The four secondary support structures were the organizational infrastructure, human resource management practices, the technology employed and its development, and methods of procurement. These basic supporting structures made it possible for an organization to add value at each of the five links in the value chain. If any of the four supporting structures were weak or unable to contribute to the five links, an organization's strategic competitiveness was reduced. Porter's view of the generic value chain is shown in Figure 8–4.

Revisions of the value chain concept recently have applied it to a larger, industry-based view. In this revised view, you trace the major value-adding activities of a class of products or services and try to analyze where the economic opportunities are and how your own capabilities and strengths apply to those segments of the chain. The automobile industry, for example, could develop a simple value chain that included mining, shipping, steel production, shipping, component fabrication, subassembly, shipping, assembly, storing, shipping, marketing, sales, financing, and service. Henry Ford was determined in the 1920s to integrate his firm to each and every step in this chain, but over the years he discovered that it was not a profitable venture. The skills, competencies, and capabilities demanded in each step of the value chain were different, and Ford Motor Company eventually narrowed its "automobile business" to focus on fabrication, subassembly (although much subassembly is subcontracted), assembly, and financing.

This broader view of the value chain of an industry or a class of products helps your management team decide where your organization's particular skills and abilities might best add value and hence better serve customers. If you analyze the economics of each of the steps in an industry value chain, you may find opportunities or, alternatively, segments of the business in which competition does not make much sense (for instance, because margins are low, barriers to entry are high, and competition stiff).

There is no magic about deciding what the discrete links in a value chain should be. Try to identify all the separate activities that add value in the series of processes from raw material to consumption and then analyze the economics of each one. If an activity has trivial impact on the overall value added throughout the chain, it might be grouped with another activity until the grouping becomes a significant link in the value chain that delivers to customers. The goal is to create a sequential list of value-adding activity clusters, each of which has a significant impact on the value of the final product or service.

With such a list in place, you can then begin to analyze each link in the chain to see where the economic opportunities are. In this analysis, you look at special skills or technology demanded by the activity, at what the cost structures in that activity are, and at what the related margins might be; then you compare these factors with your own corporate capabilities. Let us look again at our automobile industry example. If the skills and experience demanded by the mining link are inconsistent with the organization's core capabilities and, hence, ability to add significant value, then the firm should choose, strategically, to compete elsewhere. If the margins in that mining link are narrow and shrinking because competition is high, barriers to entry are high (cost of new equipment and remote location costs), and power of customers is high, then the firm should choose to compete at a different point in the value chain. James Moore, principal at GEO Consulting, has developed an analytic procedure for doing this comparison that helps organizations clarify whether they have what it takes to succeed in business at any point in a product's value chain.

Core Capabilities

A key concept in the evolving fit strategy models was that of core capabilities. First popularized by C. K. Prahalad and Gary Hamel,[6] core capabilities referred to the collection of organizational skills a firm had developed over time that enabled it to compete and made it difficult for others to imitate its success. Core capabilities were seen as clusters of skills or competencies, often intangible, that related to technology and its development, to internal organizational processes around innovation, production, and financial management efficiencies, and to marketing. One example of successful core capabilities identification and application is Canon's expertise in what they called "opto-electronics," a phrase they used to capture their ability to marry optical skills and electronic skills effectively. This ability and its application to new products took Canon from being a camera company to being the leading firm in the birth of the computer laser printer industry. Caterpillar's extraordinary capability for managing the production, financing, and distribution of first-rate construction equipment worldwide is an example of a cluster of organizational skills in design, manufacturing, global relationships, financing innovation, and dealer relations that complemented each other intricately to create the world's most successful construction equipment company. Wal-Mart's ability to manage inventories across a vast retail distribution system is another example of organizational core competitive capability.[7] Honda's expertise and innovativeness in designing and applying high-power, high-efficiency small engines led to competitive advantages in several industries including motorcycles, lawn care products, and automobiles. Disney's ability to imagine and create animated stories that appealed to children and adults was the central factor in an empire of entertainment that has grown to include amusement parks, broadcasting companies, toys, hotels, and golf courses.

The key question that this kind of strategic thinking poses to a firm's management is, "What are your unique core capabilities?" A firm that can identify something it does better than anyone else and can focus that capability onto responsive markets will have, for the moment, a competitive advantage. By definition, core capabilities take time to develop and are so complex, weaving together competencies from various divisions of an organization, that they tend to be difficult to imitate, especially in the short run. This problem was one of the key findings in Jim Collins and Jerry Porras's seminal book *Built to Last*.[8] As firms tried to find places in which their particular core capabilities might compete successfully, they found themselves fighting for increasingly narrow niches. Strategic fit thinking was ultimately limited, which caused some firms to begin thinking about ways of changing the relative mix of competitive advantages in industry according to their desires.

Intent Model

While Andrews and Porter and others emphasized finding the right time and place to compete, Hamel and Prahalad began to wonder about core capabilities as a means of developing strategic competitive advantage in the future. In this approach, they built on the ideas of Karl Weick, who wrote about the importance not just of responding to the environment, but of *enacting* it.[9] Whereas James Bryant Quinn and others had defined strategy as the path made apparent by a series of historical decisions,[10] Prahalad and Hamel asserted that strategic thinkers should be finding ways of enacting or shaping their competitive environments by investing in and creating a set of organizational capabilities that would give them, at some time in the future, a competitive advantage.

This strategic intent might take years to realize, but if carefully conceived and managed, it could reshape the economics of an industry and give a firm an advantage that would take others, similarly, years to duplicate—in the meantime, of course, the innovative firm would continue to develop its core capabilities. This more proactive approach was called the strategic intent model. One shining example of this way of thinking is manifest in the history of Komatsu, the Japanese construction equipment maker. When Komatsu decided to take on Caterpillar in the global construction market, it had neither the resources nor the core capabilities to do so effectively. Yet the company formed a serious, strategic intent and, by following that intent, by investing year by year in its targeted capabilities, was able to win major portions of its chosen business.[11]

The strategic intent model brings to the fore, first, the importance of having a vision of what the organization could and should become and, second, the determination and resources to invest in the competitive capabilities necessary to bring that vision to pass. If it takes years, even decades, to build an advantageous set of core capabilities, then only firms with the vision and resource to continue doing business will be able to achieve that goal.

Ecological Model

A third approach was emerging in the work of James Moore at GEO Consulting. Moore postulated that the concept of business industries was dying and that a more accurate descriptive metaphor of what was happening in the business world near the end of the millennium was the concept of business ecosystems.[12] Moore argued that the reality was that Company A may be competing with Company B in one region of the world, be selling to Company B in another region, and be in a joint venture alliance with Company B in third region. Each company, in this ecological view, is living and thriving in a complex relationship with the other, and the destruction of either might lead to disastrous results for the one that remains.

This view is decidedly different from the common "business is war" mentality that most managers take to their strategic planning and that usually involves finding ways to minimize or destroy competitors' positions. In the ecological view of business, putting other companies out of business may be the worst strategy for a company that has these multiple relationships around the world. The more long-lasting approach is for managers to view their businesses as ecosystems with ill-defined boundaries between industries or companies and to approach their competitors as necessary parts of the business ecosystem rather than as enemies to be exterminated. Companies who can compete on one hand and ally on the other are developing core capabilities that allow them to deal with ambiguity, contradiction, and competing internal pressures in ways that give them an advantage, are hard to imitate, and build their flexibility for the future. Those companies that persist in fighting their competitors may in fact be sowing the seeds of their own destruction.

DEVELOPING STRATEGIC THINKING

The main elements of the fit, intent, and ecological models of strategic thinking build on and are related to each other. Modern strategic thinkers work hard to understand the influential forces in the world around them, to assess and develop their relative competitive strengths vis-à-vis their competitors, to develop clear visions of where they want to go, and to maintain the flexibility and even contradictory nature of countervailing relationships in order to develop a sustainable, strategic, competitive advantage. This effort at strategic thinking is hard work. You must read about and follow trends in the general and trade presses to keep current on forces that are influencing your present and future. You must be keenly aware of the basis on which your own unit competes with others. You must be open to learning and developing new ways of competing. You must have not only the vision but the courage to choose a path and then the fortitude to stick to it over years of effort perhaps with modest results at first.

Two modern strategists, Jeanne Liedtka and John Rosenblum, call strategic conversations the building blocks of strategy.[13] In the course of these conversations, as people try to discover and develop their strategic plans, they sometimes get confused by the language. They begin to use strategy, vision, mission, business, values, and other related terms somewhat loosely or interchangeably, which this can lead to miscommunication and misdirection. One way to begin developing strategic thinking skills is to work through what we will call an organizational charter.

Organizational Charters

Charters in the colonial era were documents that outlined the purpose, scope, and range of authority for a particular expedition. These charters included geographic definitions, goals, and expected outcomes; they also delegated certain powers for implementation. Similarly, we can consider an organizational charter as a set of documents that outlines the present and future of the organizational expedition. I think of organizational charters as having five distinct and sequential parts:

1. a mission statement
2. a vision statement
3. a values statement

4. a strategy
5. a set of operating goals

American companies seem to spend most of their time and energy attending to and working on the operating goals. In fact, I have heard senior executives of a major firm telling managers from around the firm that the managers' business was to make the stock price of the firm rise to a certain figure by the end of the year and that if it did not, the senior executives would not get their year-end bonuses, so the managers needed to get their rears in gear. This announcement was the apparent sum of the senior executives' strategic thinking. Although I believe that profitability and stock performance are important, I also assert (along with Collins and Porras and others) that focusing on these measures to the exclusion of customer service and value delivered undermine the long-term viability of a firm and can actually harm the company by encouraging people to make decisions and take actions that hurt customer relationships and eventually profitability.

Mission Statement

Organizational charters begin with a clarity around what business you are in. Unless you can state a purpose or a mission for your organization, your people will wonder what they are working for. Bennis and Biederman, in their book, *Organizing Genius,* offer good examples of purpose as they describe the characteristics of seven world-class groups.[14] Perhaps the most dramatic of these groups was the Manhattan Project, which led to the explosion of the first atom bomb and brought World War II to a quick conclusion. In the early stages of this effort, the project was not going well. Members of the Manhattan Project had been sworn to such strict secrecy that they did not know, as a whole, what they were working on or why. When J. Robert Oppenheimer took a different tactic—he called the scientists all together and explained passionately, personally, and directly what they were working on and why it was important to thousands, even millions, of people—the project was galvanized, and extraordinary results began to emerge. Effective leaders who are able to articulate immediately and powerfully the what and why of their organization's existence can motivate people in remarkable ways.

Vision Statement

The second step in building an organization charter is clarifying the vision of what could be. If the mission statement outlines what business you are in and why, the vision statement is a verbal view of where you are going. Effective leaders can describe what the goal looks like and make it real for the people involved. Sometimes leaders use storytelling[15] or a powerful metaphor or simply a clear mental image that can be described easily.

Values Statement

Once the leader can identify the purpose and the future of the organization, the next important piece of the strategic thinking puzzle is some clarity around how the organization will go about its work. This values statement attempts to clarify what means will be tolerated in the organization's efforts to realize its goals. I remember one senior business meeting in which the heads of businesses for a client had assembled to discuss their strategies. During the discussion, it became apparent that one of the managers, whose company had been recently acquired, had a subsidiary that produced, among other things, adult movies. This realization was a shock to the other managers, and a huge discussion ensued about whether the company wanted to remain in that business even though the subsidiary was highly profitable. The underlying and tacit values statement of this firm was significantly enhanced that day, but obviously, the sooner a company can clarify operating values, the easier it will be for subsequent managers to make decisions under conditions of uncertainty. An effective values statement seems essential to building the kind of lasting organization that Collins and Porras, for example, describe.

Strategy

The fourth part of an organizational charter is the strategy, that is, the path of choices that management makes among all the available paths in order to move toward the company's vision. A myriad of decisions need to be made in order to build a strategy. Sometimes these decisions are made without a vision, and a strategy emerges retrospectively. Although this kind of short-sighted reactive incrementalism may result in profitable firms, eventually the organization without a strategic intent will drift. Effective leaders have a clear view of where they want to go and how they plan to get there. The first part of this chapter introduced various approaches to thinking about and conceptualizing this portion of strategic thinking.

Strategy building is difficult in rapidly changing environments. When the context is chaotic, strategic thinkers need to develop alternative, flexible courses of action. These plans will only be effective if they have a strong value base and are consistent with what Collins and Porras called the firm's "purpose beyond profits." The current turbulence in the economic world has led to a rapid erosion of trust in strategic planning departments. Many companies that developed strategic plans with strategic intent and had bet large resources on those plans discovered in the last 20 years that strategic plans could not be trusted because circumstances changed so rapidly.

Scenario Building   A proven, effective alternative to the practice of strategic planning is scenario building, a process in which strategic thinkers develop plausible stories about what could happen in the changing environmental context. True strategic scenario building is something quite different from the common practice of "best case, worst case, most likely case scenarios." In scenario building, each story is possible and has significant consequences for the firm. The challenge is to identify these likely alternatives and then discover as soon as possible which is occurring.

Strategic thinkers at Royal Dutch Shell in the late 1960s and early 1970s developed this technique to such a point that they were able to move their company from number seven among the seven major oil companies to number one or two at the end of the millennium. By reading and thinking about economics, politics, geography, nationalism, and a host of other factors, Pierre Wack, Peter Schwartz, and their colleagues identified various likely scenarios that Royal Dutch Shell might face and then specified the kinds of indicators they might see in the newspapers for each scenario.

When small articles about Middle Eastern oil producers who were meeting to discuss "international affairs" began appearing in the international papers that they scanned regularly, these strategists recognized a leading indicator of one of their scenarios, one that included the formation of an oil cartel. What was to others a trivial non-news item in the middle of the paper was to the scanners at Royal Dutch Shell a clear predictor of their "oil cartel" scenario and its enormous implications for obtaining stable supplies of crude. Because the company had already worked through what might happen if such a cartel were formed, Royal Dutch Shell, after seeing these articles, was able to change its strategic course to one of gaining direct access to oil supplies before the oil shock of 1973 hit. In so doing, Royal Dutch Shell laid the foundation for the company's dramatic rise among its competitors. Scenario planning, therefore, has a demonstrated capacity for helping strategic thinkers approach the process of strategy building with discipline and grounded foresight.[16]

Operating Goals

The fifth element in an organizational charter is composed of the periodic operating goals and milestones that management establishes to measure and monitor progress along the strategic path toward the ultimate vision. Many companies focus on these targets and pay too little attention to why, how, and where. A company that is determined to reach certain sales targets and that focuses primarily on that goal, for instance, could unintentionally encourage people to do things that were detrimental to the company. Milestones and progress indicators are important, but they are secondary to pursuing the company's primary mission.[17]

Exercise in Strategic Thinking

Obviously, a key activity in the development of good strategic thinking is wide-ranging reading and thinking. Sometimes impending opportunity or disaster can be best seen from a different and distant vantage point. Strategic thinkers are skilled at viewing situations from multiple points of view and at collecting data on and perspectives of those different points of view. One way, for instance, that we have tried to help our MBA students develop this "ability to see the alternative" is by teaching them to play the Chinese/Japanese game of GO.

GO is a played on a board with 19 horizontal lines and 19 vertical lines that altogether create 361 squares. Unlike chess players, who have many different kinds of pieces to move, GO players have only stones, black and white, which they may place as they wish on the intersections of the lines. The objective in chess is to capture or kill the opposing king; in GO the objective is to control more territory than your opponent but not to annihilate him or her. Because the board has many more squares (chess has only 64) and because the object of the game is different, GO is a more complex game than chess is. Linear thinking that anticipates several moves down the line becomes a liability. Rather, the ability to "see" the development of strong and weak "shapes" of stones as they evolve on the board becomes more important. Western students report that learning to play GO caused them to realize that the majority of the world's population, those living in Asia, might think about things in fundamentally different ways than Westerners do and that the depth of those differences is significant. I offer this game as only one example of how you can develop your strategic thinking skills.

ESSENTIAL ELEMENTS OF STRATEGIC THINKING

Jeanne Liedtka helps us summarize our discussion with her perspective on strategic thinking, which, she says, has five key elements: a systems perspective, a focus on intent, intelligent opportunism, timing, and a hypothesis.[18] Strategic thinking begins with a *systems perspective*, an ability to see how the various forces and components of an industry fit together. A systems perspective helps you rise above satisfying your own departmental goals to see how all parts of an organization or industry fit together and how changes in one will affect others.

Once you understand the various components—the parts of the value chain in an industry, for example—*intelligent opportunism* allows you to find the profitable places in which to do business. *Intelligent* refers to the ability to analyze and interpret the various parts and pieces of an industry or business segment. Apply the analytic techniques that I described earlier in this chapter. Use these tools to develop an intelligent view of where the opportunities might lie.

This analysis provides an opportunity for you as the strategic thinker or leader to make a decision about what you want to do. This choice forms the core of your *intent*. Unless this intent is clear, your strategy will vacillate and wander.

The implementation of an intent is based on some *hypothesis* about cause and effect relationships in the industry or business. Recognition of the hypothetical nature of this element is the difference between stubbornness and persistence. If things do not work out while you are implementing your intent, a hypothesis-driven perspective will give you the impetus to try something else. Sometimes this new direction means a change in method; other times, a change in intent.

Finally, as a strategic thinker, you must understand the importance of *timing*. You need to know that the right product or strategy at the wrong time will fail. You must be neither too soon nor too late, neither rushing nor delaying unduly. Develop a sense of when you should act and when you should wait.

Conclusion

Effective leaders are strategic thinkers. They have developed the skills of clarifying what their purpose is, of visualizing what they could become if that purpose were realized, and of exploring ways and means of reaching that vision. They understand the importance of investing in and developing the core capabilities that are necessary to execute and implement their strategic intent. Increasingly, they understand the importance of managing their strategic intentions with enough flexibility to allow them not only to coexist with competitors in a global market but to thrive in a symbiotic way with them.

Strategic thinking is part art and part discipline. You can develop your strategic thinking skills. This development will require effort, study, hard thinking, lots of conversations, and a wide range of reading and reflection. It will require practice in articulating what may be only fuzzy thoughts occasionally illuminated by brief flashes of insight. It will require learning to capture those thoughts and flashes in your conscious, verbal mind and on paper. And if you are to implement and realize your strategic dreams, it will require you to develop consummate skills in leadership and managing change.

Finally, note that strategy, effective strategy, is revolutionary.[19] Unless you are finding revolutionary new ways to provide for customers, you are polishing old apples. Strategic breakthroughs and their subsequent competitive advantages have mostly come from revolutionaries, from people who are thinking outside the norm, questioning the traditional ways of doing things, and pressing for unorthodox perspectives or approaches. Steve Jobs and Steve Wosniak were so revolutionary in their thinking that Hewlett-Packard refused to fund their personal computer idea while they were employees. They left and spawned a whole new industry. Walt Disney's idea of a full-length animated film was ridiculed by most of the powerful people in Hollywood at the time. Entrenched management often does not see the value in new, revolutionary ideas, yet it is often from those very ideas that the industry-founding innovations come.

Principles of Level Three Leadership

1. A strategic issue is any issue that affects your ability to develop and maintain a competitive advantage.
2. A competitive advantage has three parts: superior value added, difficulty in imitation, and enhanced flexibility.
3. Strategic thinking applies to at least three levels: organization, work group, and individual.
4. Strategic intent is either determining to build competency in order to fit in the environment or creating an environment in which you fit.
5. Each link in the value chain for a product or service has its own strategic value or lack thereof.
6. Competitive advantage is built on core capabilities that take time to develop.
7. Effective strategic thinking is usually revolutionary.
8. Strategic scenario building can help you position yourself effectively for the future.
9. Organizational charters consist of purpose, vision, values, strategy, and operating goals.
10. Effective leaders are good strategic thinkers.
11. Strategic thinking involves an ability to analyze competitive advantages and to devise means of developing and maintaining them.
12. Strategic thinkers are familiar with several perspectives, including SWOT analysis, five forces analysis, building strategic intent based on core capabilities, long-term scenario building, businesses as ecosystems, and strategy as revolution.

Questions for Reflection

1. How much time do you spend thinking strategically about your own position, your work group's position, and your company's position?
2. If you avoid strategic thinking because either your job does not demand it or you do not have time for it, what impact will this delay have on your career over the next 10 to 20 years?
3. How does your organization treat its revolutionaries?
4. How, if at all, are you revolutionary in your thinking?
5. What could you do to develop or improve your strategic thinking skills?
6. How can you allocate regular time to strategic thinking?

7. How could you develop a set of strategic documents (charters) that relate to your organization, your work group, and yourself?

8. What do you need to read in order to develop a different perspective on your industry, company, and work group?

9. What are the key competitive forces at play in your industry? Where are they headed?

10. What scenarios can you imagine that are plausible and yet potentially disrupting to your firm or work group? How could you prepare for those alternatives?

Notes

1. Robert Greenleaf, *Servant Leadership* (Mahwah, NJ: Paulist Press, 1977) 16.

2. George S. Day, "The Capabilities of Market-Driven Organizations," *Journal of Marketing* 58 (October 1994): 37–52.

3. Bruce Henderson, "The Origin of Strategy," *Harvard Business Review* (November 1989).

4. Kenneth Andrews, *The Concept of Corporate Strategy* (Homewood, IL: Irwin, 1971, 1980).

5. Michael Porter, *Competitive Advantage* (New York: Free Press, 1985).

6. C. K. Prahalad and Gary Hamel, "Core Competence of the Corporation," *Harvard Business Review* (May 1990).

7. See George Stalk, Philip Evans, and Lawrence E. Shulman, "Competing on Capabilities: The New Rules of Corporate Strategy," *Harvard Business Review* (March 1992).

8. James C. Collins and Jerry I. Porras, *Built to Last* (New York: HarperBusiness, 1994).

9. Karl Weick, *The Social Psychology of Organizing* (Reading, MA: Addison-Wesley, 1979).

10. James B. Quinn, "Strategic Change: Logical Incrementalism," *Sloan Management Review* (summer 1989), 45.

11. For further details, see "Komatsu Limited," Harvard Case Services 9–385–277.

12. See James F. Moore, "Predators and Prey: A New Ecology of Competition," *Harvard Business Review* (May 1993).

13. Jeanne M. Liedtka and John W. Rosenblum, "Shaping Conversations: Making Strategy, Managing Change," *California Management Review* 39, no. 1 (fall 1996): 4.

14. Warren Bennis and Patricia Ward Biederman, *Organizing Genius* (Reading, MA: Addison-Wesley, 1997).

15. For more on this topic, see Warren Bennis and Harry Levinson, "Two Views of Leadership," *Harvard Business Review* (January 1996).

16. For more information on scenario planning, see Les Grayson and James Clawson, "Scenario Building" (UVA-G-260), available through Darden Educational Materials Services, Charlottesville, Virginia; Paul Shoemaker, "Scenario Planning: A Tool for Strategic Thinking," *Sloan Management Review* (winter 1995): 25; Pierre Wack, "Scenarios: Uncharted Waters Ahead," *Harvard Business Review* (September 1985); and Peter Schwartz, *The Art of the Long View* (New York: Doubleday Currency, 1991).

17. To learn more about organizational charters, refer to James Clawson, "Organization Charters" (UVA-OB-600), available through Darden Educational Materials Services, Charlottesville, Virginia.

18. Jeanne Liedtka, "Strategic Thinking: Elements, Outcomes, and Implications for Planning," working paper DWP 96–29 (1996), Darden Graduate School of Business Administration, Charlottesville, Virginia; available through Darden Educational Materials Service, Charlottesville, Virginia.

19. See Gary Hamel, "Strategy as Revolution," *Harvard Business Review* (July 1996).

Part IV: Leading Others (The Northwest Axis)

CHAPTER

Leading Others

Chapter Outline

■ Classic Model of Influence

■ Exchange Model of Influence

■ General Approach to Influence

Leadership eventually comes down to influencing others. Even with a strategic vision and skills in managing change, leaders must know how to and be willing to influence others. I assert that there are two clusters of critical skills in influencing others. The first is subsumed in the moral foundation described in chapter 4. The second cluster lies in the set of leadership skills commonly discussed—skills of persuasion that involve language and interpersonal relationships. The importance of the leader-follower relationship is represented in our general model (see chapter 2) by the northwest axis that connects the *leader* and the *followers*. The quality of this relationship will determine to a large extent how willing the followers will be to respond to the leader's attempts to influence.

CLASSIC SOURCES OF POWER

Legitimate authority

Coercion

Reward

Expertise

Personal reference

CLASSIC MODEL OF INFLUENCE

Where does this influence come from? How does a person go about influencing others? The first answer could begin with the classic view of the sources of interpersonal influence developed by French and Raven,[1] who concluded that people influence others by using one or more of five fundamental sources of power: legitimate authority, coercion, reward, expertise, and reference. Legitimate influence is based on followers' recognition of the legal authority of the title of the leader. If followers believe that people should obey the boss (or the teacher or the duke or the coach or whatever title is presented), then followers will allow that person to influence them. To followers, the leader has a legitimate right to have influence.

Coercion, of course, is based on fear. Coerced followers are afraid of the consequences if they do not do what the leader wants them to do. These consequences could be physical, emotional, social or professional, like losing their job.

Reward power comes into play when the leader influences others by offering them something in return for their conformity. These rewards are usually "if-then" relationships, e.g., "if you do this for me, then I will do that for you." Reward power is based on the leader's ability to exchange something of value with followers.

Expertise influence comes about when one person knows more about a critical issue than another person does. If the job, for instance, is to build a bridge, and there is only one civil engineer in the group, that person is likely to exert the most influence and become the leader of the group. In another group or for a different goal, of course, the engineer might have no influence. Expertise power depends largely on the task at hand—and the followers' perception of the relevancy of the leader's skills.

Referent power relates to a person's ability to influence others because they admire, respect, and want to be like the leader. People who want to emulate a person's style will be influenced by that style. People who want to join a club will be open to influence by those who control admission to the club.

People can and do draw on all these sources of influence in any given situation. We do not use one source of influence exclusively. However, those leaders who use primarily referent, expertise, and reward power bases in their attempts to influence others will be more successful in the long run. Coercion may get people to comply in the short run, but it will not have the staying power of the more respectful sources of influence. In this sense, coercion is a Level One source of influence. Legitimate power can also be used to coerce. Expertise power that relies largely on skills and judgments, and reward power that relies on mutual exchanges can both be considered rational or Level Two sources of influence. When people follow because they want to emulate the leader, they are responding to a Level Three approach.

Furthermore, given my definition of leadership in chapter 2, any source of power that gets people to respond involuntarily is something other than leadership. In this view, the use of coercion moves a person out of the realm of leadership. A person may be exerting power and people may be responding, at least in the short run, but if those people are not responding willingly, then it is not, I say, leadership.

Legitimate power and coercion are common sources of influence used by people in positions of power today. Many people respond to the wishes of others because they assume that the boss has the right to ask, has all the answers, or has the power to hurt them in some form. These methods are common and well recognized as a means of getting things done,[2] but I assert that they are not leadership. Steve Covey, my first Organizational Behavior instructor, once explained that when you use your title as a means to get something done ("I am the vice president, so you need to do what I ask!"), you are using a crutch. Like a walking crutch, a leadership/power crutch is unwieldy, is not very nimble, and does not contribute much to world-class performance. Even if you *have* positional power or the means to coerce others, if you use it, you are undermining your own ability to lead. Test this concept by asking a central leadership question: "Are these people doing this task because I told them to or because they understand why we need to accomplish this task and voluntarily agree that it is the right thing to do?" If the answer is because they understand and agree with the task, then you are on the road to becoming an effective Level Three leader. If the answer is because you told them to do the task, then you might rethink the long-term consequences of your approach to influencing others. In the long run, all enduring and effective relationships—including leader-follower relationships—are voluntary and reciprocal in nature.

> In the long run, all enduring and effective relationships—including leader-follower relationships—are voluntary and reciprocal in nature.

EXCHANGE MODEL OF INFLUENCE

Allan Cohen and David Bradford[3] have taken this fundamental insight several steps further and argue that influential relationships, with or without authority, are based on reciprocal exchanges and that the currencies of these exchanges can be identified and managed. These currencies are not monetary currencies but psychological ones in which people will exchange, for example, effort for praise, work for recognition, and compromise for inclusion. Cohen and Bradford's exchange model implies a logical, six-step sequence to developing influence with others.

First, assume that the other people are potential allies in accomplishing your purposes. If you cannot make that connection, you will have difficulty giving them something they want in exchange for something you want from them. This perspective aligns with the view presented in chapter 5 that a key leadership skill is to clarify what the others can contribute to your cause.

Second, clarify your goals so that you know what you want. This step is consistent with my principle of clarifying your vision. Third—here Cohen and Bradford build on Kotter and Gabarro's famous article on managing your boss[4]—assess carefully other people's worlds so that you can understand their concerns, their priorities and goals, and their immediate needs. Through careful listening and observation you can find out how to help other people achieve what they want to accomplish. This simple construct is the basis for the highly successful careers of many people.[5] If you cannot in good conscience align yourself with the goals of another person, then you may not be able to influence using Level Three approaches.

Fourth, assess your resources to determine if you can give people what they want or need. Sometimes you must evaluate your own willingness to give recognition or praise or other forms of interpersonal currency when you otherwise might not do so.

Fifth, diagnose your relationships with other people to see if the underlying foundation will support a series of exchanges. This step is similar to my belief that you need to have the moral rock, or moral foundation, in place before you begin trying the tools and techniques of leadership influence.

Finally, select a basis for exchange and begin making exchanges in the relationship until the relationship is comfortable, ongoing, and reciprocally rewarding, much like a business relationship. If you have not established a relationship with other people that will support exchanges of mutually valuable currencies, then trades, or interactions, are not likely to occur.

The focus in the Cohen and Bradford sequence is on the medium of exchange between people, that is, on a set of psycho-social currencies that are ethereal but very real. People value these currencies differently. If you are skilled in identifying these currencies, in identifying which currencies are valued, and in exchanging these currencies, you can significantly enhance your ability to influence. Cohen and Bradford identify inspiration-based currencies, task-related currencies, position-related currencies, relationship-based currencies, and personal-related currencies.

Inspiration-based currencies include vision, excellence, and moral correctness. If your vision has a larger significance for your department, organization, community, or society, the followers may wish to be a part of that vision and therefore will do what you ask in exchange for being included. If you are part of a team that is recognized for being outstanding at what you do, the followers may be open to influence in order to associate in some way with this reputation for quality. Followers may be inspired by the moral rectitude of your activity and may wish to participate to be a part of that integrity. The inspiration currencies that the leader exchanges for followership are new views of where to go, of how good that direction could be, and of how right that direction is.

Task-related currencies include new resources, opportunities to learn, home job support, rapid response, and information. If you can offer followers additional resources like money, personnel, or facilities, they may be open to your requests. If you can offer them an opportunity to learn something new, they may respond. If you can lend them support for their work, they may be willing to support yours. If you can promise them quicker response times in your relationship, they may be willing to adjust the way they do things. If you can give them better access to key information, they may be willing to follow your lead.

Position-based currencies are recognition, visibility, reputation, insider importance, and network contacts. Your recognition of people's good work—even if they do not work directly for you—could be influential in their world and could be exchanged for their help on your work. If you have access to people who are viewed by the followers as important, trade introductions to these people (visibility) for response. If your comments on the social network of your organization have an impact on reputation in the firm, exchange reputation-enhancing comments for other people's willingness to help out. If you are a member of an "inside" group and the followers value membership in that group, trade this sense of belonging by including them in the group. If you know people who could benefit followers, exchange introductions as a means of expanding the followers' networks.

Relationship-based currencies are related to the quality of your relationship with other people and include understanding, acceptance, and personal support. If you are willing to take the time and emotional energy and have the skills of reflective listening and empathy, you can exchange your willingness to attend to and understand followers' points of view and/or situations for their willingness to assist you in meeting your goals. Further, if you can genuinely express a sense of acceptance and friendship with the followers, you will likely have more influence on them. If you can extend your friendship to include personal and emotional support in times of need, followers are more likely to help you when you need it.

Finally, Cohen and Bradford identify *personal-related currencies* like gratitude, ownership, self-concept building, and comfort levels as means of influencing others through exchange. When you express your gratitude to others, they often feel closer to you and more bonded so that when you need help, they are more likely to give it. If you can acknowledge the ways in which followers might "own" or be the key figure in a project, they are likely to be open to your influence. If you can honestly affirm their personal values, their sense of self, and their definition of who they are, followers are likely to be more responsive to your requests. If you can manage your relationships in a way that minimizes the hassles that the followers experience, they are more likely to pay attention and be willing to respond.

These currencies of exchange all provide a means for influencing other people even if you do not have a formal legitimate base of power. As you were reading through the descriptions of these currencies, you may have thought to use them in a manipulative way to get other people to respond when your own feelings might not be genuine. Although this facade may be effective in the short run, unless you have the moral foundation in place to begin with, the use of any "technique" of influence to manipulate will eventually be perceived and your ability to influence will be greatly eroded.

One major advantage of an exchange model is that it helps us to consider how we might manage our boss or others with whom we have no formal authority. The steps outlined in this section include searching for the basis of an alliance between people. In my experience, most people approach relationships with a strong, though sometimes well-masked, intention of changing the other person. A person who says, "My boss is doing the wrong thing, but I need to go in and learn my boss's way of seeing things," will typically begin trying to change the boss's mind within minutes. The tone and conclusion of such a meeting is that the boss views this person as more of an adversary than an ally. Unless you can present yourself as an ally to the other person's goals and aspirations, you will be perceived as a hindrance rather than a help.

A major, potentially negative, aspect of exchange models is that people can be resentful if they sense that you are doing favors primarily to establish influence rather than out of a genuine concern for their well-being. Recipients will feel beholden or obligated to respond in kind. Although they may meet their obligations in order to relieve their sense of duty, this effort will not be of the quality or long-term consequence that an aspiring Level Three Leader would hope for.

The primary solution for this dilemma is to have a deep, honest, and genuine interest in the well-being of others. Without this concern, your leadership will eventually be seen for what it is, self-serving and uncaring; this perception will be disastrous to your ability to influence. Perhaps you do not particularly like the people you work with or you do not have a lot of respect for the people who work for you. If so, you may have to settle for Level Two Leadership or even Level One Leadership. Remember, of course, that if you compete against an organization with a Level Three Leader, you may have a difficult time keeping up.

Mutually rewarding relationships that are built on the moral foundation develop trust and respect, and potential followers will be open to influence. In my own study of superior-subordinate pairs in a large insurance company, the level of trust and respect in the relationships accounted for more than 75 percent of the perceived learning that the subordinate experienced. To the extent that learning is a substitute for openness to influence from another person, trust and respect are essential in establishing a strong leader-follower relationship.[6]

Sometimes people resist the notion of looking at relationships as a series of trades or exchanges. Such a view seems too commercial to them. Yet there is substantial momentum behind this view that bears consideration. Stephen Covey, author of the best-selling book *Seven Habits of Highly Effective People,*[7] compares relationships to the accounts that bookkeepers use to keep track of a company's finances. Covey argues persuasively that we have "accounts" with other people. When we do something for them that they value, we make a deposit into our mutual account, and when we ask them to do something for us, we make a withdrawal. Likewise in reverse, if they do something for us, they make a deposit in our account, and we are likely to be responsive to them in the future because of this credit balance. If we ask them to do more for us than we have done for them, we may use up our credit with them, and perhaps even overdraw the account to the point at which they feel that they have been carrying us in the relationship. If they trust us, they may let us carry an overdrawn account in the short run, but this situation is unstable and probably will not last for long. The challenge in managing our relationships and our ability to influence others is at least to maintain a balanced relationship account, and if we want to have more influence in the future, to build a large credit balance.

The exchange model system of credits and debits in relationships has been used in many societies and formalized in some. In the published accounts of the Mafia, for instance, or in the nation of Japan, clear rules about exchange of favors have been established. In Japan, members of society are taught to watch carefully the balance between *on* (pronounced *own*), or bestowed benevolence, and *giri* (pronounced *geedee*), or duty or obligation. People will manage their obligations so carefully that they may not accept a random act of kindness from a stranger for fear of generating more responsibilities than they feel they can manage in the future.

GENERAL APPROACH TO INFLUENCE

If we consolidate the classic and exchange models of influence introduced in this chapter, we can create a general approach to influencing others. With this approach, you can have a lasting influence on other people if you (1) have a clear purpose, (2) are able to communicate that purpose clearly and inspirationally, (3) can garner the support of others by showing them how that purpose benefits them, (4) can manage reciprocal exchanges with others, and (5) can manage progress toward the purpose.

Clear Purpose

Most leadership fails because it has an ill-defined or weak purpose. If you are not clear on who you are and what you want to do, you will unable to inspire superior effort in yourself or in others. It is essential that you have clarified what you want to do and that you have committed your professional efforts, if not your life, to this purpose, mission, or dream. Previous chapters have discussed various perspectives on developing a strategic vision and on creating a personal dream. I only wish to remind you here that unless you can clarify that to yourself, you will not be able to engage others.

Clear Communication

Language is the primary medium through which we communicate and with which we attempt to lead and influence others. If your language is fuzzy, illogical, uninspiring, or diffuse, you will not be able to inspire others. Four basic principles govern effective leadership communications: clarity, respect, stimulation, and congruency.

Effective leadership language is clear, respectful, stimulating, and congruent.

Clarity is essential in leadership communications because you must be clear on your purpose and on the role that others can play in that purpose. If either of these two elements are fuzzy to you, they will be fuzzy to others, and your attempts to influence people will also be fuzzy. If you can describe with focus what your goal is, why others should want to work toward that goal, and how they can help make this goal happen, you have taken major steps toward enlisting others in your enterprise.

Effective leadership communication is also *respectful* of other people. This respect can take several forms. Effective leaders are not condescending or disparaging; rather, they imply by their speech the value that others have. Consider U.S. President John F. Kennedy's famous remark during his inauguration, "ask not what your country can do for you, ask what you can do for your country." On the surface this comment might seem discouraging to listeners in that it sounds like a demand, but if we consider the implied message—"you have talents and abilities and your country needs you; let's find a way for you to make your best contributions"—the statement becomes a powerful communicator of respect. There is no sense here of fooling some of the people some of the time or of manipulating the masses. Rather, this comment shows profound respect for people, respect that if they would choose to do so, they could make an enormous difference in the quality of their lives, our lives, and the nation. When you communicate that kind of respect to others, when you show respect for people, for their views, for their concerns, and for their talents, you will get a positive response.

Effective leadership language is also *stimulating*. Even if we are clear and respectful, if our message is not delivered in powerful, inspiring, dramatic ways, others may not see the significance nor appreciate the urgency of what we propose. Effective speakers present data in poignant ways, make provocative statements that jar listeners and cause them to pay attention and to think, and dramatize their points with stories, nuances of speech, and emotional connections. If people cannot remember what you have said, how can they become galvanized by your strategy or sincerity?

Many potential leaders feel uncomfortable thinking about, much less working on, improving their delivery style. They believe that the content of their message should be sufficient. The reality is that many stimulating messages with weak content have influenced innumerable human endeavors. Consider all the mediocre products that have dominated their market segments because of superior marketing. Better yet, think of the speeches and leadership invitations you can remember. What made them memorable?

Why did you respond? My guess is that many of them were memorable because of how the content was delivered.

Consider the simple eloquence and inspiring nature, for example, of Gandhi's march to the sea to make salt. Manufacture of salt by Indians was prohibited by the British Government at the time, and Gandhi's simple, stimulating act, declaring his intention to walk from the interior to the sea and make salt and then doing so, captured the attention of millions of people and presented an extraordinary challenge to the government. When you want to influence, consider carefully how you can make your message stimulating.

Congruency is another principle that many would-be leaders violate. Congruency means that you walk your talk. Refer back to chapter 4 on the moral foundation of leadership: You do not make promises that you cannot keep. Effective leaders understand deeply that unless they are willing to do what they are asking others to do, they will not be able to sustain their influence. If we ask employees to endure cost cutting and yet we take a big salary increase, our ability to influence employees is greatly undermined. If we ask people to be creative but then hammer or punish or ridicule those who try, they learn that we are duplicitous. To be an effective leader means to be at one in our speech and in our actions. If you cannot do it, do not say it!

Clear Invitation

One reason that people do not do what we would like them to do is that we do not ask them in powerful ways. Effective leaders know how to frame and extend powerful invitations. Of course, unless an invitation is based on clear purpose, clear reward, clear roles for others, and respect for others and is delivered with stimulation and congruency, it may not be accepted. Effective leaders, though, do not shrink from the asking. If they have learned how to ask powerfully, to frame the invitation in a way that is attractive and engaging to followers, their probability of getting favorable responses goes up. The very concept of leadership extending invitations rather than demands, commands, or instructions implies a different attitude toward leadership than most people in positions of power take.

An invitation is respectful. An invitation is consistent with our basic definition of leadership, which includes a voluntary response from people. When you invite people to do something, you acknowledge that unless you have done your homework and can present the invitation in a powerful way, they may say "no." Perhaps you have concluded that invitations and leadership are incompatible; if so, then I believe you will be giving instructions, commands, guidelines, and demands to followers whose mouths are saying "yes," but inside, at Level Two and Level Three, they are saying "no." I invite you to consider your ability to frame and deliver powerful invitations and then practice doing so.

Conclusion

Influencing others is a complex task. There are many ways you can go about trying to lead. If you choose to influence others by using power as a base and by using the tools of coercion, manipulation, and force, you will get a Level One response; the body may move, but the head and the heart will be fixed. If, on the other hand, you choose to work a bit harder on the front end and learn how to speak in ways that are clear, respectful, stimulating, and congruent, and if you use that language ability to extend invitations to others, you will get favorable responses, not only behaviorally, but also at Level Two and Level Three.

This approach implies that the ability to influence others, and to influence them deeply, is as much about attitude, philosophy, and motive—your attitude, your philosophy, and your motive—as it is about learning specific techniques and tips of leadership skills. If you truly want to be more effective in leading others, I invite you to consider the principles introduced in this chapter and focus on your purpose, your language, and your ability to deliver what I call Class Five invitations, invitations that invite world-class performance.

Principles of Level Three Leadership

1. In general, we use our titles, coercion, rewards, our expertise, or our group membership to influence others.
2. In reality, all relationships are based on exchanges that must be mutual and approximately equal if the relationship is to endure.
3. Language is one of the most powerful tools of the effective leader. The language of leadership is clear, respectful, stimulating, and congruent.
4. Effective leaders respect the goals of others and present themselves as an ally to the achievement of the others' goals.
5. Effective leaders know how to issue world-class invitations that get voluntary responses from the people they wish to influence.

Questions for Reflection

1. How do you most often try to influence others?
2. What are the personal goals of the people you would like to influence? If you cannot name these goals, how can you present yourself as an ally? If you are not aware of these goals, how could you find them out?
3. How could you practice making your speech and communication more clear, more respectful, more stimulating, and more congruent with the way you behave?
4. Make a list of the people or groups of people you would like to influence. Next to each person or group, note whether you have been trying to influence them at Level One, Level Two, or Level Three. If you have been trying at Level One, consider the consequence of your efforts and the results you have been getting. If you have been trying at Level Three, consider how you might make those efforts more effective.
5. The next five times you try to influence someone, listen to yourself speak; search for the clear, respectful, stimulating, and congruent invitation in what you say. Think about how you might improve your invitations.

Notes

1. Based on the classic article by John R. P. French Jr. and Bertram H. Raven, "The Bases of Social Power," in *Studies in Social Power*, ed. D. Cartwright (Ann Arbor: University of Michigan, Institute for Social Research, 1959), 150–167.
2. See, for example, the chapter on coercion in *Intentional Revolutions* by Edwin C. Nevis, Joan Lancourt, and Helen G. Vassallo (San Francisco: Jossey-Bass, 1996).

3. Allan R. Cohen and David L. Bradford, *Influence without Authority* (New York: John Wiley and Sons, 1991).

4. John Gabarro and John Kotter, "Managing Your Boss," *Harvard Business Review* (May 1993).

5. See, for example, *On the Top* by Zig Ziglar (Nashville: Thomas Nelson, 1994), in which a central point is that if you can help others get what they want, you will have a lifetime of success.

6. James G. Clawson and Michael Blank, "The Role of Interpersonal Respect and Trust in Developmental Relationships," *International Journal of Mentoring* (spring 1990).

7. Stephen R. Covey, *Seven Habits of Highly Effective People* (New York: Simon & Schuster, 1989).

CHAPTER

Leading Teams

10

Chapter Outline

- ■ Inspired Vision That Creates . . .

- ■ . . . A Powerful Sense of Mission

- ■ Getting the Right People

- ■ Distributed Leadership

- ■ Extraordinary Coordination

- ■ Creative Support

- ■ Moral Foundation for Respect

- ■ The Right Roles for the Right People

- ■ Participation

- ■ The Right Measures

- ■ Team Life Cycles

An information systems project leader wrestles to organize a massive change
effort in an urban municipal modernization program involving hundreds of
people. An account executive for a global financial services firm wonders how
to coordinate the efforts of colleagues in eight different cities on behalf of a
single global client. A wiring harness group seeks help in making up a backlog
of product that a customer needs immediately. A course head struggles to find
a way to build a cohesive teaching team among colleagues teaching multiple

This chapter was written by Greg Bevan and James Clawson. Copyright © 1998 by the Darden School Foundation, Charlottesville, VA. All rights reserved. Adapted from UVA-OB-655.

> *sections of the same course. A world-class climber tries to manage emotions*
> *as the expedition moves up the 8,000–meter mountain despite large egos,*
> *troublesome porters, and peers jockeying for position on the summit team.*

Each of these teams faces a common set of problems: how to build an effective team, especially when time is short and the consequences are significant. The answers are not easy but are increasingly important. The paradigm shift described in chapter 1 is creating more and more team-based organizations. As a result, more leaders are faced with the dilemmas and challenges of managing teams—short-term teams, project teams, program teams, special function teams, ad hoc teams, and permanent, goal-oriented, profit-motivated teams. There are even national and international conferences designed primarily to teach people how to lead teams more effectively.

Although all the skills outlined in chapter 9 about influencing others can apply to leading teams, some other principles will also help you think about how you attempt to lead teams. Effective work groups have several key dimensions and characteristics that effective leaders understand and manage. As a team leader, your challenge will be to recognize these aspects of effective teams and manage them well as the development of your team unfolds. Warren Bennis and his colleague Patricia Biederman made a very interesting study of seven of the most successful groups in history.[1] Their insights, adapted here and combined with insights from others, make a powerful outline of the characteristics of effective teams.

INSPIRED VISION THAT CREATES . . .

Bennis and Biederman found that the groups they studied shared a certain kind of leader who provided a "vision" that inspired the team. These leaders were able to paint this vision in such vivid and alluring color that others could see it clearly—and wanted to join the enterprise in order to see it realized. For example, Bennis and Biederman cite a conversation from when Steven Jobs was courting John Sculley, an executive from Pepsi, for the CEO position at Apple Computer. Jobs reportedly asked Sculley, "Do you want to spend the rest of your life selling flavored water, or do you want a chance to change the world?"

Walt Disney, as the leader of the group that produced in 1937 the world's first feature-length animated film, encountered stiff opposition to his idea, so he stood up in front of the group and acted out the entire story of *Snow White and the Seven Dwarfs*. The performance was convincing and, ultimately, spectacularly successful. Leaders who will be able to galvanize the efforts of groups of people will be able to articulate a clear and powerful vision. This vision, in turn, will mobilize the resources of the team.

. . . A POWERFUL SENSE OF MISSION

As a result of an inspiring vision, members of successful groups feel more zealous about their work than the average employee does. They feel like they are indispensable parts of a vitally important enterprise. A leader who hopes to get peak performance out of a group must make certain that this sense of mission is clear—and clear in a way that ties in at Level Three to the goals and aspirations of the members of the team.

Bennis and Biederman draw an instructive example from the Manhattan Project, the group that built the first atom bomb during the latter half of World War II. As I introduced in chapter 8, the secrecy at first surrounding White Sands was so complete that the researchers themselves were not told exactly what they were doing or why. The secrecy led to declining morale and a real climate of anger and confusion. The group floundered—until the leader, J. Robert Oppenheimer, called them together, laid all the facts on the table, and told them what the project was trying to do. He explained how each of researchers' various pieces was important to the overall mission, and he laid out in emotional terms that the survival of the free world was at stake. The project was suddenly a crusade, and productivity soared.

Corporate leaders face less apocalyptic challenges, but effective leaders share Oppenheimer's ability to instill their followers with a sense of mission. This ability was one of Steve Jobs's strengths at Apple. Jobs convinced his team that they were marauding rebels destined to defeat the IBM empire—and even flew a Jolly Roger above Apple headquarters as a playful reminder of their mission.

GETTING THE RIGHT PEOPLE

Perhaps the first step in realizing a vision is getting the right people to be part of the team. "You can't pile together enough good people to make a great one," said Bob Taylor, one of the kingpins of Xerox Corporation's Palo Alto Research Center, or PARC. Taylor looked only for great people in his recruiting efforts at PARC, which was to spend the early 1970s radically rethinking computer science. Taylor's comment points out the importance of having the right people on the team.[2]

Taylor's group of young maverick thinkers refused to let any assumption about computers go unchallenged. They were the sort of revolutionary thinkers that I described in chapter 8. The computer that PARC created was the first to boast many features we now take for granted: a graphical user interface, a mouse, a desktop display format with windows.

Unfortunately for Xerox, the company did not share its research lab's vision. Development opportunity was left open for a young visitor to PARC's facility, Steven Jobs, who was so taken by the new machine that he decided to use his small upstart company, Apple, to exploit these innovations commercially.

Whom do you look for when recruiting? Bennis and Biederman offer a list of attributes shared by the members of successful and innovative groups: original thinking, specialized skills, fresh perspective, ability to see gaps in current thinking, good problem solving, ability to make connections across broad disciplinary gaps, and broad frames of reference. The mix of these characteristics placed in the cauldron of an inspiring vision and stirred by powerful leadership has created dramatic results.

Members of a team will periodically assess their own appropriateness or worthiness to be on the team by weighing their own abilities and contributions to the group against their perceptions of the abilities and contributions of the other members. A member who feels unworthy or inappropriately included will likely participate less often out of fear of censure or lack of interest, thus damaging the group's effectiveness in the process.

Consequently, one of the first requirements of an effective group leader is to make certain the right people are on the team and, once the team is selected, to reinforce the right of each member to be on the team. This responsibility does not mean just including those with the best technical skills. More important, it means paying attention to the social, team-related skills of each person. Further, it means that the leader/organizer should help the members of the team in its early days solidify their sense of why they were included. Look, for example, at mountaineering expeditions. People who organize such dangerous trips take great care in choosing their teammates and in strengthening each member's view of why he or she was included. Lou Whittaker, renowned mountain guide and leader or member of several Himalayan expeditions, concludes after years of forming and leading teams that deal with life-and-death situations regularly, "I came back from K2 in 1975 with this understanding: the measure of a good team is not whether you make the summit, but how well you get along during the climb."[3]

DISTRIBUTED LEADERSHIP

Once membership and purpose have been determined, most groups will naturally wrestle with issues related to leadership. The natural human tendency is to try to sort out who is in charge. Effective groups have strong leadership although that leadership is not necessarily embodied in a strong leader. Increasingly, strong leadership means distributed leadership rather than a designated leader. By distributed leadership, I mean a comfortable process whereby those who have the perspective, the skills, and the motivation to deal with the situation of the moment step to the fore and assume—and are granted—influence on the group. For distributed leadership to happen, team members must be comfortable with the purpose of the team and each member's role in it. Concerns about "control" and "who is the boss" must give way to a focus on the objective. This process is not easily accomplished, but develops as a result of much teamwork experience.

The need to develop distributed leadership is one reason why many corporate clients use ropes courses or adventure challenge courses. These team-based forays into the woods for low events that occur 2 to 3 feet off the ground and high events that can occur at 60 to 90 feet in the air help team members realize that every member can contribute something of value and that the goals of the team are to efficiently figure out those valuable contributions and to develop a repeating process. This kind of learning can transfer to business settings and can allow the team members to work together more efficiently regardless of location.

EXTRAORDINARY COORDINATION

Effective team leaders may not have the specialized technical expertise that other team members have; rather, effective team leaders exhibit an extraordinary expertise in mobilizing and coordinating the efforts of the team. The leader's role is to provide the best possible environment for recruits to do their work—not to do the work personally. This hurdle is difficult for many would-be managers and leaders to overcome. Sometimes people are promoted into positions of leadership and struggle with letting go of the work and learning new coordinating and facilitating skills. A psychological leap must be made when people become responsible for work that they are not doing directly.[4] Effective team leaders do not micromanage. Instead, they have a good sense of the loose-tight paradox that allows them to guide the group without interfering with the initiative and talents of the team members.

CREATIVE SUPPORT

Effective team leaders also buffer the team from bureaucracy and bureaucratic processes. As Bennis and Biederman observe, "Great Groups are never places where memos are the primary form of communication. They aren't places where anything is filed in triplicate. Time that can go into thinking and making is never wasted on activities, such as writing reports, that serve only some bureaucratic or corporate function outside the group."

Jewel Savadelis, a former student, was confronted one day at Atari with the prospect of managing more than a dozen highly creative software programmers, people on whom the revenues from the home video game market depended. They presented her with a list of challenges and declared that if she could meet those challenges, she would be allowed to manage their team. One of the demands was that she buffer them from the paperwork of the organization. Effective team leaders figure out ways to minimize the time spent by team members in organizationally originated diversions from the primary task.[5] This incident raised for Jewel a series of questions, some of which had clear moral and ethical overtones.

MORAL FOUNDATION FOR RESPECT

Effective team leaders build their influence on the moral foundation introduced in chapter 4: truth telling, promise keeping, fairness, and respect for the individual. Jewel Savadelis knew that whatever her title was, unless she could gain the respect of the programmers, she would not be able to manage, much less lead, them.

Likewise, Bennis and Biederman report that Kelly Johnson, leader of the Skunk Works—the top-secret research group at Lockheed that created the U-2 spy plane, the SR-71 Blackbird, and the F-117 Stealth Fighter—was an irascible man who could scare away group members and clients alike with his temper. But he made up for this weakness in the immense respect he inspired in his researchers. They knew that he would not build a plane he did not believe in, because once he returned millions of dollars to the Air Force rather than do exactly that.

THE RIGHT ROLES FOR THE RIGHT PEOPLE

Having the right team members and the right leadership processes does not ensure the creation of an effective team. Team organization that puts its members in the right roles is critical for success. This organization is akin to the concept of supporting others so they

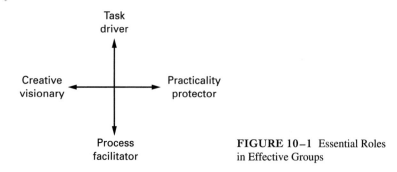

FIGURE 10–1 Essential Roles
in Effective Groups

can contribute, which was introduced in chapter 5. Thomas Carlisle, the English philosopher, once said he did not believe in the "collective wisdom of individual ignorance," yet time and time again, team decision making produces better decisions.[6] These better decisions can be improved even more if team members are organized so as to take the greatest advantage of their talents and abilities.

Effective team leaders pay a lot of attention to ensuring that the jobs and tasks assigned to members fit their talents and their inclinations. Sports coaches, expedition team leaders, project team leaders, and work group leaders all understand the value of this principle. Sometimes the person with the talent for a job does not want to do it; unless the leader can build a process that allows for each member to do the tasks he or she wants to do along the way, the success of the whole team can be jeopardized. Yet if left alone, talented team members will often find niches themselves, zeroing in on the work for which they are best suited and in which they are most interested. Some organizations leave the assignments of new employees intentionally ambiguous in the belief that talented people will create their own best way of making a valuable contribution.

I believe that four general roles are essential in effective groups (see Figure 10–1). These roles can be viewed as pairs of polar opposites, with each member of a pair contributing in a way that holds his or her counterpart in check.

Task Driver

The task driver is the results-oriented member of the group, the one who keeps the group focused on the ultimate goal of completing the task at hand. Urging his creative colleagues to get their brainchild, the Macintosh, off the drawing board and into stores, Steve Jobs was playing the role of task driver when he said, "Real artists ship."

Process Facilitator

The process facilitator, the task driver's counterpart, keeps tabs on the interpersonal dynamics of the group more than on progress toward the goal. The quality of working relationships among group members is critical—and the process facilitator watches those relationships carefully, working hard to help the group manage misunderstandings that arise in the course of the team's work.

Creative Visionary

The creative visionary is the member whose mind is most open to creative solutions, no matter how outlandish they might sound, and who is always trying to find a better way. Creative visionaries are constantly exploring the four basic kinds of creative thinking: risk taking, considering the opposites, relying on uncertainty, and looking for multiple possibilities.[7] Sometimes teams try to squelch the creative types in their midst in the name of getting things done. In so doing, the team can overlook alternative ways of doing things that might, in the end, reshape entirely the team's process or product.

Practicality Protector

The counterbalance to the creative visionary is the practical protector. This person attends to the practical realities of getting the assigned job done. Although an overattention to practicalities in finishing a job can discourage creativity and, perhaps, better solutions, an overattention to creative alternatives can strangle a team in possibilities. Practical protectors make sure that what the team asserts to do is doable.

Balance

These two paradoxes, creativity versus practicality and task versus process, are balanced and well-managed in effective teams. If team members do not naturally seem to fit these four roles, they can be assigned. I have seen the efforts of teams improved dramatically by simply assigning team members to attend to and be responsible for these four roles. The recognition by all members that all four roles are necessary and helpful contributes to the work of the team.

PARTICIPATION

Not all talented people are equally adept at collaboration. People vary in their introversion and extraversion, for example, regardless of their technical skills.[8] Some people are active in the discussions that surround the team's purpose, while others are more reticent. Effective teams have figured out ways for all team members to participate. In effect, participation is an extension of membership. If you have the right membership, everyone should be participating. If everyone is not participating, then you may not have the right membership.

Participation is not limited to the team in effective groups. Robert Kelley and Janet Caplan, in their article, "How Bell Labs Creates Star Performers," summarize seven years of research into the work strategies of standouts—and their less successful peers—at AT&T's prestigious research unit. Bell engineers all agreed on nine work strategies that influenced productivity, of which fully two-thirds—networking, teamwork effectiveness, leadership, followership, "show-and-tell," and organizational savvy—can be seen as varieties of group cooperation skills.

The importance of networking in particular became apparent when Kelley and Caplan investigated the actual work habits of average-performing and "star" teams. Although both groups agreed that a network of knowledgeable colleagues was crucial to weathering a crisis on the job, much of the star teams' success could be traced to their efforts to build networks before those crises happened. A member of an average-performing team, for example, stumped by a technical problem, may painstakingly call various technical gurus and then wait, wasting valuable time while calls go unreturned and e-mail messages unanswered. Members of star teams, however, will rarely face such a situation because they will have made valuable contacts before they actually need the help.

THE RIGHT MEASURES

The more that organizations are built around teams, the more outdated old measures of performance become. Traditional measurement systems serve the top-down power structures of the Industrial Age. These systems are what Christopher Meyer called *results measures.*[9] A results measure offers information about something that happened in the past as opposed to information about what is happening at the moment. Furthermore, results measures are usually functionally based: The marketing department monitors market share, the finance department keeps track of costs, and so forth.

The trouble with results measures is that although they may help top managers keep tabs on the company's or a team's past performance, they do not shed much light on the current processes that determine whether the company will achieve its goals. As Meyer says, "The fact that a program was six months late and $2 million over budget doesn't tell anyone what went wrong or what to do next."

Results measures are especially harmful to groups because they tend to be function-specific (market share is relevant to marketers but less so to production people) and thus undermine the advantage of group decision making in which people from different functions develop a strategic overview together. Further, results measures can divert attention away from the ongoing processes that a team is employing to produce.

Meyer cites a multifunctional group that recently presided over the development of a luxury automobile and whose measures were simply an accumulation of the measures that the individual functions had long been using. The project was delayed for several weeks by a squabble over a new door-handle design: The finance people feared it would be too expensive, while the design people stressed its importance to the overall design of the car. Hamstrung by their own measurement criteria, neither side thought to ask the overarching and crucial question: "Will the new handle help the car compete in the marketplace?"

The alternative to results measures is to use what Meyer calls *process measures:* measures that track, throughout an organization, the activities that help reach a given goal. Process measures are real-time indicators of key processes and their central contributors. For example, rather than simply knowing that the project is behind schedule and over budget, groups in which staffing is critical could benefit from tracking staffing levels during the course of the work—a process measure that could point to corrective fine-tuning.

> Process measures are like the gauges on an automobile dashboard—they indicate current status so that you know before you run out of gas or before a drop in oil pressure ruins the engine.

Process measures are like the gauges on an automobile dashboard, giving the driver and passengers current information on key processes: How much fuel is left, how far we have traveled, whether the battery is charging, and how the oil pressure is doing. All these measures are indicators of current status and necessarily so; it does not help to know that you have run out of gas after the car has already stalled.

Meyer offers four guiding principles that may help in designing a measurement system to suit the needs of a group. First, the team's process measures should be designed to help the team during the process, not to help management after the fact. The measures should be a warning system that alerts the group when corrective action is needed.

Second, the team should design its own process indicators. This principle is consistent with my assertion in chapter 1 that it is the key process contributors, those closest to the work, who know what really needs to be done. Of course, for the team to devise the right measures, it needs to be clear on the strategy of the firm; if the east-west connection in our general model is flawed, the team's ability to create good measures will be undermined.

Third, the process measures should be multifunctional and should focus on the whole work of the team, not just a few aspects of it. Along with tracking receivables, for instance, the system might also gauge the percentage of new parts to be used in a product. New parts are often an unknown quantity and thus can raise issues across a number of functions—design, inventory, manufacturing, and assembly.

Finally, teams should keep the number of process measures down. Meyer recommends no more than 15 or else the team will become paralyzed by evaluation. The challenge is to build a dashboard for the team's metaphorical car that will keep the driver and the passengers informed about how the car is doing while they travel.

TEAM LIFE CYCLES

Most of the history-making groups that Bennis and Biederman examined dissolved soon after their defining projects were done. As the authors observe, "They are like animals that die soon after they breed." But those groups were project teams, designed to do a specific job and then no longer needed.

Not all groups are so short-lived; some need to continue indefinitely. Short-lived or long-lived, groups seems to pass through a life cycle of distinct stages, each one presenting its own challenges. Perhaps you have heard the common phrase that groups go through *forming, storming, norming,* and *performing.* I would like to suggest, based on the research on group behavior and the realities of the current paradigm shift, a slightly different predictable pattern that groups exhibit and that group leaders need to understand: *forming, norming, performing,* and *re-forming.* Re-forming has become important because so many groups now need to form and re-form when a particular task is done. In fact, I argue that the organization that is able to form and re-form multifunctional teams quickly and effectively has a distinct competitive advantage.

> The organization that is able to form and re-form multifunctional teams quickly and effectively has a distinct competitive advantage.

Forming: Initiation and Orientation

When teams or groups first come together, group members spend most of their energy getting accustomed to and assessing one another. Communication is tentative as members try to answer some key questions like, "Should I be here?" "What is the purpose of this group?" and "Who is the leader?" As I said earlier in this chapter, team members often look for a leader to instill the group with a sense of purpose. If the membership, purpose, and leadership issues are not sorted out quickly, the group's efforts to do its work will flounder. Even if the group is able to jump right into its task, the membership, purpose, and leadership issues will surface again later, causing disruption and confusion.

Effective team leaders, or even effective team members who are willing to participate in a distributed leadership pattern, will work through these three fundamental issues explicitly and early in order to avoid the inefficient review of them later on. Effective teams will clarify the task and intended output of the team, the reason each member is there and how each member might contribute to that output, and how leadership of the team will evolve and develop.

Norming: The How Questions

As soon as the team has sorted out what it is supposed to do, who should be members, and how it will manage the leadership of the group, it begins sorting out the how questions: How will we work together, how will we resolve disputes, how will we relate to the outside world. Usually these questions are not so explicit; they are resolved as the group develops and spends time together. In fact, that approach is the whole point. Effective leaders are aware of these developmental stages and the tasks that a group faces in each stage, and they manage the team through the stages explicitly. Team leaders who ignore this predictable pattern of group development may feel as though they are progressing, but usually the issues come up later and bog the group down.

Effective leaders manage the early stages of group development by making the tasks of each developmental stage explicit and by talking about them. Of course, as time passes, the team may decide that some of its earlier discussions and conclusions do not work and it may argue for change; in these situations, some members may feel that the early time was lost. Nevertheless, the sooner a leader can move a group through these early stages, the sooner the group can focus on getting the work done without distraction.

Disagreements over the ground rules, the scope of the group's mission, and the best among possible courses of action make the norming stage one of the most fertile—and the most trying on the leader. Members want to know where the boundaries are and how firm the boundaries are, so they test them in myriad ways. Who speaks? How do we determine who speaks? How do we make decisions? How do we revisit those decisions? How often do we meet? What do we do before and after we meet? These questions are just some of the issues that members need to sort out so that they can focus on the task at hand.

In this creative but often volatile stage, members cultivate their ability to work together. The effective leader will not take challenges as an invitation to rule autocratically nor group upheaval as an excuse to micromanage. Instead, the effective leader uses these episodes as opportunities to point out how the skills and abilities of each member will contribute to the whole and to the achievement of the team's task.

Performing: Stabilization

Eventually, more quickly if the leader has managed it well, much of the uncertainty that hung over the group at the outset evaporates. Individual roles and interpersonal relationships become clear and accustomed. Members can now look to established precedent as they draw up their plans. The group has progressed along a collective learning curve and now, as a result, may be operating at higher levels of efficiency.

There are new dangers to face, however. Having drawn energy from the heady atmosphere of the exploration stage, members may begin to see stability as dull routine. While working with the team to ensure that efficiency is in fact being improved, effective leaders try to maintain the sense of urgency and excitement that often characterizes the early stages.

This revitalization is an ongoing dilemma. How do you reenergize long-term work groups? How do you combat the debilitating effects of day-in, day-out routines at work? One answer lies in the resonance concepts that I introduced in chapter 7. If you can help your team members revisit their team dream regularly, if you can show them how today's work fits into the plan to realize that dream, and if you have organized the structure and relationships of the team with solid foundations of trust, respect, and vision, then you have done much to revitalize ongoing efforts. In many respects, the work of the team leader becomes finding ways to remind, refocus, and rebuild the resonance.

Re-forming: Reassessment

Stable work groups often develop deep-seated working habits, almost a subculture. The more stable a group becomes, the more difficult it will be for that group to respond to radical change. Sooner or later, though, some fundamental change—declining profits, a transformed marketplace, different demands on the group from above, or just finishing the job—will make reassessment and even dissolution or re-forming unavoidable.

What makes this crossroads so difficult—indeed, life threatening—for the group is that feelings about it are likely to be wildly varied among group members. Some will vehemently oppose any change in the group's mission, some will accept it enthusiastically, and some will feel betrayed by the leader or top managers. As we discussed in chapter 8, unless the processes of understanding and dealing with change (remember that enhanced flexibility is one of the three characteristics of a competitive advantage) are built into the culture of the group, finishing the present task can easily destroy the group. The lack of flexibility can be a source of competitive disadvantage.

Depending on the culture of the team and the quality of its leadership, several reactions are possible near the end of a team's life cycle. The group may emerge from this reassessment phase revitalized and refocused, it may burst from internal dissent, it may cling to its outmoded vision and die a more protracted death, or appropriately, it may just disband and its members move on to other work. Organizations that have paid attention to and developed the processes of reassessing and re-forming productive work teams will have a distinct competitive advantage over those companies who have not.

Conclusion

Learning to lead teams is increasingly an essential skill for the modern, effective leader. As team-based organizations become more common, the challenges of leading teams become more apparent. Status hierarchies continue to break down, not only in the team-based organizations, but also within the teams themselves. Distributed leadership becomes more important. People who understand the characteristics of effective teams and how to manage them over the natural course of their development will become more effective leaders.

Principles of Level Three Leadership

1. Effective teams often display smooth processes of distributed leadership.
2. Effective team leaders understand the importance of clarifying membership, purpose, and leadership processes early in a team's life cycle.
3. Effective team leaders will find ways to revisit the team's dream or vision while the team is performing its task in order to keep energy and motivation high.
4. Effective team leaders understand and are able to manage the team's response to changing environmental and internal conditions and events.
5. Effective team leaders can manage the difficult reassessment and re-forming process that occurs when a team's work comes to an end, whatever the reason.

Questions for Reflection

1. What is your present work team's mission? Can you describe it verbally with energy and passion without reference to notes? Why or why not?
2. How can you ensure that you have the right members on your present work team? What does each member of the team contribute to the vision of the team?
3. How can you ensure that you have each team member working in a role that maximizes his or her contribution to the team's work? When the team meets, do you have a balance between task and process and between creativity and pragmatism? If not, how could you develop that balance?
4. How can you help your team periodically revisit its mission or dream and in so doing revitalize its energy and commitment? What contribution does the team make to the organization? What contribution does the team make to the organization's customers?
5. How do you envision the transition of the team from its present status to a new status once the team's work is done? What processes could you design that would facilitate this process? Under what conditions could you imagine the team's work being done? What would you do then?

Notes

1. Warren Bennis and Patricia Ward Biederman, *Organizing Genius: The Secrets of Creative Collaboration* (Reading, MA: Addison-Wesley, 1997). The seven groups were the Walt Disney studio, Xerox and Apple Computer's development groups, the 1992 Clinton presidential campaign, Lockheed Aircraft's Skunk Works, Black Mountain College, and the Manhattan Project (which built the first atomic bomb).
2. Bennis and Biederman, *Organizing Genius.*
3. Lou Whittaker with Andrea Gabbard, *Lou Whittaker: Memoirs of a Mountain Guide* (Seattle, WA: The Mountaineers, 1994), 111.

4. See, for example, Gene Dalton, Paul Thompson, and Raymond L. Price, "The Four Stages of Professional Careers, A New Look at Performance by Professionals," *Organizational Dynamics* (summer 1977), 19.

5. For more details, see the "Jewel Savadelis A" case (UVA-OB-190), available through Darden Educational Materials Services, Charlottesville, Virginia.

6. For example, in the well-known survival team exercises Desert Survival and Sub-arctic Survival, team decisions almost always are superior to individual choices, even when the individuals have had survival training and experience.

7. See James Clawson, John Kotter, Victor Faux, and Charles MacArthur, *Self Assessment and Career Development,* 3d ed. (Englewood Cliffs, NJ: Prentice-Hall, 1993), 47; the chapter titled "Survey of Behavioral Characteristics" deals with creative thinking. See also Chic Thompson, *What a Great Idea!* (New York: Harper Perennial, 1992) and Roger von Oech, *A Whack on the Side of the Head* (Menlo Park, CA: Creative Think, 1983).

8. See, for example, the Myers Briggs type indicator as one way of measuring collaboration. Another place to start is David Kiersey and Marilyn Bates, *Please Understand Me* (Del Mar, CA: Prometheus Nemesis, 1978).

9. Christopher Meyer, "How the Right Measures Help Teams Excel," *Harvard Business Review* (May 1994).

CHAPTER

Leading Organizational Design

11

Chapter Outline

■ Background Factors

■ Leadership Philosophy or Mind-Set

■ Organizational Design Decisions

■ Organizational Culture

■ Organizational Results

The north-south axis on our general model is the relationship between leaders and the organizations that they are attempting to lead. If leaders are to be effective, they must understand something about the nature of organizations and they must be insightful into how they relate to or shape any particular organization. Whereas some people might have leadership styles that would allow them to function well in many kinds of organizations, others will thrive only in a narrower range of organizational parameters.

Depending on their power bases, individual leaders may have some ability to design or redesign organizations or parts of organizations. If these efforts are made with a deeper understanding of how organizations operate and how they relate to leaders, then leaders are more likely to be effective. In essence, as Peter Senge has pointed out, leaders are designers.[1] In fact, decisions made in the designs of organizations may, ultimately, be more powerful than subsequent decisions about allocations of resources within those designs.

> Effective leaders are effective designers of organizations.

Written by James G. Clawson. Adapted from "Leading Organizational Design," UVA-OB-657, copyright © by the University of Virginia Darden School Foundation, Charlottesville, VA. All rights reserved. Reprinted with permission.

FIGURE 11–1 Causal Links to Organizational Results

An overarching view of how organizational design fits with leadership identifies five groups—background factors, leadership mind-set, organizational design decisions, organizational culture, and organizational results—as they relate to organizations and arranges them to show a rough causal linkage (see Figure 11–1).[2] Each of these groups of ideas contributes to the overall outcome of an organization's efforts and hence to the ability of an organization's leader or leaders to make things happen. Effective leaders need to understand how these groups link with each other.

BACKGROUND FACTORS

Background factors have to do with the basic building blocks of an organization, the raw materials from which an effective company is built. Sometimes background factors are taken for granted and ignored; other times, they are carefully examined and managed. These background factors include such aspects as the local labor pool, the local political and economic environment, the relative isolation from other hierarchical influence (as in the case, for instance, of a new plant), and history. Many background factors belong to the environmental factors that impinge on and affect all elements of our general leadership model (see Figure 2–3).

Garage-based entrepreneurs may not give a lot of thought to these factors as they focus their efforts on developing an idea and getting it before the public. More sophisticated entrepreneurs, perhaps working through venture capitalists, may pay considerable attention to the best place to start their company in terms of availability and cost of labor, regulatory restrictions, and local or regional tax incentives. Steve Jobs and Steve Wosniak did not travel the country to build their first Apple computer, but worked in their garage, albeit in the technology-rich area soon known as Silicon Valley, California. In contrast, General Motors, in its attempts to build a new kind of small car manufacturing plant based on the Japanese model of high quality, lean operations, and efficient processes, searched the country before settling on the relatively remote area of Smyrna, Tennessee. An important consideration in GM's decision was the relative isolation of that plant from corporate headquarters. This isolation reduced the number of managers steeped in the old way of doing things who would raise questions and inhibit innovation in process as well as product.

Effective leaders understand how these background factors are influencing their attempts to create. Bob Lancaster, for example, who was given the assignment by FMC Corporation to build a new kind of plant, chose very carefully his location so that he could create a new kind of facility without a history, based on a new philosophy, and in a place at which senior FMC management was not likely to interfere. If he had chosen to build the plant in Minneapolis, accessible to divisional executives, he might have experienced a very different outcome.[3]

LEADERSHIP PHILOSOPHY OR MIND-SET

Leaders step into a context of background factors and, using what they know and believe, begin to work. The purpose that they define for themselves and their organizations (the north-east connection in our general model), the principles that they operate on, and the style that they use in dealing with others all begin to affect the organization, sometimes intentionally, sometimes unintentionally. In chapter 8, I talked about the importance of strategic thinking and of setting a purpose for the organization and about the significance of the leadership principles that the individual uses. A person's Level Three beliefs about the purpose of the business, the way others are influenced, the appropriateness of the systems in the business, and the means of managing change have an enormous impact on the way that person approaches leadership opportunities, especially organizational design opportunities. Consequently, a significant stream of literature today encourages leaders to reexamine not only what they want others to do, but more important, what they themselves think about their work and role.[4]

A leader's philosophy will shape the kind of organization that that leader designs. If you believe that people are basically lazy and have to be supervised, your recruiting, training, supervision, performance evaluation, and information sharing systems will all reflect that bias. If you believe that all people are competitive or that people who will work in your organization should be competitive, that belief will shape the way you design the structure and systems in your organization. Conversely, the structure and systems of an organization are Level One artifacts of those beliefs. By studying an organization's major components, you can often discern many present and past leaders' Level Three beliefs about how the organization should be run.

The key issue here is that your mind-set, your philosophy about how organizations should work, will be a key factor in determining how you would create a new organization or perhaps how effectively you would be able to work within an existing one. Assessing that connection, the north-south connection, becomes critical in understanding how a situation will turn out.

ORGANIZATIONAL DESIGN DECISIONS

Structure

The first place that many people in positions of power look is to the organizational structure. Whether on paper or simply evolving in people's minds, the organizational structure is the network of relationships intended in an organization for managing coordination of decision making across many functions. Another way of thinking of organizational structure is that it is the pattern of power-based relationships that help hold an organization together. When people think of organizational structure, they often think of organizational charts. This perspective can create problems in that when structure changes, people who have become accustomed to one structure may feel betrayed or frustrated. If we accept Stan Davis's maxim that organizational structures are by definition obsolete,[5] then we can look at organizational charts as we do financial balance sheets, nothing more than a snapshot of how things are at one instant in time, and realize that they do not reflect in and of themselves the dynamic nature of what is really happening in the organization over time. (This observation suggests that the southeast relationship between task and organization in our general model is always going to be obsolete.) Yet by law and by principle of order, organizational leaders have to figure out how important decisions will be made, and this mandate is the crux of attention on the distribution of power throughout some kind of structure. A number of common structures have been used during the Industrial Age.

Military Model

One of the most common models of the Industrial Age bureaucracy was the military model developed in large part by Frederick the Great.[6] This pyramid structure helped clarify who was in charge and helped codify who could make what decisions. The military model was a hierarchical model in which each officer was responsible in turn to a higher officer. Each layer had its functional specialities, which were coordinated by the authority at the next highest level. Although the military model was a very orderly system, over time it became sluggish and slow to action.

Divisional Model

As corporations grew in size, they developed broader interests and, eventually, new organizational structures. The natural outgrowth of the pyramid bureaucracy was the M-form, or divisional, structure, which was an association of bureaucratic pyramids loosely coordinated toward common corporate goals.[7] As in the single pyramid organization, M-form organizations (so called because when you put two pyramids side by side, they look like the letter M), developed great efficiency skills but difficulties in sharing and building on skills horizontally. Redundancies in special functions like finance, marketing, accounting, information processing, and human resources and larger and larger project demands by customers led to the formation of a hybrid organization, the matrix.

Matrix Models

Matrix organizations were an answer to the problem of escalating costs on large (originally) engineering projects like space vehicles and defense weaponry. Typically, matrix organizations had two sides: a project leader side that included a list of project managers who handled various parts of the overall project and had budgets assigned to them for reaching their goals, and a functional specialist side that included technical specialty managers who had the human resources needed to tackle the various challenges that the project or program leaders faced.

Matrix organizations attacked and destroyed many widely believed bureaucratic principles like "one person, one boss." All employees in a matrix organization usually had at least two bosses: the project leader to whom they were temporarily assigned and who paid their salary, and the technical specialty boss who hired and assigned them based on their skills and availability. Matrix organizations heralded the beginning of the end for the Industrial Age functional bureaucracies.

Matrix organizations allowed people to be used more efficiently by moving them from one project to another, but also created a wave of confusion among those who were used to the simple orderliness of bureaucratic pyramids.[8] Soon, volumes of description and counsel about how to manage matrices emerged, and many companies tried to incorporate aspects of matrix organizations in their own structures.

Hybrids

Since the boom of matrix organizations in the 1950s through the 1970s, organizations have continued to evolve in a variety of directions. The major forces that have contributed to the speed of this evolution are the Information Revolution, the increasingly global nature of modern corporations, and the necessity of managing more efficiently in the face of new competition. As people become better educated and have available to them better information, they become more aware of the business processes in their organizations and how those processes work. The Internet, local area networks, and personal computing give people access to the data that are necessary for making business decisions, and better educational backgrounds help people interpret those data. As a result, the power of knowing what needs to be done in a company is rapidly dissipating downward throughout the ranks of most companies. Many senior management people are distinctly uncomfortable with this trend, but it has continued unabated for the last 20 years and likely will accelerate in the future.

This dissemination of data and the increasing reality of having to compete on a global basis has put pressure on meeting customer needs, responding to increasing competition, and doing so without raising costs. Consequently, organizations around the world for the last 15 years have been downsizing, de-layering, and reengineering in the attempt to find more adaptive, distributed, empowered organizational forms that can keep up with the rapid pace of change. These forces have spawned a variety of hybrid organizations.

Charles Handy describes four kinds of organizations that are emerging: the federalist, the shamrock, the doughnut, and the clan.[9] The federalist form is akin to the M-form organization but is spread across national boundaries in global settings. Each pyramidal bureaucracy is both independent and obliged to the holding company, working together like a loose federation with some common guidelines and goals. If these federalist structures are to succeed, leadership must work hard to ensure that the local pressures do not overwhelm the common goals and benefits that can be gained overall by cooperating among themselves. Royal-Dutch Shell, Unilever, and Johnson and Johnson are examples of federalist structures that have done remarkably well in the 1990s—and who continue to wrestle with the balance between competing interests in various parts of their organizations.

Shamrock organizations, so named because of the distribution of their employees, are about one-third full-time employees, one-third contract employees, and one-third part-time employees. This structure gives an organization more fluidity of talent, greater flexibility of managing human resource costs, and a manageable core of full-time, ostensibly dedicated employees. The challenge, of course, is to meld the efforts of the part-time and contract employees with those of the full-time force and still develop strong competitive advantages—from people who are only partially committed to the firm. As companies utilize more part-time employees, ethical issues also arise because of the nature and allocation of benefits and the impact of lesser benefits on family structures and health.

The doughnut organization, Handy says, reflects an emerging principle in which organizations are organized around a core of key people who mobilize and organize the talents of "stringers" who operate outside and around the core. A central task of the core group is to balance the energy and activities of the core group with the outside groups. Part of that task is defining the boundaries that identify the core group and those who are suppliers, contributors, vendors, and contractors working in the surrounding space. In a sense, these doughnut organizations are extensions of the shamrock organization, in which the focus is on the type of connection to the main organization.

The (clan organization) emerges from what Handy calls the Chinese Contract, a philosophical approach to relationships, including business relationships, that recognizes and values not only self-interest but also a greater common good. This Chinese Contract reminds us of our discussion in chapter 4 of the moral foundation of leadership, of the need for building a business purpose beyond profit, and of the strategic notion of a business ecosystem. A clan organization recognizes that its future lies inextricably intertwined with the futures and fortunes of other organizations and visions around it and that it must fit into this broader purpose for the well-being of all.

Perhaps the extreme form of hybrid organization evolution was described by Tom Peters when he wrote about a Danish CEO who became so concerned about his organization's inability to break through functional boundaries that he bulldozed down the walls in the head office building, put everyone's phone, computer, and other personal effects on wheeled carts, and installed electrical and data hookups all over the floor.[10] In this, what the CEO called the spaghetti organization, people group together as long as they are working on a common project and then immediately move their "desk" to another group as they move on to their next assignment.

Despite the wide and ever-changing array of options to choose from, organizational structure is only one of several design factors with which leaders as designers need to deal. Sometimes managers rearrange the boxes and lines in their structures, ignore the other design factors of the organization, and then are perplexed when nothing changes. Leaders who do not pay attention to all the key organizational design features are likely to see no results.

Systems Design

Several key systems in most organizations have major impacts on the organization's ability to perform. Effective leaders who understand the designer role in leadership will not ignore these systems. Perhaps the most important ones are hiring, training, reward, and information processing and sharing.

Hiring

Every hiring decision by a company represents a significant investment and, potentially, a constraint or an encouragement on the company's future. People with the right talent and personality to succeed at a company and to help the company succeed are hard to find and difficult to identify. Some companies go through elaborate processes to screen out inappropriate applicants; others seems to hire almost as an afterthought any warm body that comes along. Whether part-time, full-time, contract, or volunteer, each employee can become either a hindrance on the organization's strategic intent (assuming it has one) or a help that can push the company along in the direction it wants to go.

Sometimes companies use traditional methods for finding new employees without realizing the consequences of their actions. Effective leaders understand that every system in the company should support and accelerate the company's strategic intent and that if it does not, it should be a target for reengineering or surgical removal. Hiring is one such system.

Most companies who need a certain kind of skill will advertise for that skill. Usually these skills are technical skills. If a company needs a welder, for example, it advertises for welders and then screens applications for welding credentials. The same is true in accounting, marketing, and other technical areas. Usually the process involves some interviews in which the interviewers try to determine the applicant's "fit" with the company. This interviewing is often done by human resource professionals who may or may not know the working environment of the part of the company for which they are interviewing or by line managers who, although they know the working environment, may not see the value of paying attention to the "softer" criteria, the human aspects of the candidates.

One problem with this approach is that although you may get the technical skills you desire, the new hire may not have the social and leadership skills you find important. Let us say, for example, that you are trying to build a collaborative, team-based organization and you hire a skilled electrician who, unbeknownst to you, is a loner and basically distrustful of others. Although this person's technical skills may provide a contribution, the social skills will be a hindrance to the organization's goals. If you see the development of a collaborative, team-based organization as a part of your strategic intent for building a sustainable competitive advantage, the social skills of the new electrician may actually inhibit your company's development more than the technical skills help.

Because of this problem, many firms are paying closer attention to the psychological, social, and organizational skills of new applicants. At FMC Aberdeen, for instance, new applicants undergo a four-hour psycho-social testing program administered by regular employees to see if the new peoples' personal philosophies and tendencies match the organizational goals of the plant. In several cases, the company has hired people with minor technical skills and superior social skills, the philosophy being that it is easier to teach technical skills than it is to teach deeply ingrained psycho-social skills.

Training

Once a person is hired by a company, effective leaders hope that that person's growth is not over. In fact, effective leaders understand that unless people are growing, learning, and expanding their skills and talents, the firm will gradually fall into an uncompetitive position. In a turbulent environment, it has become maxim that the ability to learn is the only source of sustainable competitive advantage.

An organization's training programs are critical therefore to the realization of strategic intent. The story of IBM, including its decline during the 1980s, surely is testament to the fact that any kind of training is insufficient. For many years, IBM had a policy that all employees should receive a certain number of hours of training annually. Despite this seemingly laudable goal with the intent of ensuring an ongoing learning culture in the company, the company became increasingly out of touch with its markets.

IBM's experience points out the necessity of having training programs that are the result of and match the firm's strategic intent. At FMC Aberdeen, Bob Lancaster wanted to create an organization in which people could work without fear of their own management. He knew that such an organization meant that employees would have to understand their markets and the nature of their business and therefore how they might fear competition and the results of not meeting or exceeding customer desires, and that they would have to be able to work together in significantly more efficient and productive ways.

Consequently, Lancaster designed, with the aid of a professional consultant, a training program that began with how to relate to people. Most adults going to work for a new company and being informed that they had to go through nine days of training on how to talk with each other might think it lunacy. Lancaster, however, was convinced that unless all employees understood the basic principles of his organization and could implement those principles in their daily work lives, they would be unable to build the kind of facility he envisioned.

This nine-day specialized training program introduced the principles of respectful, fact-based communication and taught people how to avoid judging others and how to engage others in mutually respectful, joint problem solving. The program dealt with responding nondefensively to feedback as "data" and how to manage change within the self as opposed to trying to change others. Part of effective feedback included describing the potential consequences of unchanged continuation of dysfunctional patterns of behavior. The program was based on Level Three principles like "all feedback is data and no one has to respond unless he or she wants to," "we are not trying to change anyone, we think people are fine the way they are," and "if we continue behaving this way, what will happen?" Through systematic exploration, communication, and behavior of these VABEs, new employees were trained to view, to think of, and to behave in relationships in ways consistent with the organization's desired culture. Hiring the right people was an important first step in this process, and adding targeted training was an important follow-on.

Rewards

Reward systems play a big part in directing the attention of an organization's employees. Strangely, many organizations design, or allow to remain in place, reward systems that direct employee attention away from the goals of the organization or its strategic intent.[11] Unless the reward systems—including salary increases, bonus awards, promotions, public recognitions, and other forms of positive feedback to employees—are aligned with the strategic goals of the organization, people will feel confused and fragmented in their efforts and in their daily labors.

Despite the logic of this simple principle, many organizations, with good intentions, put in place and continue to use reward systems that seem at odds with their goals. Consider, for example, the company who had in place a $500 prize for new ideas. At the same time, the company had a forecasting and planning system that used demographic behavior to predict possible sales for the following year and had a system with a low base pay and a high bonus for exceeding quota, a system that, in effect, punished people for selling more or for submitting ideas that would increase quota allocations. The company's systems were working against itself.[12]

Senior management in another firm, in an attempt to improve customer service, decreed that 80 percent of all incoming phone calls were to be answered within 20 seconds. Electronic systems were put in place to monitor calls and call length by operator. Paradoxically, in order to meet management's request, employees working the phone lines began cutting their conversations short in order to answer the next incoming call. As a result, customers were cut off before they got their problems solved, and overall customer satisfaction actually declined. These vignettes are examples of unintended consequences that emerged from positively motivated design decisions intended to focus attention and reward people for behaving in one way, but which actually encouraged the exact opposite kind of behavior.

The challenge is to make sure that the reward systems in operation are reinforcing strategic intent instead of being a drag on it. Although senior management or specialists in human resources may think they have the answers, there is a strong logic to the premise that people who will be working in the system should be included in its design, especially after they have been fully educated regarding the goals and strategic intent of the firm.[13] Further, reward systems seem to be remarkably long-lived. The more a team can build flexibility into a reward system that allows it to adjust rewards for changes in behavior, the more likely it is that the organization will be able to direct employee attention to the current strategic challenges the organization is facing.

Information Technology

Information processing in this dawn of the Information Age has become a strategic design weapon. It is surprising how many senior managers still think of information systems as tools rather than as sources of strategic capability. Poor information systems can hamstring an organization's ability to bring its high quality resources to bear on market issues. Superior systems can enable and facilitate the application of highly talented individuals on key issues.

Increasingly, organizations are realizing that new information systems are literally transforming the structure, culture, and other systems of their organizations. Powerful information systems are flattening organizations, distributing key data to lower levels of the organization, and making the vertical decision-making chain obsolete. With access to data around the world, team members can communicate instantaneously with clients and colleagues in an up-to-date and informed way. More than anything else, the information revolution has caused the erosion of the bureaucratic pyramid and is replacing it with a range of organic, powerful, highly responsive organizational forms. Because superior information systems are both difficult to design and expensive to implement, as companies make that investment and learn how to manage the impact of those systems on their organizational cultures, they are developing a competitive advantage that will take others years to duplicate. Jay Galbraith and others have written extensively on how this information technology is affecting the nature of organizational design.[14]

In today's environment, information systems are strategic weapons. I am repeatedly shocked at how many managers, at all levels, view information systems as tactical tools. The reality, as we continue to emerge in the Information Age, is that the way we structure our information systems—gathering data, sifting it, disseminating it, sharing it, and making decisions based on it—will help to build or erode competitive advantage.

Aligning the Various Systems

There are other organizational systems and processes beyond the ones we have mentioned. These four—hiring, training, rewarding, and information sharing—are critical ones that bear special attention. The main point is that unless all these systems are aligned in the organization, that is, are encouraging people to think and behave in consistent ways, people will be confused, the force of the strategic intent will be dissipated, and the organization will not be able to accomplish the kind of progress it would like.

In established organizations, the leader-as-designer work that needs to be done involves reexamining key processes and systems and, if necessary, redesigning them so that they are consistent with each other and with the corporate intent. This kind of reengineering effort takes enormous courage, conviction, and stamina. Part of the difficulty is that these design factors do not have a direct impact on organizational outcomes; rather, they create an environment in which people work, and as people work, they develop a deep-seated set of guidelines about what is acceptable and what is not.

> These design factors do not have a direct impact on organizational outcomes; rather, they create an environment in which people work, and as people work, they develop a deep seated set of guidelines about what is acceptable and what is not.

ORGANIZATIONAL CULTURE

Organizational culture—the outcome of leaders' design decisions—can be enormously helpful or a huge hindrance to realizing strategic intent. According to Ed Schein, the man who is, in my view, the world's leading authority on this subject, a culture develops in response to problems that confront a group of people.[15] As the group addresses, analyzes, and solves each new problem, it develops a history of acceptable ways of behaving. If the group agrees to explain thunder and lightning as a manifestation of the displeasure of the gods, then this explanation becomes a part of the group's history and culture and is passed on from one generation to the next. If the founders of a company (e.g., Apple Computer) conclude that closed architecture is the best solution to the problem of competing with clone manufacturers, then the company develops a history and a culture that shapes its behavior in the future and distinguishes it from other company cultures (e.g., IBM). Organizational cultures, then, are the result of myriad decisions made over time that, combined, make up the pattern of VABEs that distinguish one group from the next. Figure 11–2 depicts the indirect effect that design choices have on organizational outcomes.

FIGURE 11–2 General Model Showing Leadership's Indirect Influence on Organizational Outcomes

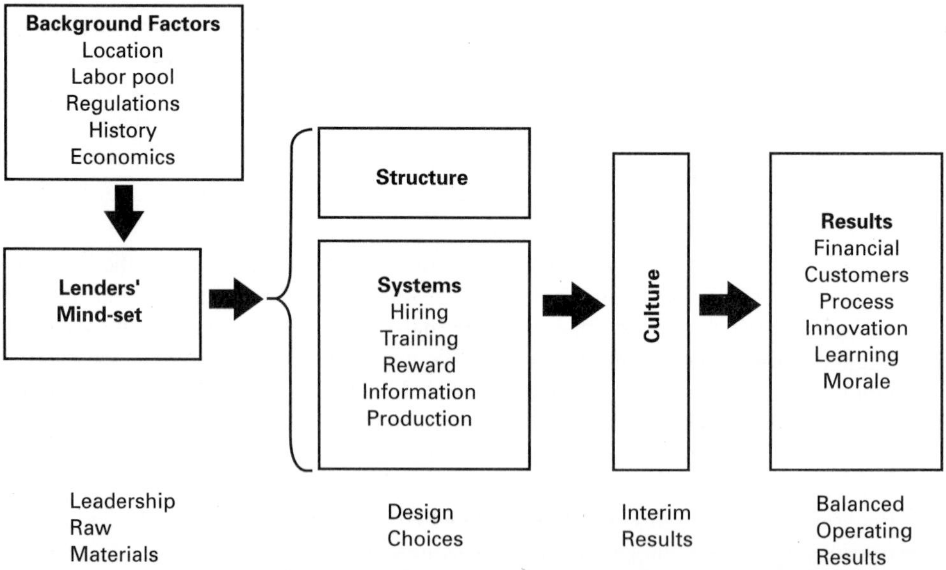

These cultures, which in the vernacular are referred to as "the way we do things around here," may be so ingrained and so deeply a part of the way we behave that we no longer recognize them as something we created but rather as just the way things are and the way things are "supposed" to be done. Often, not until someone from another culture visits do we become aware of how cultures differ and of how much we have taken for granted about the way things "should" be done.

Organizational cultures can be built consciously,[16] but usually they evolve over time as decision after decision is made and the consequences are accepted and incorporated into the daily routine of doing business. The challenge to the leader-as-designer is to anticipate clearly the impact of organizational design decisions on the culture that emerges from the other side of those decisions. What many leaders do not realize is that *design decisions do not have a direct impact on organizational behavior.* The behavior that emerges is filtered through the existing culture. If you have paid careful attention to that fact, you may be better armed to avoid unintended consequences, probably by including in the decision-making process more people in the culture who are going to be affected by the decisions.

Because organizational cultures are the result of many decisions made over time and because these decisions have become so much a part of the culture, organizational cultures are often nearly invisible to the people who work within them. Determining what your organization's operating culture is can be a frustrating effort. As Schein points out, this effort requires large amounts of courage, self-reflection, the collaboration of outsiders who can recognize aspects that insiders take for granted and do not even notice, and extraordinary skills of observation, abstraction, and articulation. If you can identify even a part of the present culture, you are then somewhat prepared to think about how that culture aligns with strategic intent; you can then begin thinking about how design decisions might impact that culture in ways that would support the strategic intent.

If you can gain some success at identifying the future culture, you face the immense task of designing interventions in the organization that will eventually shift the underlying VABEs toward the targeted ones. Many leaders during the 1980s and 1990s presumed to undertake a culture change in their organizations, but most learned that this undertaking was not an easy task, nor a quick task, nor, in the end, something that might even be feasible.

Jack Welch, for example, undertook what amounted to a major culture change at General Electric Company with his WorkOut effort in the late 1980s. His goal was to reduce bureaucracy, to increase initiative and decision making among middle and upper middle level managers, and to ingrain a new set of operating principles (speed, simplicity, and self-confidence) in the company's multiple divisions. The WorkOut effort made clear, first, that each division and various parts of those divisions had their own subcultures and, second, that managers with 25 to 35 years of experience in GE were not going to change their fundamental way of thinking and managing just because of a few announcements, a few seminars, and a few hard conversations with the boss. After several years of effort and with some good progress in hand, GE management had to accept more modest results on the goal of revamping the culture of some 200,000 employees.

Changing an organization's culture is an enormous undertaking.

In the end, culture is the *result* of organizational design efforts. A design that is conceived and implemented carefully will result in a culture that reflects more rather than less of the leaders' original intentions. A design that is not carefully thought out may cause a variety of unintentional outcomes that over time become cemented in the culture and make it even more intractable in the future.

ORGANIZATIONAL RESULTS

Organizational design decisions create a context in which people work and perform. In the midst of that context, leaders strive to encourage and guide. This effort eventually produces some results. One challenge that leaders face is to figure out what kind of results they want and whether they are focusing on the results that will accurately and comprehensively reflect how the organization is doing in meeting its mission or purpose.

Historically, the primary indicator of results has been profitability. Although many experts have suggested variations on this theme (e.g., sales, return on equity, and growth in earnings per share), the underlying focus has been on profitability. One concern that this focus has raised is the extent to which an emphasis on profitability diverts leaders and employees from the central mission of the organization. If conversations and reward systems focus exclusively on profitability, leaders can find themselves paradoxically working with an organization that is becoming less and less profitable.

Recently, scholars and leaders have been pointing out the virtues and practical productivity of a more balanced approach.[17] The balanced scorecard approach recognizes that leaders' ability to improve results is undermined if they do not understand the relationships among why people go to work every day, why it is important to meet and exceed customer expectations, and why learning and improving ways of doing business has to be a way of doing business.

The balanced scorecard approach does not ignore financial results; rather, it simply notes that there are other measures of success that, taken together, are more accurate, more predictive, and more healthy and will lead to better leadership decisions. Short-term profitability turned out to be a disastrous focus, for instance, for many overseas companies in Central and South America prior to the 1980s. When local governments grew tired of the exploitation of financial results and nationalized those investments, many companies lost millions in equity and in future income streams. A more balanced approach that included learning and development, community involvement, and reinvestment might have produced a lower level of profitability in the short run, but a larger net present value when long-term future revenue streams were considered into the equation.

The balanced scorecard approach considers not only financials, but also employee morale, learning and innovation, and regulatory relationships as key indicators of an organization's health and long-term prospects. A balanced approach would dictate that, rather than maximize profitability, we maximize an index of all four key areas, which might mean lower levels of profitability, in order to maintain steady levels of customer satisfaction, of employee learning and growth, and of innovation in products, services, and the systems we use to produce them.

Conclusion

The shape and construction of the organizations in which leaders operate have an enormous impact on the outcomes of any leadership situation. Effective leaders understand the importance of the design demands of their jobs and work hard to craft leadership philosophies that inform decisions about organizational structure and about systems that provide the context in which employees will work. Leaders also understand that they do not have direct impact on their companies' results, nor even on the development of the dominant cultures that operate in those companies; instead, they understand that they make design decisions and that each of these decisions not only addresses the immediate problem at hand, but also leaves a legacy that adds to, augments, or shifts the huge momentum exerted by the organization's cultures and subcultures. When reviewing the results that emerge from any organizational or leadership situation, effective leaders realize that a balanced perspective may not optimize profitability in the short run but will in fact produce a more stable and therefore larger net present value of that profitability over the long run.

Principles of Level Three Leadership

1. Effective leaders are effective designers of organizations and their components.
2. Effective leaders develop a clear organizational philosophy and mission or purpose and work to align the organization and its various components with that purpose and vision.
3. Effective leaders realize that their decisions about organizational structure and about the internal systems and procedures that define the principles by which work is done in the organization will have only an indirect effect on organizational outcomes and that they need to pay attention to how the organizational culture is affected by those decisions.
4. Effective leaders carefully include others in their design decisions to avoid as much as possible the debilitating effects of unintended consequences.
5. Effective leaders understand the strategic value of information systems and are designing organizations that revolve around those systems.
6. Effective leaders work hard to review and reengineer organizations or their parts (systems, processes, procedures, etc.) that divert them from achieving their visions and strategic intents.
7. Effective leaders pay particular attention to systems that often seem unimportant, like hiring, training and development, reward, and information systems, because they know that these systems all have big impacts on their people and the culture they develop.
8. Effective leaders understand that an overemphasis on profitability can actually undermine their ability to produce profits and that a more balanced approach to assessing organizational outcomes is paradoxically more powerful in the long run.

Questions for Reflection

1. Describe your personal leadership philosophy and how it relates to your vision of what your organization could or should become.
2. Review within your organization the four systems discussed in this chapter and assess on paper how those systems encourage or discourage employees from working energetically toward your organization's vision and goals.

3. Describe the core elements of your organization's culture. Use outsiders to check and confirm your description. Ponder and then describe how you think the culture should evolve if your organization is going to be increasingly competitive in the future.

4. Assess your organization in terms of its ability to learn and adapt to changing market conditions. What could you do to enhance the learning atmosphere or culture in your organization?

5. Describe how your organization does or does not use a balanced scorecard in assessing its results. What would be necessary to take a more balanced approach, and what would that approach look like?

Notes

1. Peter Senge, *The Fifth Discipline* (New York: Doubleday Currency, 1990).

2. Although this viewpoint is an older one, the connections are powerful and still generally applicable. This view was adapted from Anthony G. Athos and Robert E. Coffey, *Behavior in Organizations: A Multidimensional View* (Englewood Cliffs, NJ: Prentice-Hall, 1968).

3. For a description of Lancaster and his work in establishing this plant, see "FMC Aberdeen" (UVA-OB-385), available through Darden Educational Materials Services, Charlottesville, Virginia.

4. See, for example, Chris Argyris, *Improving Leadership Effectiveness* (New York: Wiley, 1976) and Robert E. Quinn, *Deep Change* (San Francisco: Jossey-Bass, 1997).

5. See Stan Davis, *Future Perfect* (Reading, MA: Addison-Wesley, 1987). His argument is that because all organizational designs follow a strategy in some sense, by the time the organization has been "built," the surrounding environmental factors have changed sufficiently enough that the strategy has shifted and the organization has become out of date. The challenge, of course, is to build organizations that will respond to environmental changes more quickly.

6. For more details, see chapter 1 on the context of leadership.

7. See Alfred Chandler, *Strategy and Structure* (Cambridge, MA: MIT Press, 1962) for a detailed account of how this form evolved, and William Ouchi, *The M-Form Society* (New York: Avon, 1984) for a good overview.

8. For more information on managing matrix organizations, see Stan Davis and Paul Lawrence, *Matrix* (Reading, MA: Addison-Wesley, 1977).

9. Charles Handy, *The Age of Paradox* (Boston: Harvard Business School Press, 1994).

10. See Tom Peters, *The Tom Peters Seminar* (New York: Vintage Books, 1994), 29.

11. See Steve Kerr, "On the Folly of Hoping for A While Rewarding B," *Academy of Management Journal* (August 15, 1988), 298.

12. For more details on this nonaligned system, see the "Hausser Foods Company" case written by David Nadler of Columbia University, available through Darden Educational Materials Services, Charlottesville, Virginia.

13. See C. Meyer, "How the Right Measures Help Teams Excel," *Harvard Business Review* (May 1994).

14. See Jay R. Galbraith, *Designing Complex Organizations* (Reading, MA: Addison-Wesley, 1973); Jay R. Galbraith and Ed Lawler, *Designing the Organizations of the Future* (San Francisco: Jossey-Bass, 1993); and Charles Savage, *Fifth Generation Management* (Burlington, MA: Digital Press, 1990).

15. See Edgar Schein, *Organizational Culture and Leadership,* 2d ed. (San Francisco: Jossey-Bass, 1992).

16. See again, for example, the "FMC Aberdeen" case (UVA-OB-385), which describes the intentional construction of a relatively unique organizational culture by an extraordinary leader.

17. See R. S. Kaplan and D. P. Norton, "Balanced Scorecard: Measures That Drive Performance," *Harvard Business Review* (January 1992).

CHAPTER

Leading Change

12

Chapter Outline

- General Model of Change

- The Role of Outside Help in Managing Change

- Classic Change Models

- Roles in the Change Process

- Responses to Change

- Levels in Change

- The MIT Model

L eadership is about changing. If you are not fomenting or managing change, then you are not leading. Change and its related concepts are inextricably intertwined with leadership and its concepts. Effective leaders understand and can use an effective change process. In a world that continues to change rapidly, effective leaders are comfortable with change and how to manage it. Ineffective leaders struggle with change and find that many of their efforts at managing change fail. John Kotter asserts that there are eight basic reasons why these failures occur: allowing too much complacency, failure to build a guiding coalition, underestimating the power of vision, undercommunication of the vision, failure to create short-term wins, declaring victory too soon, and neglecting to anchor the new changes in the organization's culture.[1] To be an effective leader, you must understand the change process and become a master of managing it.

GENERAL MODEL OF CHANGE

Over the course of our lives, we become comfortable with a certain set of behaviors. We have used them before, they seem to work well enough, and so they become a part of our common routines. This scenario is also true of organizations. Our set of comfortable routines becomes a box for us, a box that allows us to be productive and to move forward efficiently without testing everything we do, but it is also a box that constrains us and inhibits our thinking about and trying new things. We call this set of routines our comfort zone or our baseline behavior.

As long as we continue to get confirming feedback from the outside world about our baseline behavior, we have little motivation to change it—unless, of course, we are simply curious and want to change things for change's sake. We can, in that context, speak of internally motivated change and externally motivated change.

Again, this situation is also true in business. Many managers, especially Industrial Age managers, ascribe to the maxim, "if it ain't broke, don't fix it" and see that stable, historically successful routines contain a way of generating stable cash flows, building leverage, managing margins, and realizing returns of past investments. The danger, as we discussed in chapter 8, is that unless these investments build into our personal and organizational systems an enhanced ability to adapt to our environment, they become strategic blockades rather than sources of competitive advantage.

We all want to think well of ourselves. Our minds develop remarkable techniques for maintaining a positive self-image. If what we did in the past worked and helped us succeed in some sense, then we seek, naturally, to maintain that positive self-image. This desire to think well of ourselves connects to our view of the outside world. If, after long periods of time of receiving confirming data about our baseline behavior, we get some *dis*confirming data, we are faced with a choice of what to do about it.

Disconfirming data is a challenge to our self-concept because it says that what we just did does not work any more. This data tries to pull us away from our baseline behavior and signals to us that we should try something new. The data may be in the form of a monthly profit report, the establishment of a new competitor, feedback from a spouse or peer, angry facial expressions from a subordinate, a weak performance review, an appointment request turned down. Whatever the source of the disconfirming data, it challenges our view of ourselves and invites us to do something about it.

In a variety of ways, we can either accept or reject this disconfirming data. Accepting it can be painful because it means that we will have to rethink our self-image, perhaps change our behavior, move out of our comfort zone, and experiment with untried and unproven behaviors that also may or may not work. This movement is risky business.

Accepting disconfirming data even before it is received or breaking out of the comfort zone and trying to do difficult, somewhat painful, new things is the subject of Scott Peck's best-selling book, *The Road Less Traveled*.[2] Because most of us want to stay in our comfort zone, we persist in our baseline behavior. Breaking out of our comfort zone is uncomfortable and threatening. Peck argues that the road less traveled is the path that leads to this discomfort, to breaking out of our baseline patterns, and to trying new things; he adds that this is the road to learning and growth. Without it, he argues, we are destined to become little more than we presently are. A few people actually welcome dis-

General Change Process

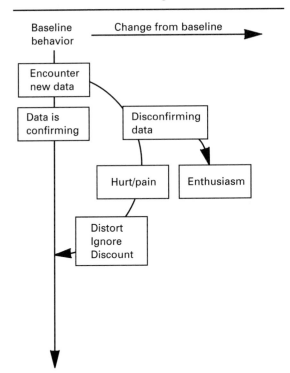

FIGURE 12–1 General Model of Change

confirming data because they view it as an opportunity to learn, to break out of their comfort boxes, and grow larger.

Many of us, however, choose to stay in our comfort zone and respond to disconfirming data by systematically discounting it, distorting it, or ignoring it altogether. If the disconfirming data are discounted, distorted or ignored, then we can continue behaving as we always did without interruption. Having encountered the disconfirming data, our behavior continues along the old baseline unchanged and undeviating. It is as if our behavior, like a rubber band stretched from the baseline, snaps back; we fall back into our old behavioral patterns. These concepts are shown visually in Figure 12–1.

Of course, the strength of the disconfirming data will have something to do with whether we can discount it, distort it, or ignore it. If the disconfirming data is very strong, we may not be able to ignore it. At the same time, we all know of people who have received enormous disconfirming data and been quite able to ignore it. Our attitudes about change and our comfort levels with change may shape our response to disconfirming data. At some level, though, we have a choice about whether to accept it.

If we accept the disconfirming data, then we have to do something about it. Acting on it will involve, by definition, some experimentation on our part. We will be electing to try things we have not done before. For most of us, being taken out of our comfort zone and forced to try something new is an experience that is threatening, scary, and undertaken

General Change Process

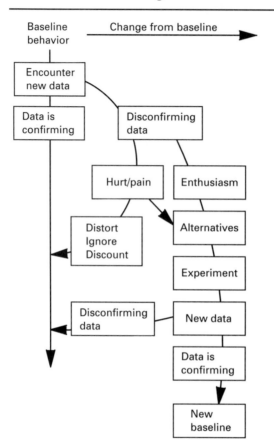

FIGURE 12–2 Creating a New Baseline of Behavior

with trepidation. We try the experiment and that, in turn, generates more feedback data. If the new data disconfirms the validity of the experiment, even if we did not do the experiment "correctly," we are likely to abandon the new approach and our behavior will snap back to the former baseline.

Think about your personal efforts to change, whether it be losing weight, stopping smoking, studying more frequently, exercising regularly, or writing to family more often. If the new behavior does not bring some positive results to you, you would probably conclude that it does not work and therefore would slip back into your former comfort zone.

If the new behavior produces positive results, though, then a new pattern begins to be established. With reinforcement, you begin to see that the new approach works. As the positive feedback continues to come in, the new baseline is established and you continue on it until new disconfirming data comes in. This evolution of our overall general model of change appears in Figure 12–2.

THE ROLE OF OUTSIDE HELP
IN MANAGING CHANGE

Outside help can greatly assist a person or an organization in recognizing disconfirming data and acting productively on it. First, assembling and presenting the disconfirming data itself is something that others can often do better than can an individual or employees working within a firm. By virtue of living *in* our own comfort zones, we have difficulty seeing that we might be overlooking (discounting, distorting, or ignoring) bits of disconfirming data. Our long-established behaviors, our habits, become invisible to us. If we tend to be defensive (again, as a person or an organization), outside infusions of information from consultants, physicians, friends, and so on, can help us view the data differently, with more seriousness and a greater sense of validity.

A second area in which outside help is of great assistance is in identifying alternative courses of action. Because we have been operating in our comfort zone, we do not see clearly other ways of doing things. Talking to a consultant or a executive from another industry can be very helpful in developing a new view of what is possible.

External viewpoints are also helpful in interpreting the data from the new experiment. If we are defensive, we may interpret the new data negatively and even subconsciously manage the experiment so that it fails. This defensive behavior happens in business, too. Outside monitors can help us be honest in our attempts to evaluate the data from the new experiments until we get our own bearings and can see things more objectively.

CLASSIC CHANGE MODELS

Historically, probably the most popular change model was the simple three-step process articulated by Kurt Lewin. He noted that a change effort began with an unfreezing process, contained a transformation process in the middle, and ended with a refreezing stage. Nowadays, with the rapid rate of change taking place around us, most observers agree that the refreezing is dangerous and that we probably should think more in terms of jelling the new processes but not freezing them. The gel image is more flexible and responsive to future change while still giving some stability. Other people argue that we should simply give up on "unfreeze-retrain-refreeze" and accept the reality of today as "unfreeze-change-change."

In our general change model, therefore, each new baseline will constantly be challenged by changing events around it. The individual or organization who does not have a deep-seated, Level Three value for change will find this new world a constant irritation filled with frustration. People who have or who develop a value for change, on the other hand, will begin to understand this process and manage it to their benefit.

A more recent, widely used change model comes from Michael Beer at the Harvard Business School. Beer offers an equation that suggests that the amount of change in a system is equivalent to the amount of dissatisfaction with the status quo times the clarity of the model of where we want to go times the strength of the change process when that product exceeds the cost of making the change.[3]

$$Cv = Dsq \times Mf \times Pc > Cc$$

where

Cv = volume of change

Dsq = dissatisfaction with the status quo

Mf = model of the future

Pc = Process of change

Cc = Cost of the change

This model is very useful because it tells us that unless people are unhappy with the way things are, they are not likely to change, and even if they are unhappy, unless they can see how to change things and how they want to change things, they are not likely to engage in the process.

Hal Leavitt at Stanford further informs this process by suggesting that the role of effective leaders in today's environment is becoming more about *creating* problems for employees so they see the need for change than it was historically, finding and solving problems.[4] Thus, effective leaders today find themselves, somewhat paradoxically, creating dissatisfaction for many employees in the hope of getting those employees to recognize and respond to changes that need to be made before it is too late. This approach is similar to Kotter's view of creating a sense of urgency to overcome complacency.[5]

ROLES IN THE CHANGE PROCESS

Other roles besides problem creator are useful in the change process: change leader, change agent, change manager, and change model.[6] Any one person may or may not play all these roles. A *change leader* is someone who initiates a change process. This initiation may come about by virtue of a significant event or a bolt of inspiration or simply from hard work in thinking about accumulating experience in the organization. Senior executives are often change leaders in corporations. They may, for instance, commission studies, request a new process for developing company strategy, or decide to acquire new kinds of businesses.

A *change agent* is someone who causes the change to begin in a person or an organization. This person actually begins the change effort. The change agent may or may not be the change leader. Consultants are often change agents, as are senior staff members; both respond to a change leader's request or initiative.

A *change manager* has the day-to-day responsibilities of implementing and overseeing the change effort. The change manager could be a staff or a line person. The change leader looks to the change manager for reports and progress. This person has to influence others in the organization to make the changes take place.

A *change model* is a person who exemplifies the change effort. These various roles have interactions. If the change leader is not a change model, that is, if the senior executive recommending an organizational change does not epitomize the requested changes, the strength of the change effort is greatly undermined. Identifying these roles in a change effort and assessing how their behavior and communications are consistent or inconsistent can help explain why many change efforts work or do not work.

We could also recognize the *changees,* the people who are being asked to change what they do and how they do it. This role is as difficult and as important as the others, yet it is often overlooked by people in the first four roles.

RESPONSES TO CHANGE

Changees often experience a predictable series of responses to change efforts, particularly those initiated from outside. When people or organizations change, they let go of some part of their historical comfort zone and embrace a new pattern. This letting go, in a significant way, is like letting a part of the self die. We can speak of experiencing change, then, as if it were like dying a little death.

There is a lot of similarity between the research of Elisabeth Kübler-Ross on the experiences of terminally ill patients and the experiences of individuals and organizational members to the change process.[7] Although neither individuals nor groups of employees go through all these stages in exactly the same way nor even in the same sequence, there is a general pattern that informs the leader desirous of managing change processes better.

People experiencing significant change typically go through periods of denial, anger, bargaining, despair, experimenting, resignation, and integration. Again, please note that not everyone experiences these stages in this order, and certainly not everyone goes through all the stages. Some people, for example, get stalled in denial.

These people react to disconfirming data by denying it. There are many forms of denial as shown in Figure 12–3.[8] We can deny the credibility of the messenger, which in effect discounts the validity of the source of the data. If, before even considering the content, we reject the message because of the source, the messenger, we can easily avoid thinking about the content of the message. If we get past this hurdle, we can deny the content of the message itself by holding on to a belief that the data is false. Again, we can easily avoid doing anything about data that we do not believe. If we are forced to accept both the message and the messenger, we can deny the relevance of the message to our own situation. "Yes," we

FIGURE 12–3 Forms of Denial

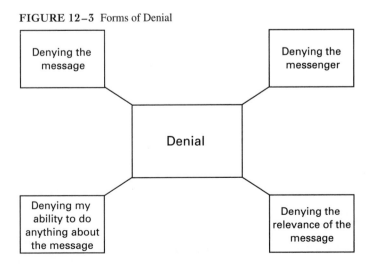

may say, "it's true, and I acknowledge that you brought this to my attention, but it really doesn't concern me." Finally, however, if we are forced to acknowledge that the data source is credible, that the data is true, and that the data relates to us, we may then deny our ability to do anything about it. These four successive hurdles to receiving and seriously considering disconfirming data are defense mechanisms that we often use to protect our self-image.

People can stay locked in denial for long periods of time. Some refuse ever to come out. Addictions are, in part, a form of denial in as much as they are an attempt to seek a short route to resonance. People who ignore health warnings from the surgeon general's office are in denial. Employees or managers who ignore competitive signals from their industries and persist in old routines are in denial.

If the disconfirming data is strong enough to pierce a person's denial, the first emotional response is typically anger. Anger arises when the changee realizes that the disconfirming data cannot be denied and must be dealt with. This realization forces us to leave our comfort zone and move into a new, unknown arena. If this arena is navigated successfully, we will be required to give up something of our old self and move on. To change, we give up an investment of time, energy, and emotion in a pattern that no longer works so well. This loss can be very angering. We do not want to give up our former investments, and our related anger may be vented at any number of targets that may or may not have anything to do with the real source of the problem. Employees may get angry at employers instead of at the competition. Clerks may become angry with customers instead of trying to serve them. People may get angry at their colleagues, their families, their counterparts in other departments, and so on. As outlined in chapter 6, people with higher EQs and CQs are more likely to manage this anger and move ahead. Moving ahead usually means a failed attempt to move backward.

Anger in response to a recognized need for change often leads to bargaining. Having been forced to recognize that the old way does not work so well anymore, we will often try to bargain our way out of the change. "Maybe if we just cut back on expenses, we could continue as we are," is one common bargaining ploy. Another is, "Maybe we can work harder, and the data will get better." We also hear, "This is a short-term phenomenon; we'll get back to the old way soon," "We've managed changes before, and we'll manage this one doing what we've been doing," "Customers don't really know what they want; we need to educate them," and so on.

Bargaining is an attempt to reverse the disconfirming data and retreat to the original baseline. In the resonance model presented in chapter 7, bargaining is related to the ping-pong effect between preparation and SOS barriers. Disconfirming data is a manifestation of barriers. Bargaining can be very dangerous if short-term bargains are made and the data begins to show some responsiveness, because people *want* to believe that things will get better without their changing. When bargaining fails, though, as it will in all fundamental change situations, we realize that we truly have to change and this realization often leads to despair.

Despair for most of us is a watershed transitional stage between attempts to go back and willingness to go ahead. In this (it is hoped) brief period, we realize that there is no going back, that the former comfort level will not be felt again, and that, however uncomfortable, we must go ahead.

Some experts argue that people need time to grieve at this point, to vent their despair, to cry, to reflect on the good old times, and to lend a sense of completion to the past before going on to the next stage. I do not disagree with this view, but at some point we must say, "Enough crying for the past. I must live in the present preparing for tomorrow." The sooner we complete our grieving for the past and begin to see possibilities for the future, the sooner progress will be made. Again, the metaphor here is that making changes in our lives is like dying a small death, and like death, these changes require some grieving and attention if we are to move ahead with psychological wholeness.

When the grieving is coming to an end, most people begin, however timidly, to see possibilities. Seeing possibilities in the future is the beginning of exploration and experimentation. As I mentioned earlier in this chapter, outside, less involved, expert assistance can be of enormous help. As we begin to see new, manageable routes of progress and as we take a few steps in that direction, we can see the possible results. These alternative directions generate in us some hope that the despair of the recent change will be replaced with a new sense of comfort and capability.

Hope is the anticipation that our efforts can yield results. If, in the midst of a major change, we cannot see how the world will get better, we will have difficulty finding something to work for in the new arrangement, and we will begin to look to the past for comfort and support. False hopes are not any help. If management deviates from the moral rock described in chapter 4 and allows or constructs false hopes, employees will soon become disenchanted, disengaged, and slip back into despair. Realistic hope, achievable hope, small-but-tangible hope is better than promises made lightly and without much expectation of fulfillment.

As hope is realized and as the data coming in from the new experiments becomes positive, we begin to integrate the new way of doing things into our network of assumptions and values. Ghosts of the old assumptions begin to fade, and the new principles take their place. Often this integration occurs so subtly that we do not even notice it. Integration, although equally as powerful as anger and despair, is much less obvious. One day, we might notice that we have been using the new principles for a while and things have been going okay. The new order seems *almost* comfortable. Celebrating this ethereal transition is an important step in helping us understand what has happened, that we are veterans of managing change and we have created a new reality.

The process that I have just described is diagrammed in Figure 12–4. It represents an oscillation between behavior and emotion, each in turn typically triggering the next. Overcoming denial leads to anger. Overcoming anger leads to bargaining. Overcoming bargaining leads to despair. Working through despair leads to new options. Working those options can generate new hope. Hope and work together produce the kind of behavior that leads to a new pattern of doing things. Effective leaders not only understand this process, but actively plan for and anticipate the reactions so that their downside effects are minimized and their upside possibilities maximized.

Figure 12–5 shows another way to depict this process of change. Here, the early complacency of past successes is represented by a smooth, flat line. Disconfirming data becomes like rocks in a river, causing chaotic rapids. Despite the evidence, people resist the need for and efforts to introduce change. If leadership is strong and good processes are put into place, short-term positive results begin to emerge. Then, lest the new efforts snap back to the old way, a new baseline is established by an iterative consolidation of the change into a new habitual way of doing things. Unless the new way includes programs for continuous change, it can, before long, become its own complacency—and the process begins again.

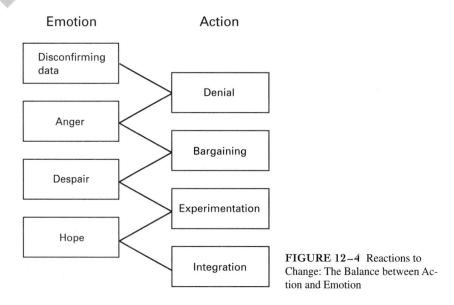

FIGURE 12-4 Reactions to Change: The Balance between Action and Emotion

---

LEVELS IN CHANGE

Like the three levels of leadership that I defined in chapter 3, change as well can be divided into Level One, Level Two, and Level Three. If the target of our change effort is behavior only, we are working on a Level One change effort, but Level One change efforts can often have unintended Level Three consequences if the formal changes requested affect us at a deeper level. Effective leaders recognize that powerful change invites people to change not only their behavior but also their thoughts and beliefs, and so those leaders target their attempts at Level Three. A Level Three change is any change that modifies the basic values and assumptions of an individual or organization.

FIGURE 12-5 Typical Change Cycle

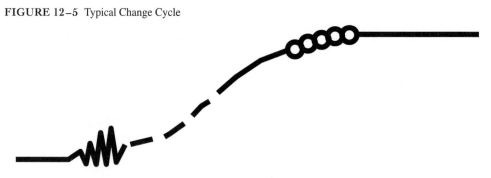

Complacency/Turbulence/Resistance/Small Wins/Consolidation/New Baseline

A Level Three change, for Kotter, would be anchoring the changes in the culture of the organization.[9] Kotter summarizes the proactive change process as follows: (1) establish a sense of urgency, (2) create a guiding, powerful coalition, (3) develop a clear and powerful vision and strategy, (4) communicate at every point possible the change vision, (5) redesign the organization to remove obstacles to change, (6) find short-term successes to celebrate, (7) consolidate short-term wins into new change initiatives, and (8) ensure that the changes are incorporated into the underlying organizational culture. These eight steps correspond well with the principles introduced in chapter 5.

Whereas Kotter has a well-informed academic view, here is a similar supporting perspective from industry. The president of the largest division of one of the most successful financial services firms in the United States has summarized the change process as the "Four Ps" of change: Purpose (derived presumably from some felt Pain), Picture, Plan, Part. These Four Ps are, in essence, a manager's view of Beer's equation: If people do not see a purpose for the change, if they do not see where they are trying to go, if they do not see a plan for how to get there, and if they do not see a part that they can play in the plan, they are not likely to participate in the change effort—and it will flounder or founder.

THE MIT MODEL

Just down the road from Kotter's Harvard office, Nevis and other researchers at MIT have developed a powerful seven-step model of managing change.[10] They suggest that change is a three-dimensional phenomenon involving a developmental process, seven tools for effecting change, and the importance of managing resistance to change.

According to the MIT team, major change efforts typically progress through four clear phases: a traditional phase, an exploratory phase, a generative phase, and an internalization phase. The traditional phase is when employees and management are just learning that the old ways are not working any more. The traditional phase allows workers to come to grips with disconfirming data coming in from the environment. Once this realization has set in, management begins searching for new approaches in the exploratory phase. In the next phase, the generative, key pieces of the change effort are generated out of new processes and approaches so that the new processes become the source of energy for change. Finally, in the internalization phase, the new processes become so well ingrained that they become a "natural" part of the organization.

Nevis and his colleagues argue well that successful change efforts utilize not one or two but seven sets of skills related to change. These seven skills are persuasive communication, participation, the use of expectations, role modeling, reward systems, structural or organizational changes, and finally, coercion. Each of these skill sets has its strengths and weaknesses, and each might be more or less appropriate at each of the four phases. The challenge for effective change managers is to understand and be able to use each of these tools as appropriate—and to avoid using them inappropriately.

THE MIT CHANGE MANAGEMENT SKILL SETS

1. Persuasive communication
2. Participation

3. Use of expectations
4. Role modeling
5. Extrinsic rewards
6. Structural and organizational changes
7. Coercion

I have argued that coercion is a use of power, but is not leadership. You may or may not feel that coercion is necessary for a short period of time. Some managers believe that people have to be forced to do what they do not want to do when the effort will eventually lead to their acceptance of the "right" way of doing things. My concern here is that if you get comfortable using coercion as a crutch, as a last means of creating change, then you risk the danger that it will become easier to use the next time. Soon you are exercising power at Level One, which is faster but in the long run, less effective.

The MIT team notes that many change efforts fail because change leaders ignore predictable resistance to change. Using the learning organization work that has been done at MIT by Peter Senge and colleagues, the MIT team suggests that a powerful way of recognizing this common feature is to encompass the principle of multiple realities. In other words, there are lots of subgroups in an organization who see the change efforts differently. Some are in favor, and some are opposed to the changes—each for their own reasons. Change leaders who can recognize that these groups each have good reasons for their viewpoints are better armed to select and use change tools that fit that group's perspective. The key to this approach is to legitimize diverse perceptions rather than to demand a singular view. Using the principle of multiple realities, management can find richer solutions and can thus reduce resistance.

Conclusion

Understanding and managing change is an integral part of effective leadership. Leaders seek to change what people do, and if leaders are effective, they will change what people think and believe. People naturally tend to settle into a comfort zone, using personal, interpersonal, and organizational techniques that have served them in the past. Changing out of or from this historical pattern usually begins with disconfirming data. Those people who attend to this data and interpret it as meaningful begin a change process. In so doing, they leave behind a part of their former self, as if they were dying a little death. Making real change, especially Level Three change, triggers a common response pattern of denial, anger, bargaining, despair, experimentation, hope, and integration. Leaders who understand and are skilled at this process can help people through these predictable stages and manage their mutual changes more effectively.

Principles of Level Three Leadership

1. Leadership by definition is about managing change.
2. Effective leaders understand and have masterful skills in managing the change process.
3. Changing is like dying a little death; one part must be let go and a new part must be born.
4. Change begins with disconfirming data. We have a choice about how we respond to that data, whether to ignore it or consider it.

5. Recognizing and managing various change effort roles—including change leader, change agent, change manager, change model, and changee—is helpful in mounting a successful change effort.

6. Disconfirming data often leads to a series of predictable reactions to the change process: denial, anger, bargaining, despair, experimentation, hope, and integration. People can get stuck all along the way, and outside help is often useful in moving through each phase.

7. People need strong and consistent reinforcement in the experimentation phase in order to settle on the new way of doing things.

8. Outside agents are often helpful in managing change because they can see things that have become invisible habits to those in the change arena.

9. Level Three, or value level change, is the most enduring.

Questions for Reflection

1. What disconfirming data have you encountered either personally or in your work group over the last six months? What was your response to it?

2. What change roles are you playing in your work group? What data do you see, that maybe others do not see, that invites you to become a change leader?

3. What support has been helpful for you in the past while you were reacting to a change process? How could you provide that support to others?

4. List the most significant changes you have made in your life. Think through the process that you used to navigate each change. How well did you manage those changes? What did you learn from them, and what would you like to know how to do better?

Notes

1. See John Kotter, *Leading Change* (Boston: HBS Press, 1996).
2. M. Scott Peck, *The Road Less Traveled,* 2d ed. (New York: Simon & Schuster, 1998).
3. See Michael Beer, "Leading Change," Harvard Case 488–037, available through Harvard Case Services, Boston, Massachusetts.
4. See Harold Leavitt, *Corporate Pathfinders: Building Vision and Values into Organizations* (Homewood, IL: Dow Jones-Irwin, 1986).
5. Kotter, *Leading Change.*
6. I credit my colleague Alex Horniman for introducing me to these ideas.
7. See Elisabeth Kübler-Ross, *On Death and Dying* (New York: Collier Books, 1993).
8. Thanks again to Alex Horniman.
9. Kotter, *Leading Change.*
10. Edwin E. Nevis, Jon Lancourt, and Helen G. Vassallo, *Intentional Revolutions* (San Francisco: Jossey-Bass, 1996).

Part VI: Conclusion

CHAPTER 13

Level Three Leadership: Getting Below the Surface

Chapter Outline

■ Summary of Basic Principles of Level Three Leadership

Level Three Leadership is about making a difference below the surface. Whereas Level One Leadership focuses on short-term behavior, Level Three Leadership attempts to influence what people think and believe. Level One Leadership has worked well enough for several hundred years, well enough to build the Industrial Age and to form large corporations that have supplied the world with a plethora of products and services. Level One Leadership gives a manager a sense of accomplishment. He or she can *see* what people are doing and does not have to worry about what they are thinking and feeling. Level One Leadership is a visible kind of leadership; managers can see what people do, and most people can see what the consequences are if they do not respond. In an orderly world, Level One Leadership works well enough.

In this turbulent, fast-changing world in which decisions need to be made throughout an organization and in which the information needed to make those decisions can be rapidly distributed, the principles and consequences of Level One Leadership are breaking down. One person, one boss, vertical hierarchies, limited spans of control, clear functional and organizational boundaries, certainty about what to do, limited sharing of information, and clear repositories of expertise are fading. Taking their place are multiple "bosses," including suppliers, customers, people from various functions, and even subordinates; much flatter organizations based on constantly forming and re-forming teams; very broad spans of influence rather than control; fuzzy boundaries between functions and organizations; mounds of uncertainty about what to do; widespread information sharing and exchange; and constantly shifting pools of knowledge and insight.

In this environment, the Industrial Age leadership notions of "command and control" or "planning, organizing, motivating, and controlling" are becoming absurdly out of date. Huge political combines in the former Soviet Union have broken down and been replaced with widely distributed, self-determined, more democratic countries. Large industrial combines have been dissembled and reorganized into smaller, more independent firms. Although the political and industrial borders will continue to be mapped and melded in various ways, the people of the world, in large part, will no longer accept circumstances in which they have less control over their lives and fewer choices of futures. "Controlling" is giving way to "coordinating," and coordinating implies a respect for underlying beliefs and values in a way that controlling did not.

The world will still contain Level One Leaders (although in the lexicon of this book, this phrase is a misnomer; I have argued that when a person with power exercises that power without regard for the followers' voluntary responses, that person is no longer a leader but merely a person who exercises power). Part of the reason for Level One Leaders will be psychological. Many people grow up with a need to control their environment and will view people as a part of that environment. I also believe that the world will still contain Level One companies run by Level One Leaders. The cultures of these companies will continue to care little for the thoughts and feelings of the people who work within them, and the companies will continue to stress short-term financial goals, many of which will focus on the rewards of the shareholders to the subversion of other worthy objectives. Many of these companies may even survive for lengthy periods of time.

But increasingly, the organizations that will thrive and grow in the Information Age will be based on Level Three Leadership. Their employees will not only do what they are asked to do, but they will do it willingly and believe in it deeply. Successful Information Age organizations will learn from the not-for-profit organizations of the Industrial Age why people work hard, yielding their best efforts for little or no pay. These Level Three organizations will understand the causal networks that encourage people to work their hardest and brightest voluntarily and will know that unless they can find ways of organizing to elicit this kind of work, they will fall further behind their competition—who will understand and find ways to do it.

People in Level Three organizations will be bonded to their companies by more than paychecks and fear of unemployment. They will believe in what the company is doing. They will have information available to them about how the company is doing. They will understand the importance of delighting the customer in a world in which alternatives sources are proliferating. Managers will understand that unless the employees are delighted, the customers will not be.

Leaders who create Level Three organizations will face many challenges. First is the historical momentum of the Industrial Age and the principles that it taught. If Thomas Kuhn is right about the nature of scientific revolutions and the time it takes to realize one, it will take one or more generations in each organization before a new Level Three model of leadership will take hold.[1] If a generation or more of leadership changes is needed in an organization before a new Level Three way of thinking can emerge, this process will spread slowly through industry. Richard Walton, a long-time researcher of high-performance workplaces, noted the slowness of this spread.[2]

A second challenge is that the poverty in many parts of the world will slow the spread of the Information Age. People who are unable to access and use computer-based information links are left to the information-sharing processes of the Industrial Age and subject to its Level One Leadership characteristics. This process will be accelerated by education and the resultant power as people access the Internet and become facile with intraorganizational networks. Already television and the nearly global coverage of satellite-based broadcasting has changed the way people in hitherto isolated areas now see the world and their personal possibilities. A major challenge of the Information Age will be to manage the increasingly obvious differences between the haves and the have-nots. Aspirations, desires, and even demands are born when people in Eastern Europe or Southeastern Asia view the "Lifestyles of the Rich and Famous" on television and see the opulent homes and the lovely vacations. Increasingly, people will insist on self-determination, first politically and then economically.

The Information Age will make this self-determination possible. Unlike the Industrial Age, in which people could be kept "in the dark" about what was possible, the Information Age will inform poor people about how others live—and therefore about how they could live. The challenge then will be to manage the perceived gaps in effort and reward, to create a world in which fairness based on contribution will guide reward systems. Level Three Leaders will understand this challenge and, with a leadership based on moral foundations, will recognize and codevelop reward systems in which all can participate.

A third challenge to face in the Information Age will be the flexibility to invade and protect people's lives. With cell phones, faxes, and Internet connections, people can work from any venue. This capability can be a help or a hindrance. Some people will allow their work to control their lives no matter where they may be. Others will face a dilemma of balancing their personal and professional lives. When we have access to growing volumes of work-related data from any location, it becomes more difficult to manage the other aspects of life—health, family, rejuvenation, and relationships. The messages sent when we say, "Hang on for a moment. The other line is ringing" or "I'll be out in a minute, dear, I just need to clear my (unspoken 58) e-mail messages" are decidedly more invasive to personal and family life than when we worked a little overtime during the Industrial Age.

Fourth, Information Age leaders will need to find ways of developing Level Three influences in an Information Age population that may not be so willing to respond. Darden's graduate school of business administration is a good example. During construction of a new building during the early 1990s, the decision was made to put Internet and e-mail connections at each seat in the new classrooms. Later, in an environment oriented toward case discussion, the entire tenor of the classroom was changed. Instructors entering the room found that they were not looking at the faces of 60 students. Rather, faces were replaced with 60 laptop lids. Some instructors joked that the students should be required to paste a photograph of themselves on their laptops so the faculty could see who they were. Further, the faculty soon discovered that the students were e-mailing each other back and forth in class. While one student was speaking, several others were simultaneously commenting and carrying on a discussion live through the local area e-mail network. In addition, students were e-mailing their friends in other sections to learn what was going on in other classes at the same time. The faculty began worrying about this loss of control, a phenomenon that has hit leaders of corporations. Whether leaders want it to or not, the Information Age has changed the face of power in institutions by distributing it wider and deeper than it ever had been before. People at lower ranks of organizations are now able to communicate with each other and to obtain information about the business, which makes it less easy for leaders to control their people or what they think and do. Orwell's fear of Big Brother should have been, according to many disgruntled modern managers raised in the Industrial Age, a fear of Little Sibling.[3] For many managers living during the present transition from the Industrial Age to the Information Age, coming to terms with this loss of control is a major career and professional issue.

Level Three Leadership also implies getting below the surface by not just taking the first acceptable solution that comes along. Although Herb Simon won a Nobel Prize for his clarification of the concept of satisficing, Level Three Leaders are not willing to settle for the first tolerable solution they hit upon. Forcing people to go to work, to break a strike, to stay late, to do anything, may be the "easiest" solution at the moment, but in the long run, this Level One approach creates much more difficulty. Level Three Leaders will think beyond the immediate and work hard, mentally and emotionally, to identify other avenues that ultimately impinge on the hearts and heads as well as the bodies of their associates. If all human interaction is some form of exchange in which the currencies may be ill defined, what kind of currency is necessary for us to exchange part of our innermost motivations?

Herein lies a paradox. On the one hand, if all human interactions are exchanges, then this phenomenon is Level One. On the other hand, if we accept that each of us is the ultimate controller of our own motivations and values and beliefs, then the question is, what currency is necessary for us to voluntarily exchange with an institution or leader a part of our central motivations and values and the efforts that are associated with them? It seems apparent to me that only when the institutional offerings are consistent with our underlying motivations and values will we give our utmost for the institution. Consider all those people who work for little compensation in rescue squads across the country. In Albemarle County, Virginia, most of the rescue squads are voluntary. People with full-time jobs volunteer their services, which often involves lengthy training and long nights and weekends, to serve on the rescue squad vehicles. Consider the "Pjs," the rescue swimmers who work with the U.S. Coast Guard, who are willing to risk their lives and their families' livelihoods (modest as they are) for the lives of others (the smart and the not-so-smart alike) at sea.[4] Consider the volunteer nurses and hospital aides throughout the world who give their own time and talent and energy to help others, many of whom are dying. Why do these volunteers give of their time? Because they believe in what they are doing. They are participating in activities that match their highest values for human life and service. Their commitments are extraordinary. Their commitments yield world-class service.

Perhaps you believe that this kind of commitment is not possible in business. In many corporations, it may not be. How can you compare saving people's lives at sea in a storm with making ball bearings or fire extinguishers? On the other hand, what is your alternative? If a competitor in your industry can create a working environment in which people can bring their bodies, minds, and hearts to work and in which they can work wholeheartedly for a bigger purpose, what will your organization do? Over time, unless you find a similar way to engage people, your company will fall behind. The service, the quality, the customer focus, the enthusiasm—all of which characterize a Level Three organization—will not be there, and your customers will, slowly at first and then more rapidly, migrate to the companies who give the superior value for the same cost.

I have written this book to outline a structure by which you can begin to think about and perhaps begin to practice leading below the surface. Level Three Leadership is not about trying out the latest fad and sticking it like an adhesive bandage over a deep wound. Rather, Level Three Leadership is about thinking beyond the superficial and developing a set of skills that will allow you to create a strong vision where none is apparent, to develop deeper relationships where none historically have been invited, and to organize in a way that will tend to perpetuate those deeper connections when you move on.

To this end, I have described in this book a changing context in which we now find ourselves. This description outlined the ways in which deep, underlying beliefs about business and enterprise are shifting. It included a consideration of the way in which rapidly changing information technology is shaping the new organizational forms. It implied the need for a sturdy, general model of leadership that would incorporate much of what we learned in the Industrial Age and yet leave room for the new realities of the Information Age.

This four-wheel drive model of leadership included four main elements: *leader, task, others,* and *organization.* I argued in this book that who you are makes a big difference as to whether you can lead or not, but that this factor alone was not enough. A big part of an effective leadership outcome was the view that the leader, you, took of the strategic tasks facing you, your work group, and your organization. I offered a summary of historical ways of thinking about strategy and some newer principles of strategic thinking, and I invited you to practice them. I argued that unless you were able to develop these strategic thinking skills, you would be at a disadvantage compared with your peers.

I went on to say that the quality of your relationships with others had a major impact on whether they would accept your view of the strategic challenges facing them. If you were able to build your attempts to influence on a moral foundation and then to communicate clearly and effectively with some stamina, you might be able to make something happen.

Finally, I said that unless you were an organizational designer, your efforts at influencing and guiding others would be hampered by the organizational constraints that every organization imposes on its employees. Unless you design organizations that fit your view of the strategic challenges and unless you understand and master the change process that is continually necessary to move collections of people from one way of doing things to another, your efforts at leadership will fail.

These three thrusts—strategic thinking, leading others, and leading by design—are presented as critical causes of positive leadership outcomes. I argued that outcomes could be measured in terms of effectiveness, efficiency, learning and growth, and satisfaction. And I argued that unless you could see below the surface and develop deeper skills in each of these three areas, your efforts would tend to be fleeting surface impacts.

My sincere hope is that the concepts, the ideas, the models, the principles presented in this book will help you become a more effective leader in your personal life, in your professional life, and in your community. I believe you can if you think about and accept the principle of Level Three Leadership—that world-class leaders are values leaders, that they think about and intend to influence the central values, assumptions, beliefs, and expectations of those they work with. Level Three Leaders understand that unless they follow these principles, their efforts will be like small meteor showers, scarring the surface but leaving no deep and lasting change.

SUMMARY OF BASIC PRINCIPLES OF LEVEL THREE LEADERSHIP

1. We are in the midst of a major managerial paradigm shift that is transforming what it means to be an effective leader.

2. Leadership is a function of many elements working together. These elements include individual characteristics, forces in the environment, strategic opportunities envisioned by the

leader, quality of relationships with followers, and appropriateness of the organization for the leader, task, and followers.

3. Leadership is the ability and the willingness to influence others to do what you want them to do willingly.

4. Leadership is about change, and change requires persistence in the development of new habits and routines. Effective leaders understand and use the mechanics and processes of managing change.

5. Leadership is also about ethics and moral behavior. You cannot be an effective leader without taking a moral stand. Effective leadership and extraordinary performance are based on a foundation of moral principles: truth telling, promise keeping, fairness, respect for the individual, and respect for demonstrated competency.

6. Leadership occurs at three levels: behavioral, cognitive, and value. Level Three Leadership is more difficult and more powerful.

7. Your personal leadership emanates from your central beliefs and your core values and assumptions. In effect, who you are as a leader defines who you are as a person.

8. Individual leadership skills can be clustered into three groups: visioning, garnering commitment, and managing progress toward the vision.

9. Motivating leadership is, in large part, a function of clear and compelling pictures of what could be. This function applies to yourself in terms of your life's dream and purpose as well as to your work group and your organization.

10. Leadership is an act of engagement. When you truly engage in something, you become a leader. Engagement is a function of personal commitments usually based on personal resonance.

11. Leadership involves mobilizing the talents of others, which means clarifying what others have to offer and offering attractive invitations to them to engage in your cause.

12. People work at things they are rewarded for; they work hard for things they believe in.

13. Leadership is closely related to time. Although many managers speak of future-oriented leadership, much of leadership is getting people to deal with the present.

14. Language is the primary tool of leadership. Effective leaders know, understand, have skill with, and can use with wisdom various forms of language.

15. Interpersonal leadership skills are based on respect for competency, trust in consistent caring, fair exchanges, and genuine willingness to be influenced.

16. Leadership is about designing organizations that support what others have to offer to the leader's enterprise. Most of these organizational forms are different from the forms developed in the last era.

17. Leaders, first, are leaders of themselves. They work hard to see a higher vision and to make it come to pass.

These principles have certain implications for your individual behavior as a leader. They suggest that if you are to be an effective leader, you will engage in the following actions:

1. Clarifying your center
2. Clarifying what is possible and desirable
3. Clarifying what others can contribute
4. Supporting others so they can work
5. Being relentless
6. Measuring and celebrating progress

The first three of these implications involve "clarifying." By this I mean bringing into sharper focus, developing, realizing, and using. Thus, the action implied here is not a one-time action, but rather is an ongoing process of discovery and utilization. As an effective leader, you do not, for instance, simply clarify your center and then forget about it for the rest of your career. Rather, you must be periodically reviewing, renewing, and recommitting to what lies at your core. I intentionally used the participle form of the verbs to imply this meaning.

Leadership is demanding and draining. It requires intense mental, physical, emotional, spiritual, and social effort. Many people retreat from these demands, and our world, our businesses, and our communities are the worse for it. I hope that your exploration of leadership through this book will have challenged you, changed you, and motivated you to reach for higher ideals and visions. I hope it will have tested and stretched your leadership skills. I hope that as a result of this effort, you see more clearly yourself, your visions, the value others have to offer, and the ways and means of combining those visions and values to make the world, your business, your community, and your life a better place. Each of us can make a difference, can be effective within our circles of influence, can make the situation around us a better one. I hope you will make the choice to do so.

Notes

1. In *The Structure of Scientific Revolutions,* 3d ed. (Chicago: University of Chicago Press, 1996), Thomas Kuhn discovered that even after irrefutable scientific evidence was had and known, scientists who had been raised in the old paradigm literally had to die off before the new paradigm was accepted and incorporated into general scientific thought. This reluctance may also be true of business organizations, especially given the larger and therefore stronger momentum of organizational culture that exists in many corporations. Whereas scientists often work in smaller organizations and even in relative isolation, corporations have a strong institutional learning process that propagates former thinking through myriads of processes and policies.

2. See Richard Walton, "From Control to Commitment in the Workplace," *Harvard Business Review* (March 1985).

3. George Orwell (really a man named Eric Blair), in his book *1984,* published at the birth of the Information Age in 1949 by Harcourt, Brace and Jovanovich, New York, told a story of how information was supposed to give control to a centralized authority, nicknamed Big Brother by the masses.

4. For a description of the training and professional lifestyles of these extraordinary men, see Sebastian Junger, *The Perfect Storm* (New York: W. W. Norton, 1997).

Part VII: Exercises

Level Three Leadership Program Workbook

General Leadership Model

Strategic Challenges I Am Facing

Leadership Implications of My Strategic Challenges

Organizations I Expect to Lead

My Core Leadership Principles

Self-Assessment on the Six Steps to Effective Leadership

Charter for My Organization

Charter for My Work Group

Charter for Myself

Managing Personal Change and Blind Spots

Systems and Processes That Need Redesigning

My Life's Dream

Activities in Which I Resonate

Ways to Bring Resonance to Work

Ways I Want to Improve My Leadership Language

Leading Change

Intelligence Self-Assessment

Building Commitment

What Do I Want to Do This Year?

Central Point

GENERAL LEADERSHIP MODEL

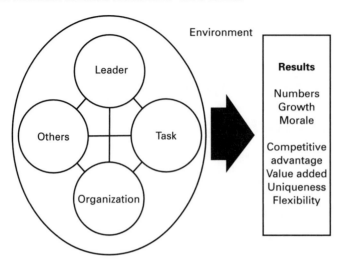

STRATEGIC CHALLENGES I AM FACING

A *strategic challenge* is any challenge that affects my own, my work group's, or my organization's ability to develop and maintain a competitive advantage. A *competitive advantage* is defined by (1) superior value added, (2) difficulty in imitation, and (3) enhanced flexibility.

Organization _____
_____
_____
_____
_____
_____

Work group _____
_____
_____
_____
_____

Self _____
_____
_____
_____
_____
_____

LEADERSHIP IMPLICATIONS
OF MY STRATEGIC CHALLENGES

What kind of *leadership traits* and abilities will be necessary to meet the strategic challenges mentioned above?

Organization leadership   _____
_____
_____
_____
_____
_____
_____
_____
_____
_____
_____
_____

Work group leadership   _____
_____
_____
_____
_____
_____
_____
_____
_____
_____
_____
_____

Self leadership   _____
_____
_____
_____
_____
_____
_____
_____
_____
_____
_____

Organizations I Expect to Lead
(from now until I pass)

My Core Leadership Principles
(that will guide me as I assume
responsibility)

1. _____

2. _____

3. _____

4. _____

5. _____

6. _____

7. _____

8. _____

9. _____

10. _____

1. _____

2. _____

3. _____

4. _____

5. _____

6. _____

7. _____

8. _____

9. _____

10. _____

SELF-ASSESSMENT ON THE SIX STEPS
TO EFFECTIVE LEADERSHIP

Give yourself an honest self-assessment on each of these personal leadership characteristics and note the basis for your assessment. Read chapter 5, "Six Steps to Effective Leadership," before responding.

Scale: 1 = am not very good at this; 2 = am below average on this; 3 = am average on this; 4 = am above average on this; 5 = am very good at this.

Clarifying my center   1   2   3   4   5

Clarifying what is possible   1   2   3   4   5

Clarifying what others have to contribute   1   2   3   4   5

Supporting others so they can contribute   1   2   3   4   5

Relentlessness   1   2   3   4   5

Celebrating progress   1   2   3   4   5

CHARTER FOR MY ORGANIZATION

Review chapter 8, "Strategic Thinking," and particularly the section on organizational charters before responding to the next three exercises.

Mission   _____

                                 _____

Vision   _____

Key operating values   _____

Strategic path   _____

Key operating goals/
    milestones   _____

CHARTER FOR MY WORK GROUP

Mission

_____
_____
_____
_____
_____
_____
_____
_____

Vision

_____
_____
_____
_____
_____
_____
_____
_____

Key operating values

_____
_____
_____
_____
_____
_____
_____
_____
_____

Strategic path

_____
_____
_____
_____
_____
_____
_____
_____

Key operating goals/
milestones

_____
_____
_____
_____
_____
_____
_____
_____

CHARTER FOR MYSELF

Mission

_____

Vision

_____

Key operating values

_____

Strategic path

_____

Key operating goals/
   milestones

_____

MANAGING PERSONAL CHANGE AND BLIND SPOTS

Letting Go

Following your class discussion of personal blind spots and the personal change process, consider your own leadership style as you now understand it and note:

Personal characteristics I would like to *let go* of or *move away* from:

_____
_____
_____
_____
_____
_____
_____
_____
_____
_____
_____
_____
_____
_____
_____
_____
_____
_____
_____

Grasping or Moving Toward

Personal characteristics I would like to *acquire* or *move toward*:

_____
_____
_____
_____
_____
_____
_____
_____
_____
_____
_____
_____
_____
_____
_____
_____
_____

SYSTEMS AND PROCESSES
THAT NEED REDESIGNING

After reading the chapter on leading organizations, think about the systems and processes in your organization that are not working well. List these systems and processes and begin thinking about how you would redesign them if given the chance.

Dysfunctional systems   A better design would be

_____   _____
_____   _____
_____   _____
_____   _____
_____   _____
_____   _____
_____   _____
_____   _____
_____   _____
_____   _____
_____   _____
_____   _____
_____   _____
_____   _____
_____   _____
_____   _____
_____   _____
_____   _____
_____   _____
_____   _____
_____   _____
_____   _____
_____   _____
_____   _____
_____   _____
_____   _____
_____   _____
_____   _____
_____   _____
_____   _____
_____   _____

MY LIFE'S DREAM

After participating in the session on resonance or reading chapter 7 on resonance and leadership, consider what your life's dream is and write it down. Do not be frustrated if you find this exercise difficult. It may take you some time, even months or years, to clarify your dream. As a way of moving toward this clarification, use the following page to note times and experiences during which you felt resonance. Remember to distinguish between dreams and goals.

_____
_____
_____
_____
_____
_____
_____
_____
_____
_____
_____
_____
_____
_____
_____
_____
_____
_____
_____
_____
_____
_____
_____
_____
_____
_____
_____
_____
_____
_____
_____
_____
_____
_____
_____
_____
_____

ACTIVITIES IN WHICH I RESONATE

After listening to the class discussion on resonance or reading chapter 7 on resonance and leadership, list activities in the past in which you have felt resonance. Note what you were doing and how it felt.

_____
_____
_____
_____
_____
_____
_____
_____
_____
_____
_____
_____
_____
_____
_____
_____
_____
_____
_____

Ways to Bring Resonance to Work

_____
_____
_____
_____
_____
_____
_____
_____
_____
_____
_____
_____
_____
_____
_____
_____

WAYS I WANT TO IMPROVE
MY LEADERSHIP LANGUAGE

After a discussion of leadership language as outlined in chapter 9, "Leading Others," think about the basic concepts of leadership language and consider how you would like to strengthen your ability to communicate.

Clear: _____

Respectful: _____

Stimulating: _____

Congruent: _____

LEADING CHANGE

After discussing CQ (leadership and intelligence) and reading chapter 12, "Leading Change," consider what things you need to change in order to become a more effective leader. Note your thoughts here.

What Needs to Change in My

Self:
_____
_____
_____
_____
_____
_____
_____
_____
_____
_____
_____

Work group:
_____
_____
_____
_____
_____
_____
_____
_____
_____
_____
_____

Organization:
_____
_____
_____
_____
_____
_____
_____
_____
_____
_____
_____

INTELLIGENCE SELF-ASSESSMENT

Following the discussion of leadership and intelligence after reading chapter 6, assess your intelligence in each of the following categories.

Intellectual Intelligence (IQ):
  Inherited abilities
  Curiosity
  Discipline
  Range of interests

Emotional Intelligence (EQ):
  Recognizing emotions in yourself
  Ability to manage your emotions
  Using productive self-talk
  Avoiding emotional hi-jackings

Social Intelligence (SQ):
  Recognizing emotions in others
  Caring about the emotionality of others
  Counseling others in managing their emotions

Change Intelligence (CQ):
  Recognizing the need to change
  Understanding the change process
  Skill in managing the change process

BUILDING COMMITMENT

After the discussion of leading organizations and of the importance of aligning organizational factors (the southern element in the general model), consider what things you can do to build commitment in yourself and those you work with.

Things I Can Do to Build Commitment in

Myself: _____

_____

_____

_____

_____

_____

_____

_____

_____

_____

_____

_____

My Work Group: _____

_____

_____

_____

_____

_____

_____

_____

_____

_____

_____

My Organization: _____

_____

_____

_____

_____

_____

_____

_____

_____

_____

_____

WHAT DO I WANT TO DO THIS YEAR?

What are the most important goals you want to accomplish this year with regard to developing your leadership skills and outcomes?

1. _____
2. _____
3. _____
4. _____
5. _____
6. _____
7. _____
8. _____
9. _____
10. _____

CENTRAL POINT

What is the most important thing you learned from this book or the course you used this book in about becoming a more influential leader to yourself, to your work group, and to your organization?

_____
_____
_____
_____
_____
_____
_____
_____
_____
_____
_____
_____
_____
_____
_____
_____
_____
_____
_____
_____
_____
_____
_____

Survey of Managerial Style

Managers constantly identify desirable behavior both in themselves and in others with whom they work. Much of this behavior takes on a characteristic pattern. Knowing something about these different patterns may help us to become more productive professionals. This instrument measures an aspect of managerial style. Please complete all items, then score and interpret them according to the instructions that follow.

Note that people will often rate questions like those included in this packet in terms of how they think they *should* answer or in terms of the way that they would *like* to be. Such answers are not what is wanted here. Please answer the items in terms of how much you agree with a statement as it applies to what you *actually do*. Give careful thought to your answers and remember that your results are only valuable to the extent that they reflect what you do, not what you think you should do. If you are a student now, consider the last job you held as you answer these questions. If you have not worked before, think about what your first job experience will be like.

As you complete the survey, please answer *all* items. You will probably note that some of the items on the survey are very similar; this is necessary to ensure that the survey information is statistically reliable. Please rate each item *independently* without regard to your responses to previous items. Finally, please note that there are no right or wrong answers on this survey.

SURVEY OF MANAGERIAL STYLE

Section I: General Information

1. How many major organizational levels are there in your organization from the chief executive to the lowest rank? In figuring the number of levels in your organization, it may help to sketch out the levels on the back of this page.

   NUMBER OF MAJOR LEVELS IN YOUR ORGANIZATION: _____3_

2. If the chief executive is at level 1 in your organization, at what numerical level are you?

   YOUR ORGANIZATIONAL LEVEL: _____3_

3. How many people report directly to you?

   NUMBER OF DIRECT REPORTS: _____0_

4. Overall, how many people are in your reporting line of authority? For example, in item 3, if you mentioned four direct reports and the first has 30 employees, the second has 49, the third has 12, and the fourth has 29, and none of their subordinates has subordinates, then the overall number in your line of authority is 120.

   OVERALL NUMBER IN YOUR REPORTING LINE OF AUTHORITY: _____

Section II: Management Style Items

Directions: For the 30 items below, read each item and rate it in terms of how much you agree that the item *describes you.* On the scale, SA = Strongly Agree; MA = Moderately Agree; LA = Slightly Agree; LD = Slightly Disagree; MD = Moderately Disagree; and SD = Strongly Disagree.

Item	Agreement			Disagreement		
	SA	MA	LA	LD	MD	SD
1. Managing company progress toward a vision represents a major portion of what I do in my job.	( )	( )	( )	( )	( )	(·)
2. I am methodical in the way that I carry out my job responsibilities.	( )	( )	( )	( )	( )	( )
3. Most of my work-related activity is in thinking about the future of my organization.	( )	(·)	( )	( )	( )	( )
4. I am a real "take charge" type of person.	(·)	( )	( )	( )	( )	( )
5. Garnering commitment in people toward meeting some organizational goal represents a major portion of what I do in my job.	(·)	( )	( )	( )	( )	( )

Item	Agreement			Disagreement		
	SA	MA	LA	LD	MD	SD
6. I am very decisive. When I must make a decision, I stick to it.	( )	(/)	( )	( )	( )	( )
7. Whenever I must present information to a group, I typically speak without notes or outlines.	( )	( )	(/)	( )	( )	( )
8. I focus my professional energies on envisioning the future of the organization.	( )	( )	(/)	( )	( )	( )
9. Whenever I must present information to a group, I write out the speech, then read it to the group.	( )	( )	( )	( )	( )	(/)
10. I am self-confident.	(/)	( )	( )	( )	( )	( )
11. I focus my professional energies on getting people in my organization to build their commitments to our organization and its goals.	( )	( )	( )	( )	( )	( )
12. I learn best by diving in and seeing if something works or doesn't work.	( )	( )	( )	( )	( )	( )
13. Most of my work-related activity is watching and managing indicators of organizational activity.	( )	( )	( )	( )	( )	(/)
14. I spend most of my professional time considering views of what my organization can become.	( )	( )	(/)	( )	( )	( )
15. Most of my work-related activity is in pulling people together for the purpose of attaining an organizational goal.	(/)	( )	( )	( )	( )	( )
16. I think that the most important aspect of my job is preparing for future needs of the organization.	( )	( )	(/)	( )	( )	( )
17. I manage my professional time efficiently.	( )	(/)	( )	( )	( )	( )
18. I think that the most important aspect of my job is persuading people to accept my vision for our organization.	( )	( )	(/)	( )	( )	( )
19. I make an effort to participate in group activities.	(/)	( )	( )	( )	( )	( )
20. I focus my professional energies on managing and monitoring my organization's progress toward a goal.	( )	( )	( )	( )	( )	(/)
21. Thinking about what my organization might look like in the future represents a major portion of what I do in my job.	( )	( )	(/)	( )	( )	( )
22. I am a predictable person. I think that people know what to expect of me.	( )	(/)	( )	( )	( )	( )
23. At work I try to foster close personal relationships with my coworkers.	(/)	( )	( )	( )	( )	( )

Item	Agreement			Disagreement		
	SA	MA	LA	LD	MD	SD
24. I spend most of my professional time in managing company progress toward a vision.	( )	( )	( )	( )	( )	(∅)
25. Solving problems in unstructured situations is an important part of what I do.	(∅)	( )	( )	( )	( )	( )
26. I would rather do something myself than delegate responsibility to someone else.	( )	( )	( )	(∅)	( )	( )
27. I learn on my own first, then apply what I have learned.	( )	( )	( )	(∅)	( )	( )
28. I spend most of my professional time convincing others in my organization to carry out a plan.	( )	( )	( )	( )	( )	( )
29. Whenever I must present information to a group, I speak while using an outline as a reference.	( )	( )	(∅)	( )	( )	( )
30. I think that the most important aspect of my job is looking at how my company is performing and determining what it needs to do to stick to the company plan.	( )	( )	( )	( )	( )	(∅)

NOTE! Do not read the rest of this note until you have completed the questions that come before!

Scoring and Interpreting Your Data

The Theory

This questionnaire was designed to measure aspects of your leadership style and preferences. Measuring leadership is not easy. Social scientists have been arguing for decades, even centuries, about the answer to the question, "What makes a good leader?" Out of this debate have emerged numerous theories about what makes a good leader. But these theories are often contradictory and confusing. We believe that, in spite of the controversy about what the concept of leadership comprises, a practical, immediate model of leadership would help focus the developmental efforts of managers on things they can begin doing now.

Given our reading of leadership studies and our observation of leaders in the world, we have concluded and suggest that leadership includes three fundamental clusters of skills and abilities: creating vision, garnering commitment to that vision, and monitoring and managing progress toward the realization of that vision.

Vision. Powerful leaders have a clear vision of where they want their organization to go. Vision is the view a person holds about what the organization will look like and be doing in the future. Obviously, some people have greater visions than others, and some have visions that extend further into the future than others. And some have visions that do not work or come to fruition. All managers can, and we believe, ought to have a vision of their organization, what it can become, where it is going, how it should be operating, and what it should be like to work within it.

Vision is an essential part of leadership. Having a vision requires creativity; leaders must be able to think and see beyond the present time frame and beyond the usual options. The ability to see ahead and to see nontraditional alternatives are creative parts of leadership. So is the ability to frame the context of a business problem in broader terms that question current assumptions. The ability to incorporate these often unusual thoughts into a cohesive vision of the future of the company defines the first set of leadership skills.

Commitment.   The ability to garner the commitment of others to that vision is a key cluster of leadership skills. A leader may have a vision of what an organization can become, but unless others receive and become committed to that vision, it is unlikely to be realized. Leaders can create visions, but commitment, on the other hand, is offered by followers. It is this commitment of a group of followers that allows leaders to build their visions into organizational realities. A key task of the leader, then, is to garner commitment from those people who are critical to his or her success.

Leaders may foster commitment in a variety of ways, for example, public communications, one-on-one interactions, involving others in the decision-making process, and modeling commitment to an idea. However the successful leader goes about it, he or she is able to develop and maintain strong commitments from others to his or her vision for the organization.

Monitoring and Managing Progress toward the Vision.   The third cluster of skills in leadership is the ability to monitor and manage progress of the organization toward the vision. For us, this cluster constitutes the bulk of "management" education today: ascertaining the right measures to monitor and using techniques and tools to get those indicators to yield the right results. This aspect of leadership focuses on the *details* of the business. That we place monitoring and management as a subset of leadership does not denigrate it. Rather, we are pointing out that although managers can indeed be leaders, they need to augment their skills with visionary and commitment-building skills. To us, management is a component of leadership. Ensuring that deadlines are met, objectives are achieved, and budgets are used appropriately are leadership skills that are valuable and necessary (but not sufficient).

Leadership and the Survey of Managerial Style (SMS)

Although some writers have drawn a provocative and dichotomous distinction between leadership and management, we believe the two are closely related and that a consideration of the fluid relationship between them is more productive. Hence, we assert that leadership is not so much a question of whether you are either a manager or a leader, but rather, how much emphasis you place on the component skills of leadership, of which management is one. Knowing something about how you tend to emphasize creating vision, garnering commitment, and monitoring and managing progress toward the vision can help you in several ways. We will outline some of those ways, but first, let us score the data you have generated.

Parts I and II of the SMS are designed to gather general information about you and to measure your self-perception of your work behavior with regard to each of the three clusters we just discussed. From these data, you can begin to construct a picture of your leadership profile, that is, how much you emphasize leadership overall and how much you emphasize the three different clusters of leadership. With these data, you can analyze the strength of your desire to be a leader and the distribution of your behavior across the three dimensions of leadership.

Scoring Your Data

Step 1. On the Section II Scoring Form on the following page, you will see that values are associated with each point on the scale used in Section II of the survey: Strongly Agree = 6; Moderately Agree = 5; Slightly Agree = 4; Slightly Disagree = 3; Moderately Disagree = 2; and Strongly Disagree = 1. For each section of the scoring form, indicate the score for each of the items listed. For example, if you checked "slightly agree" for Item 3 and "Agree" for item 8, your scores for these items would be 4 and 5, respectively. Please note that in Section II scoring, not all items are scored. The extra items in Section II of the survey are to control measurement error and are not included in the individual scoring procedure.

Step 2. Sum the scores in each column to derive scores for vision, commitment, and management.

Step 3. Sum the scores for vision, commitment, and management to derive your total score.

Step 4. Compute proportional values for vision, commitment, and management by dividing the scale score by the total score.

Section II Scoring Form

Score your responses as shown below.

Strongly Agree = 6; Moderately Agree = 5; Slightly Agree = 4; Slightly Disagree = 3; Moderately Disagree = 2; Strongly Disagree = 1

Source	Score	Source	Score	Source	Score
Item 3	5	Item 5	6	Item 1	1
Item 8	4	Item 11	6	Item 13	6
Item 14	4	Item 15	6	Item 20	1
Item 16	4	Item 18	1	Item 24	1
Item 21	4	Item 28	3	Item 30	1
Total Vision	21	Total Commitment	22	Total Management	10
VISION		GARNERING COMMITMENT		MONITORING AND MANAGING PROGRESS	

Note: Maximum Scale Score = 30, Minimum Scale Score = 5

TOTAL SCORE SECTION II (Vision + Commitment + Management) = _____53_____

PROPORTIONAL VALUES FOR SECTION II
Vision/Total Score = _____%
Commitment/Total Score = _____%
Management/Total Score = _____%

Step 5. Complete the SMS Profile on the following page. The concentric circles on the SMS Profile represent varying strengths of leadership: the larger the circle, the greater the interest in leadership. The letters associated with each circle correspond to the total score obtained in Section II of the survey. Find the circle that corresponds to your total score in Section II and trace the circle with a heavy marking pen.

Step 6. The SMS Profile contains 32 dotted line segments that you can use conveniently to create the segments of your profile. First, starting anywhere, draw a solid line from the center of the chart out to your circle (A, B, C, D, or E). Then note that each dotted pie segment represents about 12 degrees (11.25 exactly) of the 360 degrees in a circle. For example, if your V score were 40% of your total score, you would calculate .40 of 360, which equals 144 degrees. 144 divided by 12 degrees for each dotted segment equals 12, so you would count 12 segments from your first line and draw a second line from the center to the circumference. Do this for each of your other scores to produce a pie chart with three segments, one each for V, C, and M. Label each segment with the corresponding initial V, C, or M.

Note: When you have finished scoring your data, you should have a pie chart with three divisions in it. The size of the pie reflects your overall interest in being a leader. The size of each of the three wedges, one each for creating vision, garnering commitment, and monitoring and managing progress toward the vision, indicates the relative strength of each leadership skill area. When you have completed the profile, proceed to the interpretation section.

Survey of Managerial Style: Profile

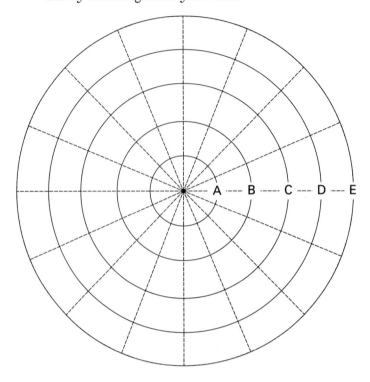

A = 15–29   B = 15–29   C = 15–29   D = 15–29   E = 15–29

Interpreting Your Profile

The first thing to note is that it is not necessarily good or bad to desire to be a leader. Leadership roles place demands on individuals just like all positions in life do; some people enjoy that set of demands, whereas others do not. Regardless of how superficially attractive the recognition and apparent influence of leaders may be, unless your personal skills and interests fit the demands of a particular leadership position, you are not likely to be happy or successful in that position. Thus, the size of your leadership pie is not a value judgment about you or your worth in your organization or in society. Rather, it is a description of your present preferences and as such can be used by you to make sound decisions about yourself and your work.

The same can be said of the relative strength of the three basic areas of leadership as proposed in this profile. Knowing something about your relative position in the areas of vision, commitment, and management can certainly help you to elaborate your leadership skills and may guide you as you make career and educational decisions. We encourage you not to treat these three clusters of leadership skills as fixed and equally desirable. It is quite possible that your scores are evenly balanced among these skills. Alternatively, you might obtain a moderate score in one area and higher scores in the others. Each profile, of course, will have different implications for your planning, your development activities, and perhaps for the way you manage your work.

We expect that scores in these leadership areas can change depending on context and the demands of your job. Patterns of response such as these remain to be researched. For now, the important thing to note is that we are talking about general leadership functions and that strength or weakness in one area is not necessarily desirable or undesirable.

Interpretive Alternatives

For each of the alternative profiles below, write your interpretation of what they might mean to the individuals or corporations that have them. See if you can identify individuals who fit each pattern.

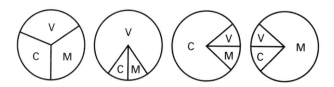

Selected Bibliography on Leadership

You may be interested in the following additional resources on the topic of leadership.

Bass, Bernard A. *Stogdill's Handbook of Leadership*, rev. ed. New York: Free Press, 1981.

Bennis, Warren, and Burt Nanus. *Leaders: The Strategies for Taking Charge and the Four Keys of Effective Leadership.* New York: Harper & Row, 1985.

Brache, Alan. "Seven Prevailing Myths about Leadership." *Training and Development Journal* (June 1983).

Burns, James MacGregor. *Leadership*. New York: Harper & Row, 1978.

Covey, Stephen R. *Principle-Centered Leadership*. New York: Summit Books, 1991.

Covey, Stephen R. *The 7 Habits of Highly Effective People*. New York: Simon & Schuster, 1989.

DePree, Max. *Leadership Is an Art*. New York: Dell, 1989.

Donnithorne, Larry R. *The West Point Way of Leadership*. New York: Currency/Doubleday, 1993.

Fiedler, F. E. *A Theory of Leadership Effectiveness*. New York: McGraw-Hill, 1967.

Frew, David R. "Leadership and Followership." *Personnel Journal* (February 1977).

Gardner, John W. *On Leadership*. New York: Free Press, 1990.

Hill, Norman. "Self-Esteem: The Key to Effective Leadership." *Administrative Management* (August 1976).

House, Robert J., and Terence R. Mitchell. "Path-Goal Theory of Leadership." *The Journal of Contemporary Business* 3, no. 3 (fall 1974).

Kouzes, James M., and Barry Z. Posner. *The Leadership Challenge*. San Francisco: Jossey-Bass, 1988.

Tannenbaum, Robert, and Warren H. Schmidt. "How to Choose a Leadership Pattern." *Harvard Business Review* (May–June 1973), Reprint No. 73311.

Tichy, Noel, and Mary Anne Devanna. *The Transformational Leader*. New York: Wiley, 1986.

Yukl, Gary A. *Leadership in Organizations*. Englewood Cliffs, NJ: Prentice-Hall, 1981.

Zaleznik, Abraham. "Managers and Leaders: Are They Different?" *Harvard Business Review* (May–June 1977), Reprint No. 77312.

Survey of Behavioral Characteristics

Researchers have identified a number of behavioral characteristics in managers that likely influence managerial learning and productivity. The purpose of this survey is to help you consider your own behavioral characteristics and the influence they might have on you as a manager. Please rate the items on the following pages in terms of how much a word or sentence describes you. When you complete the items, go on to the scoring and interpretation section. Note: Please do not read the interpretation section before you complete the items, as it may influence the way in which you complete the items.

Part I: The items in this section contain two words or combinations of words on each end of a scale. Please circle the number that most accurately describes you and your behavior.

habit-bound	3	2	1	0	1	2	3	open-minded
talker	3	2	1	0	1	2	3	listener
practical	3	2	1	0	1	2	3	innovative
exploratory	3	2	1	0	1	2	3	procedural
receptive	3	2	1	0	1	2	3	directing
factual	3	2	1	0	1	2	3	intuitive
organization person	3	2	1	0	1	2	3	entrepreneur
risk taker	3	2	1	0	1	2	3	risk averse
ritualistic	3	2	1	0	1	2	3	experimental
uninhibited	3	2	1	0	1	2	3	inhibited
leader	3	2	1	0	1	2	3	follower
poet	3	2	1	0	1	2	3	accountant

This exercise was prepared by Gail Pearl and James G. Clawson. Copyright © 1988 by the University of Virginia Darden School Foundation, Charlottesville, VA. All rights reserved. Darden School Case UVA-OB-0364. Reprinted with permission.

Part II: In this section, each item contains a sentence on each end of the scale. Please circle the number that most accurately describes you and your behavior.

I develop new ideas.	3	2	1	0	1	2	3	I use others' ideas.
I like to influence other people.	3	2	1	0	1	2	3	I am influenced by other people.
I like to know how things will work out before starting something.	3	2	1	0	1	2	3	I do not mind uncertainty in a project.
I like for plans to emerge based on what a situation may demand.	3	2	1	0	1	2	3	I like to plan in advance and stick to it.
In problem solving, I enjoy finding the one right answer.	3	2	1	0	1	2	3	In problem solving, I like to consider several possible answers.
I like doing things in new ways.	3	2	1	0	1	2	3	I like doing things in old ways.
I am attracted to change.	3	2	1	0	1	2	3	I am resistant to change.
I like to design objects.	3	2	1	0	1	2	3	I like to assemble pre-made kits.
I read one book a year or less.	3	2	1	0	1	2	3	I read twenty books a year or more.
I prefer logical step-by-step methods.	3	2	1	0	1	2	3	I prefer open-ended methods that allow unexpected outcomes.
I do not mind uncertainty.	3	2	1	0	1	2	3	I prefer predictable happenings.
I act on objective information.	3	2	1	0	1	2	3	I act on intuitive hunches.
I seek the "status quo."	3	2	1	0	1	2	3	I seek change.
I do detail work best.	3	2	1	0	1	2	3	I do creative work best.

The Theory

You have just completed survey items that measure some aspects of creativity. Creativity is important because the extent to which you are creative can impact individual, small group, and organizational productivity. We also believe that creativity is a significant component of your ability to generate vision for an organization. If you are bound by historical views of an organization's capacities and directions, then you are less likely to be able to lead the organization through the inevitable changes of the future.

In the past decade or so, numerous researchers and practitioners in business have studied creativity or have created models for developing creativity in managers. The models vary considerably but some common concepts surface in all of them.

Seeking several possible explanations. Historically, we have educated such that we seek the right answer in learning instead of looking to several possible explanations. Throughout our secondary and higher education careers, we took many exams and quizzes for which we were expected to produce the right answer. The ambiguous world does not always lend itself to one simple answer. Thus, to be innovative in our thinking, we must be open to different approaches.

Taking risks. The creative person is comfortable in risk taking. In business, for example, the creative person may make decisions that run counter to group opinion or to standards of the industry. Such actions, although not always successful, may ultimately prove useful in developing ideas in business.

Considering ambiguity in situations. Persons who are creative are comfortable with uncertainty. They are comfortable with plans that emerge based on the situation as opposed to plans that completely anticipate a project before it begins. Although ambiguity can be devastating in some situations, such as in giving directions or in creating legal documents, there are other situations in which ambiguity can foster creativity. Ambiguity forces us to consider different meanings and alternate interpretations in a creative process.

Considering the illogical. Have you ever been in a situation in which you proposed a seemingly foolish alternative? What happened? People probably laughed or discounted your suggestion. They may have said, "That's not logical." But it often happens that the illogical suggestion becomes a viable strategy. In situations in which new ideas are being generated, if all possible alternatives are quickly eliminated because of lack of "logic," then you forego potential options. Depending on the situation, the creative thinker must consider the illogical.

The instrument that you just completed was developed to awaken you to your inner creative abilities and to stimulate some thinking about how these abilities can impact on your personal and professional life. We will outline some of the possibilities later, but first, let us score the data that you have generated.

Scoring Procedure

Step 1. Remove Parts I and II from this exercise. Place Part I alongside this page and Part II alongside the next page.

Step 2. The answers that you gave in Parts I and II can be scored by circling the numbers *in the same positions* on the scales on this page and on the next page. For example, if you circled a 2 on the left for the first item in Part I, then you would circle a 2 on the first item on this page. If you circled a 3 on the right for the first item, you would circle a 7 for the first item on this page. Please note that on the scoring template, some of the scales are purposely reversed.

Step 3. After scoring all your items, calculate the subtotal for each page. Add your subtotals to derive your total creativity score.

Scoring Template for Part I

habit-bound	1	2	3	4	5	6	7	open-minded
talker	7	6	5	4	3	2	1	listener
practical	1	2	3	4	5	6	7	innovative
exploratory	7	6	5	4	3	2	1	procedural
receptive	1	2	3	4	5	6	7	directing
factual	1	2	3	4	5	6	7	intuitive
organization person	1	2	3	4	5	6	7	entrepreneur
risk taker	7	6	5	4	3	2	1	risk averse
ritualistic	1	2	3	4	5	6	7	experimental
uninhibited	7	6	5	4	3	2	1	inhibited
leader	7	6	5	4	3	2	1	follower
poet	7	6	5	4	3	2	1	accountant

Part I **Subtotal** _____

Scoring Template for Part II

I develop new ideas.	7 6 5 4 3 2 1	I use others' ideas.
I like to influence other people.	7 6 5 4 3 2 1	I am influenced by other people.
I like to know how things will work out before starting something.	1 2 3 4 5 6 7	I do not mind uncertainty in a project.
I like for plans to emerge based on what a situation may demand.	7 6 5 4 3 2 1	I like to plan in advance and stick to it.
In problem solving, I enjoy finding the one right answer.	1 2 3 4 5 6 7	In problem solving, I like to consider several possible answers.
I like doing things in new ways.	7 6 5 4 3 2 1	I like doing things in old ways.
I am attracted to change.	7 6 5 4 3 2 1	I am turned off by change.
I like to design objects.	7 6 5 4 3 2 1	I like to assemble pre-made kits.
I read one book a year or less.	1 2 3 4 5 6 7	I read twenty books a year or more.
I prefer logical step-by-step methods.	1 2 3 4 5 6 7	I prefer open-ended methods that allow unexpected outcomes.
I do not mind uncertainty.	7 6 5 4 3 2 1	I prefer predictable happenings.
I act on objective information.	1 2 3 4 5 6 7	I act on intuitive hunches.
I seek the "status quo."	1 2 3 4 5 6 7	I seek change.
I do detail work best.	1 2 3 4 5 6 7	I do creative work best.

Part II **Subtotal** _____

Total Score (from Parts I and II) _____

Interpreting Your Score

The Survey of Behavior Characteristics is a 26-item instrument with scores on each item that range from 1 to 7. Total scores (derived by adding up scores for *all* items) range from 26 to 182. A high score on this instrument means that overall you perceive yourself as a creative person. (Because the instrument is still new, "high" and "low" have not yet been specifically defined.) You probably seek activities such as brainstorming and experimentation, and enjoy situations that are open-ended and somewhat ambiguous. As a person, you probably desire change in your personal and professional life; you probably think intuitively and work innovatively.

If your score is low (which is not necessarily bad), you might be less exploratory and more procedural. In the workplace, for example, you could be more interested in following procedure, less interested in exploring new options. In problem solving, you might be more inclined to rely on tried-and-true methods than to act intuitively (on a hunch). A moderate score (high 70s or low 80s) means that you have some creative tendencies but not in all areas. For example, you may consider yourself an entrepreneurial person but at the same time feel some resistance to change and feel somewhat habit-bound.

We should stress that this instrument is new and that we are in the process of validating it. We therefore suggest that tentative conclusions be made on the basis of data obtained from it. Although we have yet to validate the instrument, we do believe that creative managers exhibit characteristic patterns. Creative managers take risks, seek change, like doing and creating new things, are avid readers, and are comfortable with uncertainty in personal and professional situations.

If you wish to learn more about individual creativity, innovation in groups, or organizational creativity, we have provided a list of resources on the following page that can get you started.

Selected Bibliography on Creativity

Adams, J. L. *The Care and Feeding of Ideas*. Reading, MA: Addison-Wesley, 1986.

Ghiselin, Brewster, ed. *The Creative Process*. New York: New American Library, 1952.

Hickman, C. R., and M. A. Silva. *Creating Excellence*. New York: New American Library, 1984.

May, Rollo. *The Courage to Create*. New York: Bantam, 1976.

Morgan, Gareth. *Imaginization: The Art of Creative Management*. Thousand Oaks, CA: Sage, 1993.

Peters, T., and A. Austin. *A Passion for Excellence: The Leadership Difference*. New York: Random House, 1985.

Ray, M., and R. Myers. *Creativity in Business*. Garden City, NY: Doubleday, 1986.

Thompson, Charles. *What a Great Idea!* New York: Harper Perennial, 1992.

Von Oech, R. *A Kick in the Seat of the Pants*. New York: Harper and Row, 1986.

Von Oech, R. *A Whack in the Side of the Head*. Menlo Park, CA: Creative Think, 1983.

Personal Engagement Project

One way of thinking about leadership is to view it as powerful *personal engagement*. When you become deeply and personally *engaged* in a cause or enterprise, leadership naturally begins to happen. When you talk about the activity you are engaged in, others begin to sense your enthusiasm, excitement, passion, and commitment and are touched by them. They then begin to listen and engage as well.

On the other hand, if you are not engaged in an effort, others will sense that lack through your speech and behavior. They will notice the lack of fire in your eyes, of bounce in your step, of electricity in your voice. Without engagement, it is very difficult to make a difference to or in others. What makes you convincing? What makes you strong? What makes you a real leader? The answers lie in the nature of and the depth of your personal engagements.

Engagement comes in different depths. Shallow engagements have little power to influence others. Moderate engagements leave space and energy for other activities. Full engagements can change the lives of people and the face of the globe. A full engagement would be represented by a complete commitment to the accomplishment of a vision, a comprehensive commitment that shapes every aspect of your life. Consider an athletic example. Bruce Jenner trained with a near-complete commitment as he approached the Olympic Games. A decathlete, Jenner moved his family next to a high school track. He awoke before sunrise each day so he could put in four hours of training before breakfast. After breakfast, he would train until lunch. After lunch, he would nap, then train again until dinner. After dinner, he was back out on the track, running, jumping, throwing, and hurdling. His life, at least for an extensive period of time preceding the Olympics, re-volved completely around his goal and his vision. His effort was rewarded with success; he won the gold medal. There was no guarantee, of course, that his complete commitment would pay off, but even so, Jenner was fully engaged in his vision. Jenner and other world-class athletes provide us with one model of deep personal engagement.

Deep, or full, engagement is inspiring to yourself and to others. People see your commitment and admire it. If they agree with the goal, they begin to want to be a part of the effort. When you are fully engaged in your projects and/or your organizations, you at-tain the essential influences of leadership. Only people who are engaged can inspire themselves and others.

Developed by Alex Horniman and Jim Clawson.

Developing engagement requires looking within. Looking within yourself can be one of the most challenging endeavors you undertake. You may or may not be able to find quickly what will command your engagement. What is sure, though, is that if you do not find something that engages you deeply, you are not going to make a difference among people.

What invites your complete engagement? Some of you may find it in aspects of work. Others may find it in avocations. For some, it may be physical activity such as sport, yoga, running, or martial arts. Some of you may find it in such spiritual dedication as religion and philosophy. The question that leaders ask and answer clearly, whether explicitly or not, is, "What is it that compels my interest and best efforts?"

Not all engagements are lifelong endeavors. We often have engagements that last for shorter periods of time. Consider something that is centrally important to you at the present or in the current chapter of your life. This exercise is designed to help you spend time and effort on that activity and in the process practice developing engagements and becoming more influential among others

Personal Engagement Project

We invite you to choose and execute a personal engagement project (PEP). The PEP is to select an action or an activity in your life that is very important to you and to spend time doing it over the course of the next six months. The goal is that you should experience what it is like to focus your efforts and engage in something of importance to you regardless of whatever else is going on in your life. While you are participating in this project, you will find that you become more of a leader. Others will observe your activity and begin to participate with you. You will see the power of engagement as a leadership principle. Of course, you will also have the benefit and a sense of satisfaction of working on something of importance to you.

We have found that many people in their studies or professions lose sight of their central purposes and goals. They describe a sense of meaninglessness to life and a sense of being on a detour or wandering from their goals. The demands of academic life, of work, of other colleagues who need your time and talents can easily divert you from spending time on what is important to you. The PEP is an opportunity to pause and consider what those neglected parts of life might be and to refocus and reengage yourself in them.

A second goal of the project is to experience the processes and techniques of managing personal change. Without an intimate understanding of personal change, it will be difficult for you to manage the efforts of others to change. Leadership is about managing change, change in self and change in others. Your PEP will represent a personal change effort that will teach you much about yourself, your levels of commitment and engagement, and your abilities to be a self leader and a leader of others.

Most of our MBA and executive program students find the PEP to be a powerful experience. As we have read and tabulated the topics of these papers, we have found that the projects people have chosen to work on fell into four broad areas: Intellectual, Spiritual, Physical, and Emotional.

Intellectual (reading, writing, learning foreign language, etc.) Intellectually stimulating projects were attractive to many students. Reading books that they wanted to read for a long time, yet for which they had not been able to find the time, was a popular project. Brushing up on or learning a new foreign language was another common project.

Spiritual (meditation, religion, balancing life, etc.) Going to church regularly and playing a more active role in nonprofessional activities was a popular project. The more engaged students became, the more frequently they took the time to pray or meditate, not only at meetings but every day at home, too.

Physical (tennis, workout, horseback riding, etc.) Many students found that physical activity invited their engagement. Having partners seemed to help them continue working out, especially when they were really exhausted from studying or other matters.

Emotional (family, expressing feeling, friendship, etc.) The emotional aspects of life can be easily overlooked and pushed onto the back burner. Many students committed themselves to improving their emotional status. Often they reported a significant increase in their sense of general well-being, in the quality of their relationships, or just in their own ability to recognize and deal with their own feelings as a result of the PEP.

You may not wish to choose an engagement project from among these headings. Feel free to choose a different project if you wish. Do not choose your engagement project lightly, though. Think carefully about your time constraints, your schedule, your energy, your other commitments. But most important, think about what in life is really important to you, something that maybe you have been neglecting lately and want to reinforce in your life. Maybe you will choose a project that you have wanted to do for a long time, but have never taken the time to work on. Pick something that will, by its nature, *engage* you as you begin to do it. If you pick something out of duty, it is improbable that you will be able to engage the effort. The objective is for you to experience and reflect on what it is like to be engaged deeply in something you love and believe in.

When you have made your selection, review it carefully in your mind. Talk about it with some close friends to see what your level of commitment will be to this project. If you find yourself hesitating or losing interest, pick something else and test it out before committing.

Once you have selected a target area, write a two-page summary of what you have chosen and why. Describe clearly what you intend to do, by when, and how you will know if you have done it or not. Be as descriptive as you can. Include the language that best portrays for you your level of engagement in this project. Anticipate that you will write a summary of your results later on.

A leadership journal will be helpful here because you can record your efforts along the way as you work on your PEP. Make entries regularly and note the key events and interactions that affect your level of engagement and your relationships with others.

When the term of your PEP is completed, we ask that you write up a two- to four-page summary of your experience. It will be useful to you to describe what you did, how you did it, how you felt, what impact you had on others, how they responded, what results you got, how you felt about the whole effort, and finally, what you learned about leadership from your PEP.

Consider this project as an opportunity to focus on a part of yourself that you have not paid decent attention to in your life recently. This assignment should *not* be busy work. We would like you to cultivate and enrich other important dimensions of yourself through recognizing your core interests and doing them.

Excerpts from Personal Engagement Project Reports

We have included here three excerpts from MBA PEP reports. They describe different kinds of personal engagement projects. We thought you might find them useful as you think about what to choose for your PEP.

Statement I

. . . Before coming to Darden (and one big reason why I got in) I was very involved in the Boston community in activities such as teaching classes to refugees for citizenship exams, working part-time in a homeless shelter, and as an elected member of the Boston International Business Society. I miss[ed] that part of my life and this assignment gave me the excuse and opportunity to "enrich this dimension of myself that has been slighted in the past." To complete this project I decided to engage in a community activity I had been considering for a long time; I joined the Big Brother/Little Brother Program of Charlottesville. In September I was introduced to Jamal (disguised name), a ten-year-old black boy from Charlottesville.

The responsibilities required of a big brother are relatively simple in theory—spend one hour a week with your little sibling in any way you like and keep the program director posted on what you are doing. In practice, however, it is quite a different story, and I quickly learned that I had severely underestimated the levels of commitment, time, patience, and emotion I would need to do a satisfactory job in this role. Jamal's needs surpass[ed] anything I could provide and I realized that my "engagement exercise" should really be a full time job.

. . . Both his sisters are in jail (he says he does not know why) but they come home occasionally on furlough and smack him around. Since his mother works and goes to school, she is rarely at home, and there is no father or other parental figure in his life. In addition, Jamal lives in a very precarious neighborhood, filled with crime, drugs, and many insolent, dangerous people.

Jamal himself is a fantastic kid. He is bright, popular, and talented musically and athletically. His grades in school have been good, and [he] wants to be a lawyer. But it is clear that, given the environment in which he lives, it is highly likely that he will be derailed from his goals and end up like his peers or sisters. This really scared me, and I found myself transformed from wanting to be a big brother that takes a cute kid to an occasional ball game to a great social emancipator—the "Catcher in the Rye" of the twenty first century.

. . . I averaged 3–4 hours a week with Jamal last semester. Very quiet at first, he opened up to me more and more although he has learned to keep his mouth shut about most things. My goal [was] to give him exposure to my life as an alternative to those around him and to help him learn to feel genuine interest in others by showing genuine interest in him. I have been only partially successful in accomplishing these goals but will get better as I learn more about how to communicate with a ten-year-old living in different universe. It is also interesting that the more I discover about Jamal, the more I discover about myself.

Statement II

It all started when a professor invited me to sit in on one of his Religions of the World classes, which he teaches for Mormon students on Main Grounds, and help him answer their questions on Hinduism. . . . I am a Hindu, though by no means very devout.

For me, the primary function of religion is to waken and give guidance to the energies of life. It is an energy-releasing and -directing system, which not only "turns you on," to borrow an Americanism, but turns you on in a certain direction, making you function a certain way—which will be one conducive to your participation in the life and purposes of a functioning social group. I made a resolve that day to read the Bhagavad Gita for at least an hour every day, for I have found that the doctrine of Karma Yoga (the Yoga of action, of dedicating yourself to the performance of your duty in accordance to your conscience) expounded in this text has been a considerable source of inspiration in the past. Since I made this resolve, I have been faithfully reading the Gita every day before I go to bed.

At the same time, I made an effort to acquaint myself with other great religions of the world. In the course of my readings, I gained a broad (though admittedly superficial) overview of Christianity, Islam, Judaism, Buddhism, Taoism, Confucianism, and the Shinto religion. I found that each of these religions was full of myths.

. . . This deference in theological perception is prominently reflected in art, and this is the aspect I chose for the final phase of my engagement exercise. I have had some opportunity to read about and see examples of Western painting and sculpture, but my exposure to Oriental art has hitherto been minimal. During the Christmas break, I traveled to India and visited some Hindu Temples in Mathura and Delhi, and a Buddhist monastery in Sikkim. Not only was I able to view the rites and rituals with a new understanding, but I also discovered some thematic patterns that distinguished Oriental art from the Occidental.

. . . My next objective is to read more on philosophies of the East, and on the myths and symbols in Eastern art and civilization. This engagement exercise has been invaluable in helping me to better understand my cultural heritage, and to reinforce my belief that there is meaning and structure to our existence.

Statement III

I developed a personal engagement project that was both physical and intellectual. The first part of the program required that I exercise each day. The second part entailed reading a non-Darden book while exercising if I worked out in the gym or listening to classical music when the gyms were closed and I went running.

I developed this program for several reasons. After having talked to my father about his career, one of his regrets was that he had not been able to stay as active as he had wanted. He regretted that he had gained weight over the years and has only now, after he has retired, begun to return to a weight which he is more happy with. I resolved, with the aid of this project, to build into my daily schedule time to stay fit. It was my hope to exercise throughout my career long after I have left the Darden community.

I also developed a list of books which I would read while I exercised. This is possible since my two primary forms of exercise were designed to be the StairMaster [exercise equipment] and Lifecycle [stationary bicycle]. My reading list was all non-Darden material and was designed to add diversity to my educational experience. The list of books on my reading list were:

The Screwtape Letters	C. S. Lewis
The Three Musketeers	Alexandre Dumas
Language in Thought and Action	S. I. Hayakawa
The Prince of Tides	Pat Conroy
The 158-Pound Marriage	John Irving
Seven Plays	Sam Shepard

Zen and the Art of Motorcycle Maintenance	Robert M. Pirsig
Rising Sun	Michael Crichton
Les Liaisons Dangereuses (translated)	Choderlos de Laclos
Caribbean	James A. Michener

I would classify my project as an overall success. At the start of the program it was difficult to exercise every day. But over the last eight weeks I have only missed two days. I have also increased my workout from an average of 24 minutes on a low setting of the StairMaster or Lifecycle to an average of three 24-minute routines in a typical workout in addition to my stretching exercises. Of my planned reading list, I have read each book except for James Michener's *Caribbean.* On the classical music front I have not been as successful. I have not found many tapes or CDs which I truly enjoy. I have fallen into a rut of listening to the one artist whom I enjoy, George Winston. Even in that selection I fear he may not be classified as classical, but I do honestly enjoy his music so it is the one selection which I have continued to play.

This process has opened me to a new perspective. Physically I am in the best shape of my life since my wrestling days of High School. I have lost weight and regained my endurance. From my reading I have been exposed to varied perspectives and experiences of the nine authors whom I have read. I feel that I have restored a balance to my life which had been missing for the past year. I am refreshed from the physical and intellectual break each day that my program allowed me to take. On the two days which I missed I found myself contemplating the book I was reading and the workout I was missing.

While Darden and my career are important in my life I have realized that there are other things which I do not want excluded and that by having them present I am more effective. It is similar to a person who believes that they can get more done by working twenty-four hours a day without rest. It is true that they will get more done in the first day or two, but eventually the person who sleeps eight hours a day will outperform the person who works twenty-four hours a day since they will be refreshed and more effective and not worn down. Exercise and reading have become like sleep to me, they are a needed break that refreshes and invigorates me for my other work.

Balancing Your Life

Leaders in the modern era face the challenge of finding the right kind of balance in their lives between work, family, self, and other interests. The constantly growing and competing demands of life on many fronts push us all to make daily behavioral decisions about how we spend our time and talents, often without taking the time to think clearly about the consequences of those decisions. Making those decisions without a clear picture of their consequences can be devastating for us all, leaders, managers, and employees.

Some people naturally seem to find a balance that fits them and their own definition of success over the years. Others have a more difficult job of it. Far too many people at middle or late middle age find that they are deeply dissatisfied with the way their lives have turned out. Erik Erikson in *Childhood and Society*, for example, outlined eight ages of humankind, each characterized by binary dilemmas. Although this approach is admittedly and primarily Western, his eighth state, in which people in their mature years wrestle with feelings of despair or integrity, is instructive. His observation is that later in life we see that it is too late to change much in our lives and we come to a realization that either life has come together much in the way that we had hoped and dreamed it would (integrity in the sense of integration into a complete whole) *or* we realize that life has not turned out like we thought it would and because it is too late to change, we begin to despair. Erikson's assertion is confirmed in the publication of books with titles like *The Failure of Success, Must Success Cost So Much? Career Success/Personal Failure, Workaholics, Work, Family, and the Career,* and *Tradeoffs: Executive, Family, and Organizational Life.* These books all examine the ways in which our daily, weekly, and yearly choices, repeated over and over again, structure our lives, sometimes in ways that we later deeply regret. The potential tragedy is that we may have made those choices without thinking or anticipating their outcomes.

What we can learn from this is not to seek a common "right" balance. Rather, we must be aware of our current choices of time and energy allocation and make adjustments that point us toward our personal definitions of success; by that we mean success in life, not just "career." The point is well-made with this oft-quoted line: How many of us on our deathbeds will gasp, "If only I had spent more time at the office!"

Prepared by James G. Clawson. Copyright © 1986 by the University of Virginia Darden School Foundation, Charlottesville, VA. All rights reserved. Revised 7/29/93. Darden School Case UVA-OB-0323. Reprinted with permission.

This exercise is designed to help you see your current behavioral allocation of time and how that allocation matches up with your personal definition of success. The exercise is built on some fundamental assumptions:

1. We all have a limited, but equal, 168 hours per week of time.
2. We all have some freedom in choosing how we spend that time.
3. We all have some talent to apply to the time we have.
4. We all have various dimensions to our lives that we choose, consciously or unconsciously, to develop or ignore.

A list of these dimensions is given in Figure 1. Some of the definitions may not be just what you immediately think, so please look at the parenthetical definitions so you will know that we mean for each dimension. The list is not necessarily complete; we all have a sexual dimension, for instance, that is not included in the list simply because most people prefer to keep their activities in that dimension private. You may think of other dimensions of life that could be added to the list. The point is that, like cut diamonds, our lives contain a number of facets; by choosing to spend time and energy and talent in some areas, we necessarily neglect others. Our colleague Alex Horniman has said that "excellence is a neurotic lifestyle," suggesting that to excel, most of us have to focus our time and attention. When we focus consciously, as in the case of an Olympic hopeful athlete, we acknowledge the sacrifice that we are making in other aspects of life and become singular in our focus. Others of us prefer to have a more rounded lifestyle and, in so doing, recognize the sacrifice of excellence in any one area.

There are several steps to completing this exercise:

1. **Clarify your personal definition of success.** Write it down. What does it mean to you now to be "successful"? Research shows that our definition of success may vary over our lifetime, but we need a place to start. You may not have thought about this before, so you may need to reflect on what it means to you to be "successful." Approach this definition broadly; that is, consider what it means to be successful in *life,* not just your career. It is your life, only you can live it, and you are the primary shaper of it. What do you want it to be?

   If you say, "I want to be happy," please take the next step and try to define what it is that makes you happy. The clarity of the definition will make the exercise more powerful for you. Again, I urge you to write this definition down. Keep it in your day planner; refer to it often; revise it as you feel it necessary. For the ship with no destination, any port will do, but the ship with a destination has a course and a purpose to its sailing. You may wish to consider the various aspects in Figure 1 again as you write your personal definition.

2. **Assess your current level of development.** On the wheel diagram in Figure 2, assess your current level of personal development on each dimension. Use a scale of 1 to 10, where 1 is completely undeveloped and 10 is perfectly developed, that is, at a world-class level. An Olympic medalist would score a 10 on the physical dimension, for example; someone who cannot walk around the block comfortably would score a 1. The zero point is at the center of the diagram. When you have marked your level of development on each dimension, shade in the area of your development across all dimensions. This will produce *your perception* of your life's balance at this point. You may find the shape of your profile revealing.

   The definitions in Figure 3 suggest another way of delineating your development. You may wish to keep these definitions in mind as you determine how to assess and shade in your development profile.

3. **Assess your current allocation of time.** Turn to the list of aspects of life in Figure 4 and estimate how much time a week you spend on each one. Without reviewing your day planner, just estimate in the first column how much time you spend on each dimension.

    If you have time, you may wish to actually keep track of your time for a week. Like our perceptions of our spending habits, our perceptions of how we spend our time do not often match up with the realities. You can use the form in Figure 5 to keep a weekly time diary and then record your results in Figure 6 to show how much time you spent during the week on each dimension. Enter the totals in the second column in Figure 4.

    As you track your time, you will notice that some dimensions overlap; that is, you could be working on more than one dimension at the same time. If you work construction, you are probably getting lots of exercise while you are working. Likewise, some aspects of work may involve new learning that stretches your mind intellectually, and spending time socially can also be emotionally powerful when you are comforting grieving friends. One way to deal with this overlap is to first allocate the 168 hours that you have each week to the dominant aspect and then return to add "shadow hours" in parentheses to indicate time spent elsewhere that had developmental impact in another area. For instance, if you find that your work required you to be learning (not just repeating what you can already do), you might assess how much of your work time is spent learning and add that number in parentheses to the Intellectual box. In this way, your week of 168 hours is leveraged; you can assess how rewarding on how many dimensions your time choices are. If you play golf with your peers, for example, you can count that time as recreation, but probably cannot include any shadow hours in parental time. If you play golf as a family, you could count recreation time and count shadow time with marital and parental aspects. You may find it interesting to see how much of your work time has shadow benefits to other aspect of life: Are you learning at work? Are you growing socially at work? You may find that you have no time, either shadow or otherwise, for a particular dimension or that the only time you have for a dimension is shadow time. It may be that your shadow time is not as productive as "hard time," in which your attention and efforts are concentrated. You decide what to include and how effective both hard and shadow times are. When you are done, add up your total hard hours and your shadow hours on the table in Figure 6.

    If you do not have time to keep a time diary (that, too, is interesting), think back on the previous week and try to allocate the time you spent on each dimension. Use Figures 5 and 6 to help you do this, and then enter your retrospective look in the second column in Figure 4.

4. **Create a profile of your current time allocation.** There are two ways you can create your profile. First, you could use the second wheel diagram, Figure 7, to mark and fill in your time allocations. This wheel is the same shape as the one in Figure 2, but the scale is now "five times the hours of time" so that 10 means you spend 50 hours a week on this dimension. Include your shadow time in this calculation. I realize that some of you may be working 60, 70, 80, or even 90 hours a week. If so, extend your Professional pie segment beyond the outer circle in scale to your current level of work.

    An alternative approach here is to use a spreadsheet graphing program to create a pie chart of how much time you spent on each dimension last week using the data from step 3. The result won't match the format of your developmental profile, but you can use it to do a mental comparison. (You could also draw this chart by hand using a compass and protractor by drawing a circle and calculating the percentage of time for each dimension (number of hours divided by 168 times 100) and multiply by 360 to get the number of degrees around the circle for each dimension. For example, if you spent 55 hours working, then 55 ÷ 168 × 100 = 33% times 360 degrees = 120 degrees of arc around the circle for that dimension.)

5. **Compare and reflect.** Now, consider the relationships between your definition of success, your self-assessed level of development, and your current time allocations. The following questions may help guide your reflection:

What connections do you see? What disparities?

Are there "flat spots" on either wheel diagram that concern you?

How do those flat spots relate to your definition of success and your allocation of time?

Do you want to do anything about the flat spots? How much time and talent will it take?

What will be the impact of your current time allocation on your development over the course of your life? That is, where logically does your present time allocation pattern take you 20 or 30 years into the future?

FIGURE 1: ASPECTS OF ADULT LIFE

Professional (working, earning in career and job)
Financial (managing money affairs)
Material (collecting things)
Recreational (playing)
Physical (exercising)
Sleep
Intellectual (learning, committing to memory, thinking)
Emotional (feeling, sensing, being aware of emotions)
Spiritual/Philosophical (praying, meditating, communing, reflecting)
Marital (with your spouse)
Parental (with your children)
Familial (with your parents)
Social (with your friends)
Societal (community work)
Political (political work)
Ecclesiastical (church work)

FIGURE 2: PERSONAL LEVEL OF DEVELOPMENT

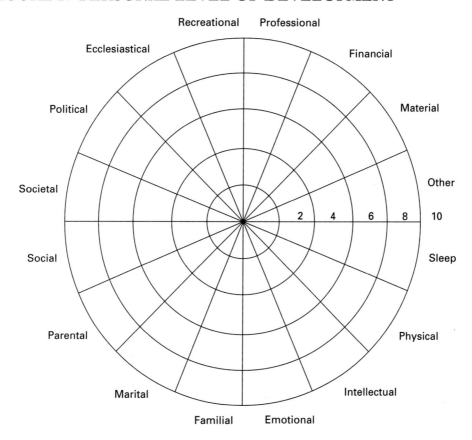

FIGURE 3: STAGES OF GROWTH

1. **Embryonic:** Unaware that the dimension exists and therefore pays no attention to it.
2. **Youth:** Aware that the dimension exists but does nothing about developing it.
3. **Adolescent:** Aware that the dimension exists but believes that it can be developed later; therefore, does nothing about it now.
4. **Young Adult:** Aware that the dimension exists and concerned about developing it; has a superficial awareness to work all along at developing it and makes modest efforts to develop it.
5. **Mature Adult:** Aware that the dimension exists and concerned about developing it; has a deep awareness of the need to constantly develop the dimension and is working hard to develop it.

URE 4: PERSONAL ALLOCATION OF TIME

Time Spent Last Week

Aspect of Life	Estimated	Total (from Figure 6)
Professional	_____	_____
Financial	_____	_____
Material	_____	_____
Recreational	_____	_____
Physical	_____	_____
Sleep	_____	_____
Intellectual	_____	_____
Emotional	_____	_____
Spiritual/Philosophical	_____	_____
Marital	_____	_____
Parental	_____	_____
Familial	_____	_____
Social	_____	_____
Societal	_____	_____
Political	_____	_____
Ecclesiastical	_____	_____
Total (168?)	_____	_____

FIGURE 5: TIME DIARY FOR ONE WEEK

Note daily your use of time in each of the following life dimensions: Working, Sleeping, Exercising, Managing Personal Hygiene (dressing, eating, bathing—you might include this in Physical if you don't want a separate look at your exercise), Reading and Learning (Intellectual), Managing Finances, Recreating (including most TV), Attending to Material Things, Parenting, Being with Significant Other, Being with Parents, Being with Friends, Working in the Community, Working in Political Events, Being in Church, Meditating/Communing/Praying. Include your shadow hours in parentheses. Then summarize the results on the figure on the next page.

Time	Mon	Tue	Wed	Thu	Fri	Sat	Sun
12:00 midnight	____	____	____	____	____	____	____
2:00 A.M.	____	____	____	____	____	____	____
4:00 A.M.	____	____	____	____	____	____	____
6:00 A.M.	____	____	____	____	____	____	____
8:00 A.M.	____	____	____	____	____	____	____
10:00 A.M.	____	____	____	____	____	____	____
12:00 noon	____	____	____	____	____	____	____
2:00 P.M.	____	____	____	____	____	____	____
4:00 P.M.	____	____	____	____	____	____	____
6:00 P.M.	____	____	____	____	____	____	____
8:00 P.M.	____	____	____	____	____	____	____
10:00 P.M.	____	____	____	____	____	____	____
12:00 midnight	____	____	____	____	____	____	____

FIGURE 6: ALLOCATING TIME OVER THE ASPECTS OF ADULT LIFE

Time Spent during the Week of   /   /

Aspect	Mon	Tue	Wed	Thu	Fri	Sat	Sun	Total
Professional	____	____	____	____	____	____	____	____
Financial	____	____	____	____	____	____	____	____
Material	____	____	____	____	____	____	____	____
Recreational	____	____	____	____	____	____	____	____
Physical	____	____	____	____	____	____	____	____
Sleep	____	____	____	____	____	____	____	____
Intellectual	____	____	____	____	____	____	____	____
Emotional	____	____	____	____	____	____	____	____
Spiritual	____	____	____	____	____	____	____	____
Marital	____	____	____	____	____	____	____	____
Parental	____	____	____	____	____	____	____	____
Familial	____	____	____	____	____	____	____	____
Social	____	____	____	____	____	____	____	____
Societal	____	____	____	____	____	____	____	____
Political	____	____	____	____	____	____	____	____
Ecclesiastical	____	____	____	____	____	____	____	____
Other:	____	____	____	____	____	____	____	____
Actual Total	24	24	24	24	24	24	24	168
Shadow Time	____	____	____	____	____	____	____	
Total Time	____	____	____	____	____	____	____	

FIGURE 7: TIME SPENT WHEEL DIAGRAM

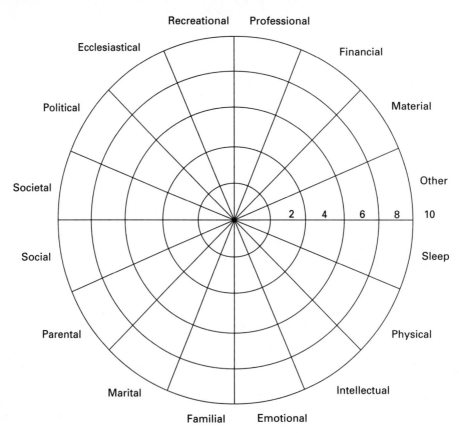

References

Derr, Brooklyn. *Work, Family, and the Career.* New York: Praeger Special Studies, 1980.

Evans, Paul, and Fernando Bartolome. *Must Success Cost So Much?* New York: Basic Books, 1980.

Greiff, Barrie S., and Preston K. Munter. *Tradeoffs: Executive, Family, and Organizational Life.* New York: New American Library, 1980.

Korman, Abraham K. *Career Success Personal Failure.* New York: Prentice Hall, 1908.

Lee, Mary Dean, and Rabindra N. Kanungo. *Management of Work and Personal Life.* New York: Praeger Special Studies, 1984.

Marrow, Alfred. *The Failure of Success.* New York: Amacom, 1972.

Machlowitz, Marilyn. *Workaholics.* Reading, MA: Addison-Wesley, 1977.

Selected Reading List

General Perspectives

Schein, Edgar. *Organizational Culture and Leadership.* 2d ed. San Francisco: Jossey-Bass, 1992. *Superb* insight; requires careful reading.

Savage, Charles M. *Fifth Generation Management.* Burlington, MA: Digital Press, 1991.

Gardner, John. *On Leadership.* New York: Free Press, 1990.

Hersey, Paul, and Ken Blanchard. *Management of Organizational Behavior,* 4th ed. Englewood Cliffs, NJ: Prentice-Hall, 1982. General text.

Wheatley, Margaret J. *Leadership and the New Sciences.* San Francisco: Berrett-Koehler, 1992.

Individual Perspectives

Covey, Stephen. *The 7 Habits of Highly Effective People.* New York: Simon & Schuster, 1989.

Viorst, Judith. *Necessary Losses.* New York: Ballantine, 1996.

Peck, Scott. *The Road Less Traveled.* 2d ed. New York: Simon & Schuster, 1998.

Miller, Alice. *The Drama of the Gifted Child.* New York: Basic Books, 1990.

Goleman, Daniel. *Emotional Intelligence.* New York: Bantam, 1995.

Fassel, Diane. *Working Ourselves to Death and the Rewards of Recovery.* New York: Harper, 1990.

Kranzler, Gerald D. *You Can Change How You Feel.* Eugene: University of Oregon, 1974.

Ellis, Albert, and Robert Harper. *A Guide to Rational Living.* North Hollywood, CA: Wilshire, 1975.

Kouzes, James M., and Barry Z. Posner. *The Leadership Challenge.* San Francisco: Jossey-Bass, 1987.

Csikszentmihalyi, Mihalyi. *Flow: The Psychology of Optimal Experience.* New York: Harper & Row, 1990.

McCarthy, Kevin W. *The On-Purpose Person: Making Your Life Make Sense.* Colorado Springs: Pinon Press, 1992.

Fromm, Bill, and Leonard Schlesinger. *The Real Heroes of Business and Not a CEO among Them.* New York: Currency Doubleday, 1994.

Vision and Task (Strategic) Perspectives

Porter, Michael. *Competitive Strategy.* New York: Free Press, 1980.

Hamel, Gary, and C. K. Prahalad. *Competing for the Future.* Boston: HBS Press, 1994.

Davis, Stanley M. *Future Perfect.* Reading, MA: Addison-Wesley, 1987.

Schwartz, Peter. *The Art of the Long View.* New York: Doubleday Currency, 1991.

Von Oech, Roger. *A Whack on the Side of the Head.* Menlo Park, CA: Creative Think, 1983.

Thompson, Charles. *What a Great Idea!* New York: Harper Perennial, 1992.

Interpersonal Perspectives

Cohen, Allan R., and David L. Bradford. *Influence without Authority.* New York: Wiley, 1991.

Bennis, Warren. *Organizing Genius.* Reading, MA: Addison-Wesley, 1997. Analyzes seven effective teams in recent history.

Keirsey, David, and Marilyn Bates. *Please Understand Me.* Del Mar, CA: Prometheus Books, 1984.

Tannen, Deborah. *You Just Don't Understand.* New York: Ballantine, 1990.

Organizational Perspectives

DeGeus, Arie. *The Living Company.* Boston: HBS Press, 1997.

Beer, Michael, Bert Spector, Paul R. Lawrence, D. Quinn Mills, and Richard E. Walton. *Managing Human Assets.* New York: Free Press, 1984.

Senge, Peter. *The Fifth Discipline: The Art and Practice of the Learning Organization.* New York: Doubleday, 1990.

Schein, Edgar H. *Career Dynamics.* Reading, MA: Addison-Wesley, 1978.

Tichy, Noel M., and Stratford Sherman. *Control Your Destiny or Someone Else Will.* New York: HarperCollins, 1994.

Galbraith, Jay R., Edward E. Lawler III, and Associates. *Organizing for the Future.* San Francisco: Jossey-Bass, 1993.

Managing Changes

Quinn, Robert. *Deep Change.* San Francisco: Jossey-Bass, 1997.

O'Toole, James. *Leading Change.* San Francisco: Jossey-Bass, 1995.

Nevis, Edwin E., Jon Lancourt, and Helen G. Vassallo. *Intentional Revolutions.* San Francisco: Jossey-Bass, 1996.

Hammer, Michael, and James Champy. *Reengineering the Corporation.* New York: Harper Business, 1993.

Schein, Edgar. *Process Consultation.* Reading, MA: Addison-Wesley, 1969.

Watzlawick, Paul, John H. Weakland, and Richard Fisch. *Change.* New York: Norton, 1974.

Cases That Apply

This list is intended as a sampling of some cases available at Harvard and Darden that apply to various aspects of the general model introduced in this book. This list is not comprehensive, but is a good starting point for building a course or a series of discussions around the topical areas introduced by the book. Darden School cases can be ordered from Darden Educational Materials Services (DEMS), Box 6550, Charlottesville, VA, 22906 (804 – 924 – 3009). The Darden Case Bibliography is online at http://www.darden.edu/case/bib. Harvard Business School Cases can be ordered from Harvard Case Services, Harvard Business School, Soldiers Field, Boston, MA 02163 (1 – 800 – 545 – 7685).

Introduction

Peter Browning and Continental White Cap A, B, and C (HCS-9-486-090, 091, and 092)
Secom Company, A and B (new case, please see DEMS for number)

Self

Peter Woodson, A and B (UVA-OB-390, 391)
John Wolford, A, B, and C (UVA-OB-167, 168, 169)
Jackie Woods, A and B (UVA-BP-330, 331; with CD-ROM)
The Life and Career of a Senior Executive Officer (UVA-PACS-023; with videotape)
Hassan Shahrasebi (UVA-OB-590; set in Iran)
Greenland (UVA-OB-581; set in Greenland involving Scandinavians)
Tetsundo Iwakuni: The Case of Japanese Leadership (UVA-OB-627)
The Hyundai Group's Chung Ju Yung: A Profile in Leadership (UVA-OB-555; Korea)

Task and Strategic Thinking

Walt Disney Productions, A (UVA-BP-259)
The Walt Disney Company: The Arrival of Eisner and Wells, B (UVA-BP-0339)
Stewart-Glapat vs. Caljan, A, B, C, and D (UVA-OB-628, 629, 630, and 631)
Charlotte Beers at Ogilvy Mather (HCS 495-031)

Leading Others

Warner Cable, A, B, and C (HCS 9-489-092, 093, 094)
Alvarez, A and B (new case, please get number from DEMS; set in Venezuela)
Great Expectations, A and B (new case, please get number from DEMS; set in Nepal)
Old Colony Associates (HCS revised case, 495-034 with individual cases associated)

ding Teams

Subarctic Survival (available from Human Synergistics International, Plymouth, MI)
Crossroads, A and B (new case, please get number from DEMS; set in England)
Meeting of the Overhead Reduction Task Force (HCS-9-478-013; with video)
GE FANUC NA, A and B (UVA-OB-437, 438; with videotape)

Leaders as Designers

FMC Aberdeen (UVA-OB-385)
Organizing the Comanche Program, A, B, and C (UVA-OB-432, 433, 434)
Park Nicollet (video case available from DEMS)
Charge of the Nueces Task Force, A and B (UVA-OB-304, 305)
The Kao Story: A Case Study (*International Management Journal,* June 1992)

Managing Change

Chicago Park District, A, B, C, and D (UVA-OB-618, 619, 620; with CD-ROM)
NYT PUB COM, A, B, and C (UVA-OB-591, 592, 593; with CD-ROM)
Big Sky Company: Magasco Mill, A and B (UVA-OB-396, 411)

Index

A

Accounts, relationship, 120
Activity, human
　Level One, 34
　Level Three, 33, 34–35
　Level Two, 33, 34
Activity, organizational, 41
Age of Enlightenment, 73
Alcoholics Anonymous, 89
Amygdala, 76–77
Andrews, Ken, 102
Anger, 160
Apple Computer, 126, 140
Argyris, Chris, 40–41
Aristocratic model, of leadership, 2–3
Assumptions, 62–63. *See also* VABEs
Atari, 129
Authority, legitimate, 5, 116

B

Bacon, Sir Francis, 73
Baker, Mark, 57–58
Balanced scorecard approach, 150
BancOne, 65–67
Bargaining, 160
Barriers, 92
Beer, Michael, 157
Behavior, 32–33, 34
　baseline, 154–56
Behavioral leadership, 40
Behavioral psychology, 33
Beliefs. *See* VABEs
Bennis, Warren, 10–11, 109, 126, 127, 133
Biederman, Patricia Ward, 109, 126, 127, 133
Boston Consulting Group, 102
Box (leadership strategy), 26, 27
Bradford, 117–19
Built to Last (Collins and Porras), 12, 107

Bureaucracy
　defined, 4
　demise of, 11
　leadership in, 36
　mind-set of, 2
Bureaucratic model, of leadership, 4–6
Burnout, 39–40

C

Canon, 106
Capabilities, core, 106–7
Caplan, Janet, 131
Caring, 79–80
Carlisle, Thomas, 130
Carrot and stick method, 36–37
Caterpillar, 107
Center, clarification of, 57–60
Challenges, strategic, 101
Change, 26, 27
　agent of, 158
　classic models of, 157–58
　emotional impact of, 82
　exponential rate of, 7
　external viewpoints, 157
　general model, 154–56
　in Information Age, 168–69
　Level Three, 41, 162–63
　MIT model, 163–64
　process of, 82, 155–56
　quotient, 81–82
　responses to, 159–62
　roles in, 158–59
　timing and, 13
Changees, 159
Character development, 59–60
Charters, organizational, 108–11
Chinese Contract, 144
Clan organization, 144

225

M